THE BLACK HAND

ROBERT M. LOMBARDO

The Black Hand

Terror by Letter in Chicago

UNIVERSITY OF ILLINOIS PRESS

URBANA AND CHICAGO

♾ This book is printed on acid-free paper.

Library of Congress Cataloging-in-Publication Data
Lombardo, Robert M.
The Black Hand : terror by letter in Chicago / Robert M. Lombardo.
p. cm.
Includes bibliographical references and index.
ISBN 978-0-252-03488-6 (cloth : alk. paper)
ISBN 978-0-252-07675-6 (pbk. : alk. paper)
1. Black Hand (United States)—History.
2. Gangs—Illinois—Chicago—History.
3. Extortion—Illinois—Chicago—History.
I. Title.
HV6448.L66   2010
364.10609773'11—dc22   2009020142

It is not important whether or not the interpretation is correct—if men define situations as real, they are real in their consequences.

—W. I. Thomas, *The Child in America*

Contents

Preface

The idea for a study of the Black Hand began in 2003 when I was gathering information for a book on organized crime in Chicago. The prevailing belief is that organized crime came to America in the form of the Sicilian Mafia and, to a lesser extent, the Neapolitan Camorra. One of the cornerstones of this theory is the argument that the Mafia and the Camorra came to America's immigrant communities in the form of the Black Hand, yet we know little about this so-called group. What was the Black Hand? Who were its members? What did they do? Finally, what was the societal response to Black Hand crime? As I attempted to answer these questions, I realized that a thorough study of the Black Hand in Chicago was a book in itself.

The more I read about Black Hand crime in Chicago, the more I became interested in the subject. As a former police officer, I was attracted to the Chicago Police Black Hand Squad, a group of six Italian American police officers who dedicated their careers to fighting Black Hand criminals. As an Italian American, I was intrigued with the White Hand Society, a group of Italian American business and community leaders who risked their lives and fortunes to fight Black Hand crime. Lastly, as a sociologist, I was fascinated with the way society responded to Black Hand crime. The press and the American public blamed Black Hand activity on the criminality of the southern Italian immigrant. Only the White Hand Society challenged this belief, arguing that Black Hand crime was the result of conditions in American society.

This research began with the recognition that we know little about Black Hand crime in Chicago. Up until this book, the only scholarly

account was that of John Landesco, who included a chapter on Black
Hand crime in his book *Organized Crime in Chicago*. There are numerous other references to the Black Hand in popular books written about
organized crime. Most, however, are fanciful, literary accounts that are
not constrained by the rules of careful scientific investigation. *The Black
Hand: A Chapter in Ethnic Crime*, written by Thomas Pitkin and Francesco Cordasco, is the only book available about the subject. Published
in 1977, Pitkin and Cordasco's book centers on Black Hand activity in
New York City with some mention of Black Hand crime in other parts
of the country. Written from a historical perspective, their book is an
important contribution to the literature and does an excellent job of
defining and recounting Black Hand crime. My book differs from Pitkin
and Cordasco's in that it provides a sociological explanation for the Black
Hand phenomenon.

Although this study uses historical data, it is truly a sociological
analysis. It would be impossible to understand Black Hand crime without studying Italian immigration and the social structure of nineteenth-
century American society. In fact, history is so critical to sociological
study that some argue that history and sociology are one and the same.[1]
We simply cannot explain society as it is without studying the decisions
that have shaped our social world.

A qualitative research design was used to conduct this research. I
collected the data without any preconceived deductive scheme and developed the findings during the process of the research. Primary sources
were used whenever available. One problem with studying historical
events is that data is limited. The Black Hand crime wave occurred in
Chicago nearly 100 years ago, and there is no one alive to provide information about the Black Hand phenomenon. Relying solely on newspaper
accounts can give a distorted image of what has occurred. Newspaper
reporting can reflect the biases and beliefs of those who write the news.
Nonetheless, this analysis relies on newspaper accounts because they
were often the only source of data available. In fact, newspaper accounts
were critical to establishing the societal response and its consequences
for the history of Black Hand crime.

This study involved the content analysis of 280 newspaper accounts
of Black Hand crime occurring in Chicago from 1892 to 1931. I collected the data from four Chicago newspapers, the *Chicago American*,
the *Chicago Daily News*, the *Chicago Daily Tribune*, and the *Chicago
Record-Herald*. The *Tribune* was especially helpful because it has a full-
text computerized index beginning in 1847. The *Record-Herald* was also
helpful. It published a printed index from 1904 to 1912 that identified

all Black Hand stories reported by the newspaper. This review led to the identification of 117 alleged Black Hand offenders. Of these, I obtained the court records of forty Black Hand defendants, four from the United States District Court, Northern District of Illinois, and thirty-six from the Cook County Circuit Court.

I also used another primary source, *Studies, Actions, and Results*, the report of the White Hand Society in Chicago, in this analysis. The White Hand Society never published this report and few copies exist. I found it in the Harvard University Library archives after an exhaustive search. The White Hand report is vital to this analysis. The report is the only empirical study of Black Hand crime ever conducted. Other primary sources that are used include Italian-language newspaper accounts of crime during the period translated into English for the Chicago Foreign Language Press Survey and the records of the Local Community Research Committee of the University of Chicago, housed at the Chicago Historical Society.

Some secondary sources were also used. I based the sections on the Mafia and Camorra on the scholarly work of a number of historians and sociologists who have dedicated years to studying these groups. Their work represents the best information available in the English language about these topics. I also used Harvey Zorbaugh's classic book *The Gold Coast and the Slum*. Chapter 8, titled "Little Hell," provided background information on Chicago's Little Sicily neighborhood, where many Black Hand crimes occurred. A lesser-known book titled *Little Sicily*, written by Bruce Zummo, also provided a substantial amount of information about the Little Sicily community.

One difficulty encountered in conducting this study was the careless manner in which the press reported Italian names. Accounts of the same incident appearing in different newspapers often spelled the names of the offenders, victims, and witnesses differently. Although I have made every effort to obtain the correct spelling, there is no guarantee that all names in this work are correctly spelled.

In preparing this book, I benefited greatly from the support of Loyola University, Chicago. A summer stipend allowed me to reduce my teaching load and concentrate on writing and gathering data. I also benefited from a semester in residence as a fellow of the Center for Ethics and Social Justice during the fall 2006 semester. There I did a good deal of the writing and, through participation in a series of meetings with other center fellows, refined many of the arguments presented in the text. Special thanks goes out to my graduate research assistants Elizabeth Berkhout, Stephanie Lambert, Jessica Rosati, Rachel Sterk, and Daniela

Steffenino, whose many hours viewing microfilm contributed greatly to this project.

I would like to thank the faculties of the departments of sociology at the University of Illinois at Chicago and DePaul University, whose guidance over the years formulated my understanding of our world and gave me the sociological insight needed to write this book. Many thanks also go out to Rosemary Tirio for editing my grammar and Arthur Bilek and Dominick Candeloro who reviewed the final draft of this book. I am also grateful to Joan Catapano, Danielle Kinsey, Ann Youmans, and all the people at the University of Illinois Press who worked to make this book possible. Finally, I would also like to acknowledge C. Wright Mills, who reminded all sociologists of their responsibility to "deliberately present controversial theories and facts and actively encourage controversy."[2]

THE BLACK HAND

Introduction

On February 23, 1908, the *Chicago Daily Tribune* reported that one-third of Chicago's Italian immigrants were paying tribute to an organization of extortionists, blackmailers, and assassins known as the Black Hand. Hundreds of families were living in fear because of the death threats sent to them by Black Hand criminals, and hundreds of other families were preparing to leave the city unless the government could find some means of controlling these criminals.[1] The Black Hand was a crude method of extortion used to blackmail wealthy Italians and others for money. Blackmailers would send a letter stating that the intended victim would come to harm if he did not meet the extortion demands. The term *Black Hand* came into use because the extortion letters usually contained a drawing of a black hand and other evil symbols such as a dagger and skull and crossbones.

The following is a Black Hand letter received by Benedetti Cairo on August 18, 1908:

Dear Sir,
We are four persons and you must excuse us if we seem to bother you. The time is hard. You must keep this to yourself and your wife. You must obey these demands. You can pay. We ask of you $1,000.

You have until Aug. 18 at 8 P.M. You must go to Eighteenth street and Cottage Grove avenue. At the right hand there is a corn patch. At the corner, under a wood sidewalk, there is a cigar box. You take a look around and you will see a man who will make a signal to you with a red handkerchief. When you have seen the signal immediately put the money in the cigar box and go right straight home without looking back. Do no make any mistake. Otherwise you pay for it soon.

Beware to not fall and also keep quiet. Otherwise you will pay for this bad! We mean what we say. You think this over well and Saturday we will wait for you at the designated point and I tell you again not to tell this anybody, otherwise it will cost you dear! This is all, and, believe me, and the four of your good friends. Excusing us. Good-bye. Do not fail or you will pay for it.

THE BLACK HAND

Black Hand crime occurred in Chicago for a relatively short time. Most Black Hand crimes occurred in a five-year period between 1907 and 1912, although isolated incidents occurred as early as 1905 and as late as 1931. Two Italian communities suffered significantly: Little Sicily in Chicago's Near North Side and the Italian settlement on the Near West Side, but it was Little Sicily that became the hotbed of Black Hand crime.

There is a consensus about the major characteristics of Black Hand crime. First, Black Hand crime originated in Italy. Second, members of the Sicilian Mafia and the Neapolitan Camorra committed Black Hand crime in the United States. Third, only southern Italians and Sicilians committed Black Hand crime. Finally, only southern Italians and Sicilians were Black Hand victims.[2] This was the public perception of Black Hand crime during the last century and it continues to be the perception today. In fact, a whole literature has developed supporting this position.

The literature supporting the Italian origins of Black Hand crime is extensive. It includes magazine and journal articles as well as published volumes. For example, an April 1911 edition of the *Literary Digest* reported that members of the Camorra operated all over the world under the picturesque title of the Black Hand. A 1921 edition of *Current History* argued that the Black Hand was an extension, or offshoot, of the Mafia that came to the United States after World War I. In their landmark study of cultural assimilation, noted sociologists Robert Park and Herbert Miller reported that the spirit of the Mafia and the Camorra developed into Black Hand activities in the United States, which had a paralyzing effect on the development of Italian immigrant life. A 1967 book on the history of the Mafia concluded that by 1904 the Black Hand had reached the status of an organization, with branches in every part of the United States and ties to Sicily, and that the American Mafia sprang from the loosely organized Black Hand to become the highly organized Cosa Nostra.[3]

In spite of the popular belief that the Black Hand originated in Sicily and the south of Italy, there is considerable evidence arguing against the Italian origins of Black Hand crime. Italian community leader Gaetano

D'Amato argued that the term *Black Hand* was never heard of in Italy until long after it had been used in the United States and then only in reference to American crime. D'Amato called the alleged association between the Camorra, Mafia, and the Black Hand a "myth." The United States Immigration Commission also supported the position that the Black Hand was unheard of in Italy. The Commission reported in 1911 that upper-class Calabrians and Sicilians were refraining from migrating to the United States for fear of the Black Hand and that others had actually returned to Italy to find safety from it. Diego Gambetta, studying the Sicilian Mafia, concluded that although Americans historically used the name Black Hand to represent a criminal organization of Italian immigrants, it was unknown in Italy then and now.[4]

There is also substantial evidence arguing against the belief that members of the Sicilian Mafia and Neapolitan Camorra committed Black Hand crimes in the United States. Italian journalist and attorney Gino Speranza, writing in a 1904 issue of *The Survey*, described the Mafia, Camorra, and Black Hand as "popular or journalistic creations." The so-called Black Handers, he argued, belonged to no organization or society. They were members of what the Italians called *"la mala vita"* or "the evil life"—the criminal element that exists in every country. Arthur Woods, the former New York City deputy commissioner of police, agreed. Woods wrote in a 1909 edition of *McClure's Magazine* that the Black Hand was not a cohesive, comprehensive society working with mysterious signs and passwords. Given the number of Italians with money, two or three ex-convicts were all that were necessary for a first-rate Black Hand campaign. That same year, the *Cosmopolitan* reported that the Black Hand society was a myth and that "there is no central organization. There are no blood-sealed oaths. There is no international association. The Black Hand is the generic name of innumerable small groups of criminals operating under its flag to blackmail and murder . . . As it is the police have to deal with individuals."[5]

Writing in *McClure's* magazine, Arthur Train also argued that Black Hand offenders were not members of the Camorra or Mafia. Train, a former district attorney of New York County, added that many Black Hand offenders were not even of Italian birth. Train believed that the majority of Black Hand criminals were second-generation Italians who were born in the United States. In fact, he argued that they were typical delinquents: "As children they avoid school, later haunt 'pool' parlors and saloons, and soon become infected with a desire for 'easy money' which makes them glad to follow the lead of some experienced *capo maestro*" (leader).

Train challenged the belief that Black Hand crime was the direct result of the criminal tendencies of the Italian immigrant and placed the blame squarely on social conditions in American society.[6]

In spite of evidence challenging its Italian origins, the belief that the Black Hand was a criminal organization that originated in Italy with the Mafia and the Camorra has persisted. In 1951, nearly forty years after the end of the Black Hand crime wave in Chicago, the Special Congressional Committee to Investigate Organized Crime in Interstate Commerce, better known as the Kefauver Commission, tied the Black Hand to the evolution of organized crime in American society, arguing, "There is a sinister criminal organization known as the Mafia operating throughout the country with ties in other nations. . . . The Mafia is the direct descendant of a criminal organization of the same name originating on the island of Sicily. In this country, the Mafia has also been known as the Black Hand and the *Unione Siciliano*. . . . The Mafia is a loose-knit organization specializing in the sale and distribution of narcotics, the conduct of various gambling enterprises, prostitution, and other rackets based on extortion and violence."[7]

The Kefauver Commission summary is a classic statement of what has come to be known as the alien conspiracy theory. The alien conspiracy theory argues that organized crime evolved in a line beginning with the Mafia in Sicily, emerging as the Black Hand in America's immigrant colonies, and culminating in the development of the Cosa Nostra in America's urban centers. It did not emerge out of American culture but was thrust upon the American people by alien newcomers. The roots of organized crime lie in values contrary to the American way of life. These values are tied to the cultures of specific ethnic groups who brought organized crime with them when they immigrated to the United States.

Belief in the Italian origins of Black Hand crime continues today. In fact, the alien conspiracy connection between the Mafia, the Black Hand, and American organized crime is the official position of the Federal Bureau of Investigation. The following descriptions of the Cosa Nostra and Italian organized crime were taken from the Web site of the FBI in September 2006:

> Since the 1900s, thousands of Italian organized crime figures have come illegally to the United States, most of those being Sicilian Mafiosi. Many of those Mafia members who fled here in the early 1920s helped establish what is known today as the La Cosa Nostra or American Mafia.
> The American Mafia has undergone many changes. From the Black Hand gangs around 1900 and the Five Points Gang in the 1910s and 1920s in New York City, to Al Capone's Syndicate in 1920s Chicago.[8]

Modern research, however, has challenged the alien conspiracy theory and has shown that the Black Hand was not an organization at all but simply a crude method of extortion carried out by small independent gangs. Research has also challenged the idea that organized crime in American society evolved from the Sicilian Mafia or the Neapolitan Camorra. Sociologists such as Joseph Albini, Daniel Bell, Robert Merton, James O' Kane, and others argue that organized crime is the result of social-structural conditions within American society. Commonly referred to as ethnic-succession theory, this view holds that traditional organized crime was not imported by alien newcomers but was the direct result of conditions in America, and that criminal groups have played an important role in the social differentiation of American society. Based upon Daniel Bell's functionalist argument that crime serves as a means of social mobility, the ethnic-succession argument sees organized crime as a vehicle for social advancement. Deprived of traditional opportunities for achievement, newly arriving immigrants use crime as a means of acquiring wealth and gaining status in society. Organized crime allows successive waves of immigrants, who are on the bottom rungs of society, a means of economic and social mobility that transcends the involvement of any particular ethnic group.[9]

Some have gone so far as to claim that the alien conspiracy theory is a myth derived from a combination of press sensationalism and nativist sentiments at the turn of the last century. They attribute the emergence of organized crime in American society to the advent of Prohibition and widespread political corruption. According to author Michael Woodiwiss, not even J. Edgar Hoover believed in the alien origins of organized crime; he considered such activities to be associated with local political corruption. In his book *Gangster Capitalism*, Woodiwiss argues that the view that a secret criminal brotherhood was transplanted to urban America at the end of the nineteenth century worked to produce a formula that lazy, ill-informed journalists would regularly turn to when writing about organized crime in America. The idea of a foreign conspiracy absolved the United States from any responsibility for its organized crime problems.[10]

This book challenges the belief in the Italian origins of Black Hand crime, and argues that the development of Black Hand extortion was not related to the emergence of the Sicilian Mafia or the Neapolitan Camorra but rather was rooted in the social structure of American society. Addressing this topic is important for criminology. Black Hand crimes occurred at a period in history before social-structural explanations of crime were common. Black Hand crime was tied to the alleged criminal tendencies of the southern Italian and Sicilian immigrant. Such reasoning was consistent with the state of criminology at the time. Early positivist theorists tied criminality to the biological and cultural characteristics of the individual offender while ignoring environmental influences on crime. In contrast, the White Hand Society, a group formed in Chicago to oppose Black Hand crime, argued that Black Hand extortion was the result of conditions in American society. One can understand why the public ignored the White Hand Society's position when it became public in 1908. They issued their report twenty-one years before Clifford Shaw's 1929 work that tied delinquency to the social structure of urban areas. How is it that this view persists today in spite of advances in criminology such as social disorganization, strain, and conflict theories?

This book also challenges the belief that Black Hand crime was limited to Italian victims and Italian offenders. Park and Miller report that Black Hand criminals never molested or threatened wealthy continental Italians or those of other nationalities, while the Sicilian who had shown any outward signs of prosperity would almost invariably receive extortion demands. Although southern Italians and Sicilians were the major targets, other groups were also victims of Black Hand extortion. For example, Black Hand criminals shot northerner Andrew Cuneo, the richest Italian in Chicago, after he ignored numerous Black Hand demands. Another non-Sicilian, Tracey Drake, the owner of Chicago's famous Drake Hotel, received a Black Hand letter threatening death if he did not meet a demand for $100,000. There was even a Greek Black Hand episode. Kris Koumeks, a fruit merchant living in the Near West Side, received a letter, written in Greek, demanding $500. The press estimated that during the height of Black Hand activity, wealthy Chicagoans received an average of twenty-five such letters from various Black Hand gangs each week.[11]

Although there is widespread consensus that Italians caused the Black Hand threat, there is overwhelming evidence that other ethnic groups carried out Black Hand extortion as well. For example, William Walters, an African American servant, sent his employer Mrs. J. H. Van Housen a Black Hand letter demanding $100. In another case, police arrested six German Americans for sending threatening letters demanding $2,000 to cement contractor Joseph Kornfeind. The extortionists signed the last letter *"Die Schwartze Hand"* (the Black Hand). So many Black Hand crimes were incorrectly attributed to Chicago's Italians that U.S. district court judge Kenesaw Mountain Landis publicly challenged the idea that Black Hand crime was peculiar to the Italian race, stating that most of the Black Hand cases that came before his court did not involve Italian criminals at all. Judge Landis argued that it was natural to think of the Black Hand as an exclusively Italian form of crime because it was first given publicity in the Italian quarters of New York and Chicago. However, if it had its origin among Italian criminals, the criminal fraternity quickly adopted it, and it was an injustice to hold the Italians in America responsible for every Black Hand offense.[12]

Of the 280 Black Hand crimes identified here, 60 of the 267 identified victims (22 percent) were not Italian, nor were 20 of the 117 identified offenders (17 percent). These findings were not limited to Chicago. A review of 71 out-of-town occurrences of Black Hand crime reported in Chicago newspapers revealed that 19 of the 65 identified victims (29 percent) and 10 of the 30 identified offenders (33 percent) were not Italian. In fact, of the 280 recorded incidents of Chicago Black Hand crime, 78 (28 percent) had no evidence of extortion nor did 24 (34 percent) of the 71 out-of-Chicago cases, yet the press attributed these offenses to the Black Hand. Why? How did the crimes of a small number of Black Hand gangs become defined as the acts of an international criminal conspiracy? The answer may lie in the process by which the social reality of crime is constructed.

The White Hand Society blamed the American press for the improper definition of Black Hand crime. They argued that every crime committed by an Italian was incorrectly described as the work of the Black Hand, the Mafia, or the Camorra and that the term *Black Hand* had become a generic name for the Italian immigrant in this country. Why were Italians singled out? Every time a mysterious crime was committed anywhere near an Italian neighborhood, the newspapers attributed the offense to the Black Hand. Such an attitude on the part of the press brought all Italians into disrepute and caused suspicion of the group in spite of the fact that not all Black Hand offenders were Italian. Why did the press treat the Black Hand as a secret criminal organization, made up exclusively of Italians, even though there was no hard evidence that such an organization existed? Certainly, Italians participated in Black Hand extortion, but most crimes of violence perpetrated by Italian criminals were in revenge for some personal injustice or to protect their families' honor. In fact, Italians were so underrepresented in misdemeanor and felony crime that in 1915 the Chicago City Council reported that Italian involvement in crime was "so small as to be negligible."[13]

The association of Italian Americans with the Black Hand and the Mafia had real consequences for Italian American immigrants. In his study of American nativism, John Higham writes that antiforeign sentiment filtered through a specific stereotype when Italians were involved. In American eyes, they "bore the mark of Cain"—being Italian suggested the Mafia and impassioned violence. One implication of the criminal stereotyping associated with Black Hand crime was that it prevented the orderly assimilation of Italian immigrants into American society. In an article titled "How It Feels to Be a Problem," Gino Speranza argued that Italians resented the way they were treated in the United States, and the constant headlines about the Mafia and abuses by corrupt politicians, bankers, and rough police officers left Italians without any desire to become American citizens.[14]

From New York mayor Fiorello LaGuardia to vice presidential candidate Geraldine Ferraro and Supreme Court justice Samuel Alito, being Italian has raised suspicion of ties to the Mafia. To quote Alexander De Conde, "In the popular mind, the connecting of Italians with crime was as American as associating Jews with shady business deals, Irishmen with boss politics, or Negroes with watermelons."[15] Why? Every man and woman who migrated to the United States from the south of Italy could not possibly have been a criminal. Although this prejudice has subsided as Italians have been assimilated into mainstream American culture, the cause of this prejudice has rarely been examined in a scientific manner. Studying the Black Hand provides a unique opportunity to identify the cause and social construction of this prejudice. It was the initial classification of Black Hand crime as the work of the Mafia that led to the later development of the alien conspiracy theory, forever tying Italian Americans to organized crime.

In the pages that follow, I will present a view of Black Hand crime that will challenge the traditional narrative. Chapter 1 of this book begins with a brief review of Italian immigration and settlement in Chicago. The chapter also examines the social Darwinist view that southern Italians are different from northern and that they possess character traits that prevent them from building a rational and orderly society, whether in Italy or in the United States. The chapter examines early Italian immigrant participation in crime including the emergence of the so-called Mafia, Camorra, and Black Hand in Chicago.

Chapter 2 is a history of Black Hand crime in Chicago. It is organized around the activities of the White Hand Society, a group of Italian American business and community leaders who organized to fight Black Hand crime. The chapter includes an in-depth history of the formation of the White Hand Society, background information on its leaders, and a description of the efforts of the Chicago Police Department to hire "secret service agents" to fight Black Hand crime.

Chapter 3 continues the history of Black Hand crime, centering on the activities of the Chicago Police Black Hand Squad, a group of Italian American police officers organized to fight Black Hand extortion. After the demise of the White Hand Society, the Black Hand Squad became the primary group responsible for combating Black Hand crime in Chicago.

Chapter 4 concludes the history of Black Hand crime in Chicago and includes a review of the Black Hand crimes that occurred during the Prohibition era and a discussion of the alleged Black Hand extortion of Big Jim Colosimo.

Chapter 5 examines the underlying causes of Black Hand crime. The government and the public alike generally blamed Black Hand crime on the Mafia, the Camorra, and the alleged criminal tendencies of southern Italian and Sicilian immigrants. This position was unsuccessfully challenged by the Italian community, who argued that Black Hand crime was not the result of a transplanted criminal society but the work of individual Italian criminals and social-structural conditions within American society itself. The White Hand Society identified these conditions as the isolation of the Italian community, the Italian immigrant's distrust of formal authority, the existence of saloons and saloonkeepers with powerful political connections, and a criminal justice system that was ineffective in repressing crime. This chapter also provides an alternative view of the origins of the Mafia. It argues that the Mafia in Sicily at the turn of the last century was not an organized crime group in the American sense of the word but a form of social organization that developed in Sicily in the absence of formal state government.

Chapter 6 argues that the definition of Black Hand crime as the work of the Mafia and the Camorra was the result of newspaper publicity and the state of criminology at the time. Both not only led to the identification of Italians as the folk devils of American crime but also to the development of the alien conspiracy theory, forever equating Italians with organized crime in American society. In particular, this chapter argues that newspaper and magazine accounts that tied the Italian immigrant to the Mafia and the Camorra coalesced around three major topics. These were the murder of David Hennessy, the New Orleans chief of police; the murder of New York police lieutenant Joseph Petrosino; and a series of articles on Italian immigration written by anthropologist George Dorsey for the *Chicago Daily Tribune*.

The final chapter synthesizes the earlier discsussion and reviews what has been learned about the social construction of deviance and its implications for public policy. Attributing Black Hand crime to the cultural traits of the Italian immigrant prevented state and federal governments from adequately addressing the real causes of Black Hand crime. This failure to properly define the causes of deviance has had real consequences for real people. One of the consequences of anti-Italian prejudice fueled by press accounts of Black Hand crime was the eventual destruction of the Little Sicily community. Ostensibly done in response to the need for urban renewal, it is clear that the reputation of the neighborhood as tied to Black Hand crime was partially to blame.

Although Black Hand crime only existed for some twenty years, it had a major impact on the history of crime in Chicago. The activities of the Black Hand ended any doubts in the minds of Chicagoans about the existence of the Mafia. It is the conclusion of this book, however, that social conditions in Chicago bore more responsibility for Black Hand extortion than any foreign criminal group. The isolation of the Italian community, political corruption, and an ineffective criminal justice system allowed Black Hand criminals to operate with some degree of immunity. Black Hand crimes were not related to the emergence of the Sicilian Mafia but were the product of America's disorganized urban areas.

1 *Italians in Chicago*

Between 1819 and 1910, over 3 million Italians immigrated to the United States. This was the largest and longest European migration in modern times. The first Italian immigrants came mainly from the more advanced regions of the north where they had gained experience as merchants, shopkeepers, and business owners. During the 1880s, emigration began to shift to southern Italy and Sicily. During the eleven-year period between 1898 and 1909, nearly 2 million southern Italians migrated to the United States.[1]

The causes that initiated and sustained the mass migration of Italians from the south of Italy were rooted in the defects of its agricultural system. Most southern Italian farmers were landless peasants tied to the estates of absentee landowners through tenant-lease contracts. Recurring drought, pestilence, and burdensome taxation plagued the people of the Italian south. In addition, a dramatic increase in the Italian population also contributed to emigration. The Italian population grew by over 5 million people during the years between 1871 and 1901. The island of Sicily alone added over 1 million people to its population during this period.[2]

Although once fertile, the south of Italy had become an impoverished land by the end of the nineteenth century. Much of the arable soil had been stripped away by erosion caused by insufficient rainfall. In addition, trees had been cut for fuel and timber and forests cleared for cultivation. Denuding the hillsides led to massive landslides and affected drainage: stagnant pools of water formed that became natural breeding grounds for malaria-bearing mosquitoes. As late as 1904, malaria killed 20,000 people a year. In order to avoid the bite of malaria-carrying mosquitoes that typically struck between dusk and dawn, Italian farmers were required to spend their nights high in the hills, where mosquitoes could not exist because of the cooler climate. Unlike American farmers, southern Italians did not live on the land but in hillside towns that were often miles away from the fields that they cultivated. Living on the land, as American farmers did, was relatively unknown to the Italian immigrant.[3]

Another cause of emigration was the heavy taxation of peasant farmers. There were national and provincial land taxes whose burden was often passed on from the landowner to the tenant farmer. In addition, there were taxes on movable wealth (income), nonagricultural buildings, and purchases such as salt, tobacco, and alcohol. So harsh were conditions of life in Sicily that Booker T. Washington remarked, "The Negro is not the man farthest down." Washington reported that the conditions of the colored farmer in the most backward parts of the southern United States were incomparably better than the condition and opportunities of the agricultural population of Sicily. He encountered whole families living in dirt floor, windowless, single-room houses that doubled as shops and shelters for livestock.[4]

In spite of the hardships of life in the south of Italy, many Italian emigrants intended to return home after improving their financial condition in America. The U.S. Immigration Commission reported that 44 percent of all Italian immigrants who came to America in the years between 1887 and 1907 returned to Italy. Those who stayed in the United States faced many of the hardships that they had known in their native land. Few continued in the agricultural occupations they had known in their mother country. Unlike Italians who had migrated to Argentina, Italian farmers coming to the United States found that earlier immigrant groups had already settled the land. Lacking other occupational skills, most were attracted to America's major cities where work for unskilled laborers was plentiful.[5]

Italians could be found in Chicago as early as the 1850s when a group from the northern region of Liguria settled in the downtown business district. Centered at Clark and Polk streets, Chicago's first Italian colony grew to 15,000 people by 1890. Paul Baijonotti, the Italian consul in Chicago at the time, reported that two-thirds of the people came from Genoa, Tuscany, and Piedmont, while the remaining one-third came from the Naples area. The *Chicago Daily Tribune* described Chicago's Italian settlers as patient and steady workers who were filling the ranks of unskilled workers left vacant by the Irish, who were moving up into politics and the police force.[6]

During the 1880s, many of Chicago's northern Italian immigrants migrated to the area north of the central business district around Franklin and Orleans streets. There they founded Chicago's first Italian Catholic Parish, the Assumption of the Blessed Virgin Mary, which is still in existence today. From the 1870s on, Chicago's role in the westward expansion of the nation's railroads drew increasing numbers of Italian workers, mostly from the south of Italy. These new immigrants settled within walking distance of the Dearborn Street Railroad Station at Polk and Dearborn streets. This area was known among the Italians as the Polk Depot and served as an area of transition for newly arriving immigrants. The Polk Depot was in the midst of the city's vice district. Known as the Levee, it contained over 200 saloons, gambling rooms, brothels, dance halls, and penny arcades.[7]

The Polk Depot settlement was a mother colony that spawned a number of other Italian settlements. As their numbers increased, the Italians expanded west across the Chicago River and south into the Near South Side of the city. Citing the 1898 Chicago Public School census, *L'Italia*, Chicago's leading Italian-language newspaper, reported that there were 23,061 Italians living in the city. By 1910, the West Side settlement had become the largest of the city's Italian colonies, stretching as far west as Halsted Street. The southward expansion, however, was blocked by the relocation of the city's red-light district. After 1890, because of the growth of Chicago's downtown business district, the Levee had been relocated to the area bounded by Nineteenth and Twenty-second streets, from State to Clark. As a result, Italians diverted their southern expansion along Archer Avenue and moved south into the Armor Square community.[8]

The northern Italian settlement at Grand and Orleans streets also acted as somewhat of a mother colony as newly arriving southern Italian immigrants expanded westward along Grand Avenue and into the Near North Side of the city. By 1914, over 150,000 Italian immigrants and their children were living in the city of Chicago. Most were from the *Mezzogiorno* ("land of the midday sun"), as the south of Italy was called. Sixty percent of Chicago's Italian population could now be found in four wards: the First, the Seventeenth, the Nineteenth, and the Twenty-second. They formed a semicircular belt that surrounded Chicago's central business district.[9]

The settlement of Italian immigrants in Chicago often corresponded with their residence in Italy, as people from the same towns settled near one another. For instance, Italians from the regions of Campania, Basilicata, Calabria, and Abruzzi settled in the First Ward in the Near South Side. Southern Italian and Sicilian settlers went to the Seventeenth Ward on the Near Northwest Side. Italians from southern and central Italy including the areas of Bari, Abruzzi, Salerno, and Avellino settled in the Nineteenth Ward in the Near West Side. The Twenty-second Ward in the Near North Side was largely Sicilian. The establishment of four new Italian Catholic parishes in each of these areas also reflected the early movement of the Italian population.[10]

Italians began migrating to the United States at a difficult time in the nation's history. The depression of 1893 had reduced the number of available jobs. The frontier was closing. Free land was running out, and the western states had little need for immigrant labor. Immigrants were linked to problems in the big cities. Members of the temperance movement strongly opposed all newcomers because of their links to big city political machines. Immigrants were also the target of nativist hostility. Many believed that Italians and other immigrants of the day—Greeks, Syrians, Armenians, Poles, and Hungarians—were inferior to the original Nordic stock that had emigrated from the north of Europe. Furthermore, they were Catholic. In his widely acclaimed book *Strangers in the Land*, John Higham writes that by far the oldest and most powerful form of antiforeign tradition in the United States came out of Protestant hatred of the Roman Catholic Church.[11]

The hostility against Italian immigrants was directed largely at southern Italians and Sicilians. This hostility, strangely enough, originated in Italy where southern Italians were viewed as having a different cultural heritage than the Italians of the north. Northerners believed that southern Italy's location at the crossroads joining Africa, Europe, and the Middle East had given birth to a people who were racially inferior. Northern Italian propagandists described southern Italians as biologically lazy, incapable, criminal, and barbaric. Italian criminologist Giuseppe Sergi used skull measurements to argue that northerners descended from superior Aryan stock while southerners were primarily of inferior African heritage. Sergi asserted that the resulting savage tendencies of the southern Italian culminated in violent crimes and criminal associations such as the Mafia and Camorra, and that these tendencies made them unable to live in a civilized society.[12]

The "southern question," as it was often called, was classically defined by Italian criminologist Alfredo Niceforo in his book *L'Italia Barbara Contemporanea* (Contemporary Barbarian Italy). Niceforo stated that two separate Italies existed, the modern and civilized north and the inferior and primitive south. He argued that Sardinia, Sicily, and the *Mezzogiorno* contained peoples who were still primitive, not completely evolved, and less civilized and refined than the populations of the north and center of Italy. He also argued that the criminality of the *Mezzogiorno* was violent, brutal, individualistic, and an eruption of brute force while the crime in the Aryan north was refined and evolved.[13]

Sergi and Niceforo were followers of the Italian school of criminology. Founded by Cesare Lombroso (1835–1909), the Italian school argued that criminals were "atavistic," or throwbacks to an earlier stage of evolution. Lombroso's "criminal anthropology" broke with the Enlightenment belief that crimes were committed by immoral individuals who freely chose to commit criminal acts. Lombroso was the first to relate biological characteristics to crime. D'Agostino, in his study of Lombrosian criminology, argues that Lombroso's racial doctrines provided a launching pad for theorizing about the southern Italian. In fact Lombroso himself argued that an "inferior civilization" marked by a "criminality of blood" existed in the south of Italy.[14]

Based on the work of Sergi and Niceforo, the 1911 *Reports of the U.S. Immigration Commission*, commonly called the Dillingham Report, argued that northern and southern Italians differed in language, physique, and character. The Commission reported that while the northerner was cool, deliberate, patient, practical, and capable of great progress in the political and social organization of modern civilization, the southerner was excitable, impulsive, highly imaginative, impracticable, and had little adaptability to highly organized society. The U.S. Bureau of Immigration was so completely influenced by these beliefs that it began distinguishing Italian immigrants by categorizing them as either northern "Keltic" Italians or southern "Iberic" Italians. In their *Dictionary of Races or Peoples*, the Immigration Commission further singled out Sicilians, stating that they were "at bottom Ligurian or Iberic, but much modified by the many invading peoples, including even North Africans," and that they were "vivid in imagination, affable, and benevolent, but excitable, superstitious, and revengeful."[15]

The influence of Sergi and Nicefero could also be found in the work of American sociologist Edward Ross. In his 1913 study of immigration, Ross repeated the position of the Italian criminologists that northern Italians differed dramatically from southern Italians. Ross also reported that the two regions differed in crime. While northern Italy led in fraud and chicane, crime in southern Italy revealed a "primitive stage of civilization" where homicide and brigandage excelled. He even argued that the children of the southern Italian immigrants born in the United States were inferior, stating, "It appears that these children, with the dust of Saracenic or Berber ancestors showing on their cheeks, are twice as apt to drop behind other pupils of their age as are the children of the non-

English speaking immigrants form northern Europe." Ross concluded that as long as the American people consented to assimilate great numbers of southern Italian immigrants, they must resign themselves to "lower efficiency, to less democracy, or to both."[16]

Such beliefs undoubtedly had an effect on the American public. For instance, Appleton Morgan, in an article appearing in an 1890 edition of *Popular Science Monthly,* asked, "What Shall We Do with the 'Dago'?" (The word "dago" is a disparaging term used to describe an Italian, Spaniard, or Portuguese. It is derived from the Spanish word *hidalgo* referring to a man of lesser nobility.) Morgan argued that jail was not a deterrent to Italian crime because Italians "live better and work about as much, have warmer clothing and better beds in the meanest jail in the United States than they experience out of it." Morgan based this opinion on the fact that he once saw Italian railroad-camp workers make soup with the bones left behind by circus lions and tigers.[17]

The Immigration Commission also argued that an alarming feature of Italian immigration was the fact that it included many individuals belonging to the "criminal classes, particularly of southern Italy and Sicily." In fact, the Commission reported that in southern Italy crime had greatly diminished because most of the criminals had gone to the United States. The Commission also reported that crimes of personal violence, robbery, blackmail, and extortion were peculiar to the Italian people. Accompanying the tendency to commit these crimes, the Commission added, Italians possessed the ability to avoid "arrest and conviction." In addition, the homicidal tendency of the Italian immigrant was proven by the fact that in certain provinces of Italy, which furnished the greatest number of immigrants, there had been a "remarkable decrease in the number of murders and homicides," while at the same time there had been a "startling growth of Italian criminality of the same nature in the United States."[18]

Such statements lent themselves to the belief that certain types of criminality were inherent in the Italian race. Sentiment was so strong against the Italian immigrant that the National Origins Act of 1924 restricted Italian immigration to 2 percent of their population at the time of the 1890 census, which in effect ended large-scale Italian migration to the United States. In the years from 1900 to 1910, Italian immigration averaged nearly 200,000 people a year. With the imposition of the quota, the United States government allowed fewer than 4,000 Italians per year to enter the country, while countries like Great Britain were allowed to send 24,000 emigrants a year. The law remained in effect until it was replaced by the Immigration and Naturalization Services Act of 1965.[19]

In spite of popular beliefs about the criminal tendencies of the southern Italian and Sicilian immigrant, few Italians in Chicago were actually involved in crime. *L'Italia* reported in 1892 that of the 22,449 persons arrested in Chicago that year, only twenty-six were Italian; of the fifteen hundred inmates in the Illinois State Prison, only five were Italian immigrants. Similarly, an 1894 survey of the twelve hundred inmates in Chicago's city jail failed to find one Italian among them. The Department of Public Welfare of the City of Chicago reported in 1919 that Italians ranked fifth behind immigrants from Germany, Austria-Hungary, Poland, and Russia in numbers of people arrested; the number of Italians arrested was not very high when considered alone or when compared to that of other nationalities. In addition, Italians were free of vice, drunkenness, and mendicancy. The City of Chicago attributed the offenses committed by Italians to two things: ignorance of the law and the importation of Old World standards into American life, mainly the distrust of government. Father Edmund Dunne, the first pastor of the Near West Side Holy Guardian Angel Parish, supported this view of Chicago's Italians. In his book the *Memoirs of Ze Pré* (Uncle Priest) Dunne reported that southern Italians were "honest, industrious, and temperate, pure in their domestic lives and law-abiding in their civil relations." In addition, Dunne found that "they had a keen sense of right and wrong."[20]

Although southern Italians in Chicago failed to live up to their criminal reputation, there were a number of cultural practices that distinguished them from other immigrant groups. The south of Italy was notorious for its lack of government-sponsored mechanisms of social control, resulting in a cultural system that favored retribution as a means of settling grievances. As a result, violent crime was not unknown in the Italian American community. In addition, many early Italian immigrants entered the United States under a labor agreement controlled by a labor contractor, or *padrone*. These padrones became the subject of much suspicion and the targets of newspaper and government investigations. More importantly, southern Italians and Sicilians brought with them an understanding of the existence of the Camorra and the Mafia, concepts that were completely alien to the American people.

Historically, the vendetta, or blood feud, was characteristic of societies that lacked a strong central government. In modern times, the vendetta has persisted in places where public justice cannot easily be obtained and private means of settling grievances are a much simpler recourse. The vendetta typically involved exacting vengeance on a killer or one of his relatives for the murder of a family member. The absence of effective state government in Sicily and the south of Italy allowed the vendetta to linger in these regions longer than in other parts of Western Europe. It was particularly widespread in Corsica and Sicily, countries that had experienced extensive foreign domination. The practice continued among southern Italian and Sicilian immigrants in the United States. In Chicago, for example, the widows of fifteen Italian laborers who were killed in an Alaskan mine disaster assaulted the padrone who had employed their husbands and stolen the men's wages after their deaths.[21]

The padrone employed or found work for Italian immigrants. The word was also used to describe persons who exploited child labor. Take the example of Emmanuel Mallelo, of South Clark Street, who was arrested by the Chicago police in January 1877 for "slave dealing" in Italian children. Mallelo had allegedly rented a child for twenty-five dollars a year to walk daily through the streets of Chicago with a harp on his back and play music. The child then gave the money he collected to Mallelo each evening. If the child did not collect the minimum amount required, he was sent out into the dark to raise the sum. A subsequent court proceeding revealed that Mallelo had kept eight boys in similar bondage.[22]

An 1893 investigation of the padrone system by the *Chicago Daily Tribune* detailed similar abuses. According to the newspaper, parents in Italy allowed their children to come to the United States to work as street musicians and beggars. The parents entrusted the children to the padrone, who provided the parents with a small sum of money and was responsible for the children's care. Once they arrived in the United States, the children were required to earn a certain amount each day as musicians, most of which was kept by the padrone for the "living expenses" of the child. Those who did not earn the required amount of money were allegedly tied to a bedpost at night and beaten. Other children were reportedly trained by the padrone to stand on street corners at night and cry piteously. When questioned by passersby, the children would explain that they must sell all their newspapers before they could return home or face a severe beating. Feeling sorry for the children, the sympathizers would purchase a paper and provide a generous tip.[23]

Complaints against Italian labor contractors were not limited to child labor. In February 1886, a man named Caesar Moreno appeared before the House of Representatives Labor Committee in support of a bill outlawing the padrone system. Moreno testified that the traffic in "Italian slaves," as he described them, began in 1869 when Ferdinand Deluca was consul-general of Italy in the city of New York. Ever since that time, the Italian consulate there had been the headquarters of the infamous business that also extended to a number of other major American cities. In Chicago, he alleged, the chief offender was also the Italian consul, whom he claimed was the principal owner of 5,000 slaves in and about the city. When confronted with the accusations, the Italian consul in Chicago replied that such claims were nonsense and that Moreno was a liar. In fact, he argued, there were scarcely 5,000 Italians in Chicago to begin with.[24]

Investigators did find a man in Chicago named "Stephano" who found work for Italian immigrants. He was described as "a banker, grocer, beer-seller, contractor, builder, money-lender, philanthropist, lodging-house keeper, steamship agent, broker, capitalist, and politician." Stephano owned a building in the heart of the Italian colony on South Clark Street where he rented rooms to those for whom he had found jobs. The ground floor of the building housed a saloon and a store. During the winter months when there was no work, Stephano said that he supported the men and their families. During the summer when the men worked, they repaid him whatever he was owed. When asked how much he charged for securing employment, he replied "not a cent."[25]

In spite of Stephano's denials, there is ample evidence of unscrupulous practices among Italian labor agents. *L'Italia* reported in September 1894 that twenty Italian laborers, who had each paid six dollars for a job to an Italian track boss, arrived at their destination to find that the promised jobs did not exist. In May 1901, a man posing as a railway employment agent collected three to five dollars from each of three hundred Italian laborers. He told them to meet him at the railway depot in Chicago at 8 o'clock the same night, but he never arrived with their railway passes to the section camp. In yet another case, forty-five men were shipped from Chicago to a work camp after paying three to eight dollars per man. When they arrived at the site, they were informed that they would receive $1.25 a day as opposed to the $1.35 a day that they were promised. When they refused to work for the reduced wages, they were sent to do another job draining and leveling an awful swamp. Those who did not have the money to return to Chicago were forced to work in the swamp, under armed guard, until they had earned enough money to purchase a train ticket home.[26]

An investigation of the padrone system in Chicago by the U.S. Commissioner of Labor found that among 1,860 Italians interviewed, 403 (22 percent) worked for a padrone. Of these, 379 (94 percent) reported that they paid a commission to the padrone. The average amount paid was $4.84 for eleven weeks of labor, or forty-two cents a week, at a time when Italian men in Chicago were earning, on the average, $10.89 weekly. In those instances where the men were taken out of the city to work, they were compelled to purchase all or part of their food from the padrone, often at prices that were double those charged in Chicago. There was no mention of child labor in the federal report. These findings were challenged by the *Tribune*, which charged that the Commissioner of Labor's report only told half the padrone story. Sending reporters into the streets of Chicago, the newspaper identified in a single evening four separate dens of children who were under the control of a padrone.[27]

In spite of the frequent investigations of the padrone system, nothing made Italians more sinister in the minds of the American public than the mysterious stories of the Camorra and the Mafia. Chicagoans were exposed to the Camorra of Naples as early as 1877 when a *New York World* article, reprinted in the *Chicago Daily Tribune*, described the Camorra as a sort of freemasonry of crime that dated back to the Middle Ages with branches in every city in Sicily and the south of Italy. The membership reportedly swore on the crucifix to secrecy and resorted to every sort of violence and fraud to obtain money. They infiltrated every class and part of Neapolitan society in order to further their interests and attempted to force tribute from those not of their membership.[28]

On October 24, 1888, an article appeared in the *Chicago Daily Tribune* asking the question, "Has Chicago a Mafia?" The article was written in response to two earlier reports of Mafia activity in New York City. On October 22, the *Tribune's* New York office reported that a secret Sicilian society known as the Mafia had murdered Antonio Flaccomio because of his betrayal of several Italian counterfeiters. According to the story, the murder of Flaccomio "brings to the notice of the American people" the existence of an organization of Sicilian cutthroats, counterfeiters, and malefactors of all sorts known as the Mafia. The purpose of the Mafia was to protect criminals from the authorities, settle disputes, and punish traitors with death. On October 23, a coroner's jury investigating the Flaccomio murder determined that there was no doubt that the Mafia existed in New York, New Orleans, and other American cities.[29]

The next day, the *Tribune* answered the question of the existence of the Mafia in Chicago by announcing, "Wherever there are Sicilians there also is the Mafia." It described the Mafia as a secret Sicilian organization, closely related to the Camorra of Naples, that is worldwide in its operations, levying blackmail on even the poorest of Italians. Not everyone agreed that the Mafia existed in Chicago. In fact, Emilio De Stefano, one of the alleged sources of the Mafia story, objected to the manner in which the newspaper portrayed the information that he had provided. De Stefano recounted that what he had said about the existence of the Mafia and Camorra was only what he had read in romance novels many years ago when the south of Italy was under the rule of the Bourbon kings, but these societies no longer existed. De Stefano asked why the press described an Italian charged with murder as an Italian brigand or Italian Camorrist, as opposed to just reporting the offender's name, location, and profession. Why did the press build crimes committed by Italians into sensational stories as if only Italians could commit such crimes?[30]

In spite of the initial concern about the existence of the Mafia, it was two years before an alleged Mafia incident again came to light in Chicago. In spite of the local dearth, the press continued to report Mafia activities in other cities. For example, there was a report in 1890 that *"La Mafia"* had marked Boston police officer John Rosatto for death because of his efforts to bring several Italian murderers to justice. There was also a report that Dominico Gaituchi was murdered in New York City by Antonio Chialadano on the orders of the Mafia. It should be noted that Chialadano admitted the stabbing but claimed it was in self-defense.[31]

In October 1890, David Hennessey, the chief of the New Orleans Police Department, was murdered. There had been considerable Sicilian migration to New Orleans after the Civil War. Two factions had developed among the Sicilians, the Provenzanos and the Matrangas. Both were engaged in a struggle for control of the stevedore business on the New Orleans waterfront and each accused the other of being part of the Mafia. During the struggle, Hennessy was murdered. A number of Italians were tried for the murder, but they were acquitted. After their acquittal, a mob stormed the jail and lynched eleven of the defendants.

For the next year, weekly newspaper articles introduced Chicagoans, and people throughout the country, to the depredations of the Mafia and the criminal tendencies of the Sicilian immigrant. The impact of the New Orleans affair on the reputation of Italian Americans cannot be underestimated. In fact, it has been argued that the New Orleans incident gave birth to the American stereotype of Italian Americans as criminals and the idea that Italians started organized crime in the United States.[32]

Three weeks after the Hennessey murder, there was a report from St. Louis that Joseph Gazzolo had been condemned to death by the Mafia. Gazzolo received a letter postmarked in New Orleans that read, "Notice of Condemnation: You have been duly tried by the judicial tribunal and found guilty of many crimes charged against you, and sentenced. The order has been given for your execution. Repent, and prepare for a future state, as you will receive no further warning. This is by order of the Mafia." Some months later, Gazzolo entered a Chicago police station asking to see the local inspector. When the desk sergeant told him that he would have to return in the morning, Gazzolo and his companions reportedly began to "jabber wildly in Italian" and reluctantly left the station. Returning the next morning, Gazzolo related to Chicago police that he had sold a fruit stand to another man, knowing that the lease on the property was no longer valid, and that he suspected that the victim of the fraudulent sale was sending him threatening letters. A second letter read, "Tempus Fugit. Having failed to comply with the demand for restitution of that which you swindled, justice will be dealt out to you. Vendetta never fails." The word vendetta and three cross marks were written in blood. Below the crosses was a postscript written in Italian: "The sons of Italy never forget. The vengeance of the vendetta is sometimes slow but always sure."[33]

The Gazzolo incident brings to mind a number of important issues. First, obvious acts of personal vengeance were being attributed to the Mafia. Second, local Italians invoked the name of the Mafia to frighten other members of the Italian immigrant community. Finally, statements such as they began to "jabber wildly in Italian" suggest that the press took a condescending view of the Italian immigrant.

An 1891 article titled "Hyde Park in a Panic" classically expressed the sometimes condescending and even comical view of the Italian immigrant taken by the American press. The *Chicago Daily Tribune* reported that the residents of Hyde Park had barred their doors and taken sanctuary on their rooftops because of a rumor that the Mafia was out looking for trouble. The alarm was caused by the Italian chef of the Columbian Hotel, who had tripped over a dog while delivering a bucket of cranberry sauce to the local police station. Covered with red berries and screaming in Italian, the chef was seen by a police officer, who came to his aid thinking that he had been the victim of foul play.[34]

October 1892 brought notice of a new, sinister criminal organization in Chicago. Calogero Di Martino and Giovanni Ciaciro were shot during a card game in an Italian saloon on Tilden Avenue. The murder of Di Martino and the wounding of Ciaciro were proclaimed by the Chicago press as the work of the "Mafia and the Black Hand." *L'Italia*, however, reported that the shootings were the result of a quarrel over women and money, and had nothing to do with either group. Oscar Durante, the newspaper's editor, challenged the Mafia theory, stating, "This fable of the Mafia is an unreasonable stupidity, an imbecility pure and simple. Every small quarrel between Italians gives rise to the cry of the 'Mafia.' This organization does not now and never did exist." This incident not only established the use of the term *Black Hand* in Chicago as early as 1892, but also defined the continuing debate between the American press and Italian community regarding the existence of the Mafia and the Black Hand.[35]

Whether the Mafia existed in Chicago or not, stories of alleged Mafia crimes continued to appear in Chicago newspapers. Shortly after the murder on Tilden Avenue, as the case became known, the press reported that the Mafia was again active in New York City. Little had been heard of the Mafia in New York since the attack on Antonio Flaccomio and the subsequent suppression of the alleged Mafia group responsible for his murder. The latest allegation charged that the wife of Italian businessman Marzio Gondice had been poisoned and her body stolen by members of the Mafia in an effort to gain control of property that she owned in Italy. Two months later, a story that the leader of the New York Mafia had come to Chicago again raised concerns about the existence of the Mafia. Chicago police responded that they could not trace any crimes committed in the city directly to the Mafia. Chicago detective Charles Arado, himself an Italian, agreed. Arado was intimately familiar with crime in the Italian community and did not believe that the Mafia existed in Chicago.[36]

In October 1894, a man named De Bartolo drew a gun and, "shouting threats of Black Hand vengeance," fired point-blank at newspaperman Oscar Durante during a meeting of the McKinley Club, an Italian American Republican political organization. It is unclear why De Bartolo invoked the Black Hand name. The incident was probably politically motivated. Durante was among the leaders of an effort to swing Italian voters away from the Democratic Party, which, he charged, had broken with the working man and caused the Civil War and slavery. Four months after the shooting, Durante reported that he had received two letters from a woman, or somebody pretending to be a woman, professing burning love for the young editor and inviting him to come to Columbus, Ohio. Durante also received a third suspicious letter from a man named Mantello urging him to come to Columbus to obtain new subscribers for his newspaper. Suspecting foul play, Durante turned the matter over to the police. When confronted, Montello admitted that he knew who wrote the letter, but he refused to reveal the author's identity and added that Durante was his enemy.[37]

Little was heard of the Black Hand in Chicago for a number of years. There was, however, an occasional report of Mafia activity. In March 1901, for example, the *Chicago Daily Tribune* published a feature story titled "Most Dangerous Neighborhood in Chicago," referring to a small Sicilian colony on Grand Avenue near the Chicago River.[38] The *Tribune* described the neighborhood as the headquarters of the Mafia. The Mafia allegedly held its meetings in a building next door to a saloon owned by a man named Frank Morici. Two blocks from the Morici bar was the House of Blazes, a boarding house where many of Chicago's Mafia members reportedly lived. An elaborate system of alleys, back gates, and sunken walks under the houses provided a safe means of escape for the boarders when sought by the police. More vendettas were said to be settled there than in any other part of Chicago. Whether it was the actual number of acts of vengeance or simply the foreign nature of the people, the article clearly demonstrated the sinister view that the Chicago press held of Sicilians.

Two months later, Felix Labriola reported that he had received a number of letters from the Mafia warning him to stop searching for his estranged wife Mary.[39] It seems that Labriola's wife had run away with another man, Geatano Bergamo. The letters were written in red ink and they bore a picture of skull and crossbones, a hand holding a dagger dripping blood, and a bulldog with a bone in its mouth. There was no demand for money, only a threat of violence if he did not end his search. What was interesting about the Labriola letter was that it bore many of the characteristics that would come to be associated with Black Hand crime.

In September 1904, the Black Hand was back in the news. Three Sicilian railway workers were attacked near Riverdale, Illinois. Andrea Scaezia and Antonio Veriuso were murdered in their beds. A third man, Bruno Binzenza, was left critically wounded. They were killed by two masked men who had invaded the railroad shanty where they were sleeping. Although robbery was the apparent motive for the murders, the acts were soon attributed to the Mafia and the Black Hand. Both men were immigrant workers who had announced that they were going to return to Italy that very day with the money they had saved working in America. In fact, $485 was recovered from one of the victims—a large sum of money at that time—that apparently had been overlooked by the robbers. Two months later, Natale Selafini was found murdered in Chicago. His death was also attributed to the Mafia and the Black Hand.[40]

Responding to the Selafini report, L'Italia questioned why the American press was again disparaging the Italian good name by carelessly attributing the death of Selanfini to the Mafia and the Black Hand. Although infrequent, suspicious crimes in the Italian community were increasingly being attributed to the Mafia and, to a lesser extent, the Black Hand, even though most of these crimes were robberies or acts of personal vengeance for some purported wrong or act of betrayal. Then in 1904, the term Black Hand began to replace the use of the word Mafia to describe crimes attributed to Italians in Chicago. A study of Black Hand crime in New York City by Pitkin and Cordasco reported that the term came into use there in August of 1903.[41]

There was another alleged Black Hand crime in February 1905. Luigi

Caprelli of South Chicago received a letter sent by members of the "Black Hand" society in the neighboring Pullman district.[42] The letter gave him a month to leave the city. Caprelli originally thought that laborers whom he had fired from his work crew had sent the letters. One week later, however, he received a second letter instructing him to leave the wife of Michael Gorila. Gorila had left his wife sixteen years before, and, believing him dead, she had remarried. Caprelli thought that the author of the letter was his wife's former husband. Interestingly, similar letters were sent to two different Louis Caprellis who both lived in South Chicago. Apparently, Gorila was not sure which Caprelli had taken up with his wife. Like the word *Mafia*, the term *Black Hand* was now being used as a means of intimidation.

Some months later, Justice A. J. Sabath received a threatening letter stating, "Black Hands are after you and they will get you." The letter was written in Bohemian and signed the *"Zabarni Mafie."* The incident clearly established that groups other than Italians were using the words Mafia and Black Hand as forms of intimidation. In September 1905, Mrs. David Hartshorn of South Indiana Avenue received a letter directing her to place $50 on the gate in front of her home. The letter was signed the "Three Black Hands." Police believed that the note was a hoax but assigned detectives to investigate the incident anyway. The incident contained all the elements that would come to be known as Black Hand crime.[43]

Two months after the Hartshorn incident, five persons were burned to death in an Italian tenement house fire on East Seventy-third Street. Three of those who lost their lives were reportedly kneeling in prayer when the fire consumed them. The lessee of the building told the police that the "Black Hand Society" had recently sent him letters demanding $2,000. Although the letters did not threaten arson, police began an investigation in the belief that the writers of the letters may have started the fire.[44]

The use of threatening letters to extort money was not unheard of. In August 1904, Antonio Sbarbaro, a prominent Italian undertaker, was threatened with death unless he paid $10,000 to an organization called the Five Skeletons. Sbarbaro, considered a leader among the members of Chicago's Near North Side Italian community, ran a funeral home on North Wells Street. The letter instructed Sbarbaro to deliver the money to a designated location and threatened death if he did not comply. In addition, the letter informed Sbarbaro that many of his countrymen had recently met their deaths by violence as the result of their failure to comply with the demands of the Five Skeletons gang.[45]

On July 10, 1906, Salvatore Sarafina of 11 Milton Avenue, in Chicago's Near North Side Little Sicily neighborhood, received the following letter:

> Dear Friend
> With these few words we let you know that you are charitable and we know that you will not refuse what we ask as friends. If you do not give what we ask on July 10 look out, for your life is in danger. Our society says you should give what we want. The person that we will send will meet you and ask "Cigar Spagnioli," and if you do not give him $500 you will be murdered. We mean business.
> THE BLACK HAND SOCIETY[46]

The letter, written in Italian, was decorated with crude-looking skulls and crossbones and long daggers. Police announced that the letter was the most conclusive evidence of the existence of the "Black Hand or Mafia Society" among Chicago's Italians that they had ever seen.

Two months later, a Black Hand letter demanding $300 was received by John and Joseph Gannello of 83 Gault Court (now Cambridge Avenue), in Little Sicily.[47] The brothers, one a city employee and the other a railroad section worker, were instructed to indicate their willingness to pay by carrying a closed umbrella under their left arm while walking near their home. Similar letters were received by others in the area and were said to be the work of a shrewd Italian lawyer. For a fee, the lawyer would drive the writers out of the city and nothing more would be heard from the Black Hand.

Little Sicily was not the only community to experience Black Hand crime. Italians began reporting Black Hand extortion in the Near West Side and in South Chicago. Little Sicily, however, became the center of a bombing campaign that brought increased attention to the Black Hand problem. On April 8, 1907, Black Hand agents bombed the home of Giuseppe Mancusco, a grocer at 92 Milton Avenue. Luckily, no one was injured. Mancusco had received several letters from a society of "Six Friends" demanding payment of $500 under penalty of death. He took the letters to the police, who instructed him not to pay. The police told Mancusco to paste a newspaper in his front window and place a tin can (filled with paper instead of money) on his sidewalk as directed by the extortion letters. On the night specified, four detectives laid in wait, but no one came to collect the tin can. As a result, police dismissed the crime as a prank, claiming that a large firecracker caused the explosion. Mancusco then received two more letters from his tormentors. The last read, "We instructed you to leave the money on the sidewalk at 60 Milton Avenue. You notified the police. Get ready for death at once, for you have defied the society and must die."[48]

Black Hand criminals next exploded a bomb in the front of a two-story building at 903 Milton Avenue, the home of Leonardo Digiocanno. They also fired revolver shots through the windows of the house. Digiocanno had received three Black Hand letters demanding $500. The next victim was an Italian banker who received a package of parts needed to assemble a bomb. The recipient, Salvatore Genovese, found the "infernal machine" after having received several requests for $2,000. Genovese took the package to the authorities, where it was examined and found to contain several fulminating caps, revolver cartridges, and other materials for making an explosive device, but all disconnected and harmless. In the box was a crude drawing of two men in the act of killing a third. Genovese regarded the package as a warning of what he might expect if he did not pay the amount demanded by the blackmailers.[49]

The press responded to the series of bombings in the Italian community by calling for the addition of Italian-speaking detectives to the police force. As it stood, the police knew nothing of Black Hand extortion until an explosion or assault had occurred. The police department needed to make changes in the detective division that would allow police officers to gather information on an extortion threat before the injury occurred. One way to do this would be to develop informants in the Italian community, something that Italian-speaking police officers could more easily do. When asked about New York's plan to organize a police "secret service" to fight Black Hand crime, Chicago police chief Shippy responded that he did not believe that foreign "secret societies" were at work in Chicago and that he did not think that the city needed such a plan.[50] Although the Chicago Police Department was not yet convinced that it was a serious problem, Black Hand crime as a method of extortion was now firmly established in Chicago.

There are probably incidents of alleged Mafia and Black Hand crime other than those reported here. Nevertheless, the cases cited demonstrate a pattern of progression beginning with threats of Mafia violence and ending with Black Hand extortion as we have come to know it. The data suggests that criminals did not import Black Hand crime from Italy but that it evolved over time. Letters threatening Mafia violence merged with those demanding money and, as the words Black Hand began to replace the term Mafia, Black Hand extortion was born.

Why Italian criminals chose the words Black Hand to distinguish their crimes is not certain; however, there are several explanations for the origin of the Black Hand name. The most likely is that the name was taken from an anarchist group that killed wealthy landowners in Spain during the late 1800s. It was later learned, however, that the local provincial police chief might have invented the name in order to incriminate the leaders of the anarchist movement. The use of the words Black Hand in the United States, under the Italian name *Mano Nera*, has been associated with the publicity given to the Spanish society. In 1902, a series of articles appeared in newspapers throughout Europe exposing the Spanish Black Hand trials as a miscarriage of justice. Shortly thereafter, the term was used in the United States by a small group of blackmailers who were attempting to extort money from a New York bank.[51]

Another explanation attributes the name Black Hand to a society in Puerto Rico that came to the attention of American forces in 1898 during the Spanish-American War. This revolutionary society committed atrocities against the Spanish governors of the island and those who collaborated with Spanish authorities. Still another explanation argues that the name was borrowed from a secret organization founded in 1911 by Serbian nationalists to unite all of the areas containing ethnic Serbian populations that had been annexed by Austria-Hungary. Although there is no direct association between these groups and American crime, the fearsome-sounding name could have been adopted from either group. It should be noted, however, that criminals called themselves the Black Hand in Chicago as early as 1892, making these explanations unlikely.[52]

Terrence Powderly, chief of the Division of Information of the U.S. Immigration Bureau, provided a different explanation. Powderly reported in 1908 that he had learned in Italy that the term *Black Hand* represented an Italian custom. In Italy, a man who wronged a woman and failed to right the injustice was driven from among his fellows as the "Black Hand" of ostracism was raised against him. Although originally used to describe a noble purpose, the term was converted to one less noble when brought to the United States and applied to crime.[53] Powderly's interpretation suggests that the words Black Hand were used to describe a form of retribution that could be applied to almost any type of situation.

Other explanations attribute the creation of the label to the media. The name has been attributed to Carlo Barsotti, the editor of New York's *Il Progresso Italo-Americano*. Barsotti reportedly coined the phrase Black Hand in order to avoid using the word *Mafia* when referring to Italian crime in the hope that the offenses would be viewed as resulting from conditions in American society. Italian commentator Gaetano D'Amato, writing in the *North American Review*, provided yet another explanation. D'Amato argued that the Black Hand name was probably first used by some "Italian desperado" who had heard of the exploits of the Spanish

Black Hand society and considered the combination of words to be "high sounding" and "terror inspiring." After one or two crimes were committed under the Black Hand symbol, he continued, American newspapers began to apply the term to all crimes committed by Italian criminals in order to attract public attention.[54]

Whatever their origin, the words Black Hand were now used to signify a particular type of crime. The Black Hand had become a method of extortion that routinely used blackmail letters, one that was not strictly tied to the Italian community. Whether it was the use of the terror-inspiring words or the sensational attention paid to blackmail cases by the press, the words Black Hand had taken on a completely new meaning that would have a lasting effect on Italian immigrants in Chicago and, in particular, the residents of Chicago's Little Sicily.

2 The White Hand Society

In November 1907, Dr. Camillo Volini, of 388 Halsted Street, received a letter threatening the lives of his four children unless he paid $8,000 to the Black Hand.[1] Ten days later, he received a second letter that contained the words "Look Out!" and a picture of a black hand. About the same time, Dr. Peter Cutrera, a physician at Milwaukee and Grand Avenues, received a similar letter demanding that he pay $8,000. So did Dr. Joseph Damiana and several other prominent Italians. Banker Pasquale Schiavone, also at 388 Halsted Street, received two Black Hand letters. After the second letter, a man presented himself at Schiavone's bank and attempted to collect the money.

Until this time, Black Hand offenders had mainly targeted the poorer class of Italians—usually peddlers and merchants. They were now becoming bolder, attacking the leading merchants and professional men of the community. Aroused by the increasing boldness of Black Hand criminals, a group of prominent Italians met with Guido Sabetta, the Italian consul in Chicago, to discuss the growing crime problem.[2] Present at the meeting were Drs. Camillo Volini and Peter Cutrera, attorney Stephen Malato, *Unione Siciliana* president Joseph Mirabella, and a number of other leading men of the community. Together they proposed the formation of a "White Hand Society" to fight what the "yellow press" of Chicago called the Black Hand. (The term *yellow press* was used to describe newspapers that emphasized the sensational side of the news through the outrageous use of stories about murder, sex, and crime.) Sabetta endorsed the formation of the White Hand, as did the Italian-language newspaper

La Tribuna Italiana, which promised to place itself at the White Hand's disposal.

Reacting to Sabetta's active support of the establishment of the White Hand Society, Black Hand criminals sent him the following letter, which was obviously an attempt to prevent the members of the Italian community from taking action against Black Hand crime.[3]

> Chicago free country Nov. 14, 1907.
> Friend of a revolver shot.
>   I had already heard of the 16th floor of the Masonic Temple where a Gentleman lived who occupied the position of consul for the ignorant Italian people. Well I did not believe it and wanted to see for myself whether they were really telling me the truth. In fact I found the words true spoken by that man worth listening to and the applause given by the hearers all right.
>   Well if the people are in the habit of making show in the halls by holding meetings, I am not a part of that numerous class, but although my party is small but strong enough to destroy such rabble as you. You are too small compared to what we are looking for, and do not deserve to be mentioned with such, but as you have worked against us we will not fail and kindly warn you.
>   This trembling hand which scribbles this sheet is that strong arm which is sure to make a hole in the most sensitive part of your breast.
>   Good by till an opportune time.
>   Friend Beniamino and Co.

Because many Black Hand offenders were Sicilian, Chicago's Sicilian community felt duty bound to bring Black Hand offenders to justice.[4] As a result, the two leading Sicilian organizations in Chicago held meetings to organize a crusade against Black Hand crime. The 1,400-member *Unione Siciliana*, the largest Sicilian society in Chicago, met on November 18, 1907, to endorse the White Hand effort. More than a thousand people attended the meeting. That same day, the 800-member *Societa Trinacria* met and endorsed the White Hand Society. The 250-member Italian Chamber of Commerce also lent its support to the effort.

Stephen A. Malato, attorney and former state legislator, condemned the acts of Black Hand criminals at the *Unione Siciliana* meeting, arguing, "As Sicily has given the largest contingent of these bands of rascals, it is our duty to wipe them out. There is no general organization of the Black Hand in Chicago, but there are small groups who are becoming bolder and unless we wish to have the experience of New York and New Orleans, they must be wiped out quickly. In the case of the notorious criminals who have fled from Italy, they must be sent back."[5] Malato's speech firmly established the position of the Italian community that the Black Hand was not an organized criminal society, a position that ran contrary to the picture of the Black Hand portrayed by the American press.

The White Hand believed that the press viewed Black Hand extortion as the activity of a single criminal organization because Black Hand criminals, in Italian communities throughout the country, used the same methods of extortion. Additionally, Black Hand criminals may have exchanged introductions and solicited financial contributions to help offenders in need. The result was not a vast organization but a casual bond established by mutual interest and by virtue of the fact that one became the accomplice of the other when needed. The Black Hand existed as a type of crime, and though it was not an organized society, there was often cooperation among those who engaged in Black Hand crime.[6]

To supervise the activities of the White Hand Society, Chicago's Italians organized an executive committee composed of local bankers, merchants, lawyers, and physicians. Among them were Stephen Malato, Pasquale Schiavone, Camillo Volini, Joseph Mirabella, and Guido Sabetta. The White Hand established its headquarters in the Masonic Temple Building in downtown Chicago next to the offices of the Italian consulate and the Italian Chamber of Commerce. The society announced that it would secretly receive information about the activities of Black Hand criminals and that it would provide protection to all those threatened with Black Hand extortion. A fund of $10,000 was set up to begin the work. Dr. Camillo Volini began the subscription drive with a donation of $250. The money was to be used to hire private investigators, attorneys, and interpreters to assist the police in arresting and prosecuting Black Hand criminals.[7]

Within a day, Chicago's Italians reported nearly twenty cases of Black Hand extortion to the White Hand Society. Stephen Malato was so sure of the success of the White Hand that he announced that they would end Black Hand crime within a month. In addition, the White Hand formed a committee of 100 local Italians to call on Chicago's mayor, the state's attorney, the Chicago postmaster, the U.S. attorney, and the head of the Secret Service to enlist their support in the White Hand effort.[8]

Two days after opening its doors, the White Hand Society announced that it knew the identities of the leaders of the more than fifty Black Hand criminals who were operating in Chicago.[9] Surprisingly, the White Hand believed that many were minor politicians who were under the impression that they had the protection of city and county authorities. The White Hand also believed that a half-dozen of the blackmailers were either ex-convicts or fugitives from justice in Italy. One of the first aims of the White Hand Society would be to ensure that these fugitives would be returned to Italy to serve out their sentences.

By the end of its the first week of operation, the White Hand Society had hired twenty local Italians to serve as White Hand investigators under the supervision of attorney Stephen Malato.[10] These new "secret agents" were local peddlers, clerks, and laborers. Only Malato and two other members of the White Hand knew the identities of the "White Hand Police," as they were called. Their first assignment was to watch the movements of the eleven suspected leaders of Chicago's four Black Hand gangs. So strong was the support of the Italian community for the White Hand effort that nearly 500 local Italians applied to become investigators for the White Hand Society.

On November 23, 1907, the White Hand Society placed the following notice in *La Tribuna Italiana*, a local Italian-language newspaper, concerning Black Hand crime:

1. We publicly notify all persons who send extortion letters to stop such nefarious proceedings for the good of the Italian name.
2. We beg the public in general and the press of Chicago particularly to refrain from blaming the Sicilians for such deeds.
3. We beg the public and the American press to cease mentioning the "Black Hand Society," because no organization of that kind exists in America or in Italy.[11]

It is doubtful that the White Hand Society really expected Black Hand criminals to cease their activities, but the organization hoped that the press and the public alike would recognize that Sicilian criminals were not the only ones committing Black Hand crime. The White Hand also hoped that the press would use more discretion in reporting Black Hand extortion. Few paid attention to the White Hand's argument that there was no Black Hand organization in Chicago. Soon every crime in the Italian community, involving extortion or not, was attributed to the Black Hand. It appears that federal authorities also failed to understand the nature of Black Hand crime. Although there had been an increasing number of Black Hand demands sent through the U.S. mail, James Stuart, the chief postal inspector in Chicago, announced that he attached no importance to the letters, regarding them either as jokes or as feeble attempts at blackmailing the recipients.[12]

Seven weeks after the White Hand was established, it announced that it had driven ten of Chicago's most dangerous Black Hand criminals out of the city.[13] Dr. Camillo Volini explained their success by telling how his agents kept track of suspected Black Hand offenders. When the White Hand identified an offender, they let it be known that he was not safe in Chicago. If the suspect offender left the city, thinking it would be safe for him to operate somewhere else, the White Hand sent his record to the authorities in his new place of residence. Volini said the White Hand would not rest until the offender returned to an honest life. Because of the actions of the White Hand Society, word was received that Black Hand criminals intended to "lie low" for a time in the hope that the White Hand campaign would blow over.

Although they believed that they had the Black Hand on the run, the White Hand thought it important to continue to be vigilant against Black Hand crime.[14] As a result, they hired a former detective for the Italian secretary of state in Rome to act as an operating director of the White Hand Society. Volini and the other members of the executive committee had businesses to manage, and it was difficult for them to involve themselves in the daily activities of the organization. The new official, Godfrey Trivisonno, described as an "Italian Sherlock Homes," was also responsible for meeting with the Italian fraternal societies. He gave lectures on how to detect the passwords used by Black Hand criminals, how to keep secret the fact that you had discovered a Black Hand member, and how to reveal the information about Black Hand crime to the White Hand Society without exposing yourself or your family to retribution.

The White Hand Society filed the following articles of incorporation in the State of Illinois on December 6, 1907:

1. There is founded in Chicago, and incorporated according to the laws of the state, an association called "The White Hand," which responds to the need of action, for the peace of the colony and for the good name of Italians, against certain forms of crime.
2. Its purpose is in a special manner:
   a) To cooperate with the duly constituted authorities by proper and lawful means, to paralyze and eradicate individual and organized crime which exists in the midst of the Italian colony, forcing it to submit to threats and violence.
   b) To remove from the atmosphere the burden of mystery and terror.
   c) To rid public opinion in America of its preconceived notions and prejudices, reestablishing the truth concerning Italy and the Italians, frequently misrepresented by incorrect reports, and by interests not openly avowed.
3. The White Hand makes use of the following means, to pursue the above-mentioned goals:

a) The analysis of the conditions within the Italian community that have made possible this peculiar form of organized crime.
b) Involvement in the legislative process in order to prevent and repress the previously mentioned form of crime.
c) Informing the police of people recognized as being capable of criminal behavior and the locales needing special surveillance.
d) Requesting information from Italian authorities about newcomers whose lifestyles and social connections may raise reasonable suspicion.
e) Providing legal counsel to assist in criminal prosecutions in order to ensure that the real nature of the motive is uncovered and to gather information that would assist the purposes of the White Hand.
f) Promoting cooperation with the police in those cases where such cooperation was necessary for the successful outcome of the judicial verdict.
g) Providing swift and efficient assistance to victims who cooperate with the White Hand Society.
h) Promoting the use of all means and measures to encourage our fellow countrymen to resist the menaces of criminals.
i) Promoting communication with the press in order to ensure truthful and accurate reporting about criminal activity carried out by Italians or ascribed to them.
j) Promoting and encouraging pride in being Italian.
k) Providing the Italian community and the public at large with news and information regarding the existence and activities of the White Hand Society.[15]

So successful was the initial work of the White Hand Society that it received national and international attention. In New York City, the Italian community began a similar organization. Led by Frank Frugone, the editor of the Italian newspaper *Bolletino della Sera*, over 300 New York Italians enrolled as members of the Italian Vigilance Protective Association, whose purpose was to protest against Black Hand crime. In Washington, D.C., Baron Mayor Des Planches, the Italian ambassador to the United States, also endorsed the work of the White Hand, as did the Italian minister of foreign affairs in Rome. The director of the National Liberal Immigration League wrote in a letter to the White Hand Society that such action by the Italian community was the best way to wipe out the slander that the Black Hand had brought upon the Italian name. White Hand members hoped that this recognition would lead to a nationwide effort, headquartered in Chicago, to rid the country of Black Hand crime.[16]

The success of the White Hand also became apparent when the "su-

preme council" of the Black Hand sent Camillo Volini the following
letter notifying him that he must die:

> Dr. C. Volini
> 382 South Halsted street:
> The supreme council of the Black Hand has voted that you must die.
> You have not heeded our warnings in the past, but you must heed this.
> Your killing has been assigned and the man waits for you. He must do
> his duty. Prepare yourself for death. We will kill your body, but we do
> not want to kill your soul.[17]

The threats did not deter Volini, who the *Chicago Daily Tribune* described as a "big, practical looking physician, with a keen zest for life."
Volini responded that he was not afraid and it would take a brave man to
attack him; even if the Black Hand did kill him, the cause was a good one,
and it would go on without him. Although steadfast in his beliefs, Volini
had stopped making night calls and, as a result, his medical practice had
dwindled. In addition, he was suspicious of every visitor who came to his
office. He only allowed those whom he recognized past the clerk. He also
carried a revolver, and his friends guarded him when he traveled.

Volini was no stranger to conflict. He had served in the Italian Navy
during the Italian-Abyssinian war, and his volunteer efforts during the
1886 cholera epidemic in Venice earned him a medal from that grateful city. During his early years in Chicago, his horse and buggy were a
familiar sight as he traveled over the rutted streets of the city to visit
patients. His office was crowded with those who could pay for his services and those who could not. Volini also opened a drug store at Taylor
and Halsted streets and worked tirelessly with Jane Addams at nearby
Hull House. With the support of Addams, Volini led an effort to enlist
Italian-speaking probation officers to supervise Italian youth under the
jurisdiction of the juvenile court. Volini's favorite counsel to his friends
and patients was, "Be a good citizen, be industrious, and give your children an education."[18]

Black Hand criminals challenged the initial success of the White
Hand Society when they murdered Joseph Concillo in the rear of his home
on Gault Court in Little Sicily. Concillo's murder climaxed a blackmailing campaign directed at the wealthier residents of the district. Those
targeted included Dr. Antonio Lagorio, undertaker Antonio Sbarbaro,
and cigar manufacturer Mariano Zagone. Although Black Hand criminals had committed several bombings and had fired shots through the
windows of their victim's homes, the killing of Concillo was the first
murder associated with the blackmailing campaign. The gravity of the

Concillo murder attracted the interest of the White Hand. Not only did the society assist in the investigation, but it offered a $300 reward for information leading to the arrest of the killer.

The rising number of blackmailing cases led to the permanent assignment of two Italian American police officers to Black Hand crime. Detectives Gabriel Longobardi and Julian Bernacchi were assigned to Assistant Police Chief Herman Schuettler's office to work on crime in Chicago's Italian community. Detective Longobardi, born in Naples, had been a member of the department since 1906. He had immigrated to Chicago after serving in the Italian army and worked as a real estate agent until joining the police department. He was originally assigned to the Maxwell Street district, where his acquaintance with the residents of the Near West Side allowed him to successfully conduct a number of important investigations and win promotion to detective. Schuettler described Longobardi as a "first class man," and commented that the Chicago Police Department needed more men like him. Detective Bernacchi also joined the department in 1906, and, like Longobardi, he had investigated a number of important crimes in the Italian community.[19]

Detectives Longobardi and Bernacchi raided the home of Black Hand suspect George Morici in Little Sicily in February 1908. Recovered in the raid were a box of rubber stamps and a bottle of red ink. The find was particularly significant because many of the letters sent under the name of the Black Hand contained a skull and crossbones printed with rubber stamps. The rubber stamps and red ink found at the Morici home directly connected him to the Concillo murder. Concillo had received a threatening letter that bore a red stamp. Although he was a young man of small means, his uncle, Guiseppi Bruiscato, was well off, and the blackmailers intended that Concillo get the $300 from him. Black Hand criminals had demanded money from Bruiscato and dynamited his home the previous summer. The murder was believed to have occurred after Morici's accomplice, Giovanni Scardini, observed Concillo in Sarciti's Saloon at 66 Milton Avenue. From witnesses, police learned that Concillo had entered the saloon half an hour before he was killed. When Concillo saw Scardini, he turned on his heels and left the saloon by the rear entrance. Police were unable to determine whether Scardini had left the bar immediately after him. When questioned by the police, all who were present responded that they knew nothing. Refusing to provide information to the authorities was common. People were afraid to cooperate with the police for fear of retaliation.[20]

Police also implicated Morici in a number of other Black Hand crimes. George Gundura, who also lived on Gault Court, received several threatening letters, each bearing a red stamp. One of the letters contained a demand for $500 and was signed with a drawing of crossbones. Morici had gone to Gondura's home and demanded $300 to settle the extortion demand. Gondura refused to give Morici the money, and the meeting ended in a brawl. In another case, Lucian Tomaselli, a wine merchant at 111 Gault Court, received a Black Hand letter demanding $500 and threatening to kill his children if he failed to pay. Two days after Tomaselli received the letter, Morici appeared at his home in the company of Giovanni Scardina. Morici was told about the threatening letter and agreed to look into the matter for Tomaselli. He returned later and told Tomaselli that he could settle the matter for $300. The next night, three shots were fired at the Tomaselli home. Because of the shooting incident, Tomaselli's wife went to Morici and begged him on her knees not to harm her family. His reply was, "You must pay $300 or I'll do what I must do."[21]

Morici was eventually tried for murder and several bombings near Gault and Oak streets in Little Sicily. Three months later, a jury in Judge Windes' court returned a guilty verdict against Morici for his part in these crimes.[22] Morici's conviction was thought to be the first ever obtained in a Black Hand case in Chicago. The conviction of Morici was so important that the members of the White Hand Society predicted the end of Black Hand extortion in Chicago. Stephen Malato, who aided the state in securing the conviction of Morici, announced that the guilty finding would serve as a lesson to all Black Hand criminals who had threatened the lives of Chicago's Italians. He hoped that Morici's conviction would also teach them that they were living in a civilized society that would not permit these crimes to go unpunished.

During the course of the Morici investigation, Archie Guerin received a Black Hand threat decorated with drawings of several skulls and crossbones. Archie Guerin was the brother of Webster Guerin, whom Dora McDonald had murdered the year before. Dora was the wife of Mike McDonald, "boss gambler" and Chicago Democratic Party heavyweight. McDonald headed an organization of saloon and gambling interests known as "Mike McDonald's Democrats." They had elected their own candidate, Harvey Colvin, as mayor of Chicago in 1873. With Colvin in office, McDonald organized the first criminal syndicate in Chicago composed of gamblers and compliant politicians. It is important to note that McDonald's activities firmly establish that syndicated or organized crime existed in Chicago prior to the alleged arrival of the Mafia, Camorra, or Black Hand.[23]

Although the arrest of George Morici proved that the White Hand Society and the Chicago police were making progress against Black Hand crime, there were as many as thirty other Black Hand criminals still operating in the city. Then in April 1908, Stephen Malato received an anonymous letter that provided the names of seventeen active Black Hand criminals and detailed information about their crimes. Many were the same people who had already come to the attention of the police and the White Hand Society. Most of the Black Hand suspects were small tradesmen and laborers. Camillo Volini turned the list over to Assistant Police Chief Schuettler for investigation. What the police learned from the letter was that the guilty persons were often "grafters" who attacked their own friends and acquaintances. The letter also confirmed police suspicions that the worldly "friend" who happened along and arranged for the terms of the extortion settlement, in so many Black Hand crimes, was really part of the extortion scheme.[24]

While the police were calling for a grand jury investigation of the information received by Malato, Black Hand criminals threatened to abduct the eleven-year-old son of Antonio Lumia, a jeweler and watchmaker in Little Sicily. The blackmailers instructed Lumia to deliver $800 to the area of Halsted and Hooker streets the following Thursday night to prevent the kidnapping. Lumia told the police that he did not suspect anyone in particular, but a number of suspicious-looking men had been in his store on several occasions. Working with Chicago police, Lumia delivered a dummy package to the designated location, but no one retrieved it. A few days latter, Black Hand criminals sent another letter to Lumia warning him that any further attempt to betray the plot would end in his death. Still defiant, Lumia turned the letter over to the police. Not long after, his antagonists discharged two loads of buckshot into his jewelry store. Lumia, who had been sleeping in the shop, returned the gunfire, shooting a dozen bullets at the assailants.[25]

One week later, detectives observed a man loitering in the doorway of the Lumia home. Knowing that Lumia had been the target of Black Hand extortion, the officers attempted to question the man. Seeing the approach of the officers, the man, Joseph Lapaglia, fled. The police apprehended him after a short chase and found a small bottle of nitroglycerin that they believed was to be used to bomb the Lumia home. Newspaper headlines attributed the Lumia extortion attempt to the Black Hand. Apparently frustrated by the headlines, Detective Bernacchi told the press that he had worked on hundreds of these cases and was positive that the robbers were friends of the victims who acted as go-betweens to pass the extortion money to a mythical third party. The truth was, "There is no Black Hand in Chicago."[26]

In spite of the success of the White Hand Society and Chicago's Italian detectives, an editorial appearing in the *Chicago Record-Herald* noted that extortion letters were still appearing in the homes of prominent and wealthy families, especially in the Italian community.[27] The solution, the newspaper argued, was continued pressure by the White Hand Society and the assignment of Italian detectives and "secret service" men to the investigation of Black Hand crime. In what the Italian community must have viewed with relief, the editorial argued that Black Hand criminals were not part of an organized criminal conspiracy. They were, rather, members of small gangs who lacked the organization or means of executing their terrorist threats, and some of the extortion letters were even of "crank" origin. Nevertheless, the editorial concluded that the occasional kidnapping, explosion, or assault was a reminder that the people of Chicago should not take Black Hand crime lightly.

The crimes committed by Black Hand criminals were not only violent, but they created tremendous fear among Chicago's Italians. On April 25, 1908, a rumor spread through Little Sicily that Black Hand criminals would dynamite three local schools in retaliation for the determined efforts of the better class of Italians to do away with Black Hand crime.[28] Residents of the district allegedly had received a half-dozen letters threatening to blow up the Jenner Elementary School at Oak and Milton streets, the Adams Elementary School at Chicago and Townsend streets, and the Two Sisters School, an Italian-language school in the same area. At the Jenner school, twelve hundred panicked students fled into the streets following a report that three members of the Black Hand had placed a nitroglycerin bomb, set to explode at 2 o'clock in the afternoon, in the basement of the school building. School officials believed that the letters were the work of local hoodlums who were seen waiting outside of the building telling the pupils that an explosion would soon occur.

One month later, a similar incident occurred at the Near West Side Washburn School. A rumor circulated that twelve-year-old Abe Cohen had seen two tall men with "enormous black moustaches" creeping around the corner of the school.[29] The men had reportedly dug a great hole under the building and filled it with 500 pounds of dynamite, ready to be touched off if Principal Charles Thompson did not pay $2,000 to the Black Hand. The tale soon spread to nearby Garfield School, where a story circulated that four men had called on Principal James Walsh demanding $4,000. After Walsh refused their demands, the criminals allegedly placed a thousand pounds of dynamite in a hole that they had dug under the building in order to blow up the school that afternoon.

The next day, the panic spread to Jackson School. Principal Hedges blamed the bomb tales on an article that had recently appeared in an Italian-language newspaper describing a Black Hand threat against schoolchildren. The incident was repeated at Dante School a few days later when students spread the rumor that members of the Black Hand had prepared to dynamite the building. Residents near the school said that most of the children rushed panic-stricken into the street at 3 o'clock in the afternoon, although the school principal denied that this had occurred. Although Black Hand criminals could have started the rumors to further the terror inspired by the Black Hand name, it is more likely that the stories resulted from the rumors published in the Italian press.[30]

Fear of the Black Hand was so great that even the police began attributing almost every crime committed by an Italian or in the Italian community to the Black Hand. When six Sicilians attempted to abduct Giovannina Ognebene as she left work in downtown Chicago, police described the offenders as Black Hand bandits, even though the offense had nothing to do with Black Hand crime.[31] In fact, the incident was a case of "bride kidnapping" or "marriage by abduction," a common practice in southern Italy and Sicily. Typically, the kidnapping would occur, and, once the couple consummated the relationship, marriage became a necessity. One of the would-be Lotharios, Salvatore Forestiere, had known the Ognebene girl and had asked for her hand in marriage. When spurned by the girl's father, Forestiere enlisted the help of his friends to spirit her away. The plot ended when the driver of the carriage that the kidnappers had hired became suspicious and called the police. The fact that Sicilians had carried out the plot led the police to suspect Black Hand involvement.

Fear also allowed criminals to use the Black Hand name to further crimes that had nothing to do with Black Hand extortion. For instance, Mrs. J. B. Smith received a Black Hand letter demanding $1,000. Failure to pay, the letter threatened, would result in the dynamiting of her home and the murder of her daughter. Police believed that the letter was an attempt to force Smith to sell her property at Division and Townsend streets in Little Sicily.[32] In a similar incident, Joseph Telser was the victim of a bombing when a gallon jug filled with explosives and small stones exploded in the doorway of his saloon, also located in Little Sicily. Tesler suspected the Black Hand although he had not reported a Black Hand extortion attempt. He believed that a group of men who were trying to lease his saloon might have been involved in the bombing.

Not everyone feared Black Hand criminals. Not only did Chicago's Italians fight back through the efforts of the White Hand Society, but individual Italians also refused to pay Black Hand demands. The case of Sam Sapienza provides an important example. After receiving a number of Black Hand letters demanding $1,000, someone exploded a dynamite bomb under the front porch of his home in Streator, Illinois.[33] After arranging a meeting with Onafrio Puccio and Mike Rizzio, the suspect Black Hand offenders, Sapienza shot Puccio. Fleeing to Chicago, Puccio entered the German-American hospital and Rizzo went into hiding in Little Sicily. Police arrested both men after a neighbor, Antonio Accomando, informed them of the offenders' whereabouts.

In spite of the initial successes of the White Hand Society, the *Chicago Daily Tribune* announced in August 1908 that the White Hand was "practically dead." Through intimidation and bribery, Black Hand criminals were often able to suborn witnesses and corrupt government officials. Pardons also bore some degree of responsibility for the continuation of Black Hand crime and contributed to the audacity of Black Hand criminals. Those convicted of murderous conspiracies were often released after a few months at the insistence of "mysterious influences." For example, state officials released three of the five extortionists sent to the Joliet Penitentiary through the efforts of the White Hand Society after they had served only a portion of their sentences. In addition, the White Hand was bankrupt. It had spent all of the money that had been raised during the first burst of enthusiasm on investigations and other efforts to bring Black Hand criminals to justice. Unwilling to sacrifice large sums of money with uncertainty of success, the Italian business community dropped its financial support, forcing the White Hand Society to disband. Dr. Camillo Volini, the president of the White Hand, moved indefinitely to Montana with his family after increasingly ominous threats against his life. Stephen Malato, attorney for the society, left for Italy.[34]

Although started in the name of the Italian people of Chicago, the Italian community did not support the White Hand Society. In fact, the White Hand complained that the wealthy Italian community in Chicago poorly supported the one movement that sought to defend it against an alarming form of crime. The White Hand attributed this apathy to the fact that it had accepted money from the Italian fraternal societies, which was mostly the money of poor working people, to defend the lives and wealth of the prominent men of the community. For instance, the *Unione Siciliana* contributed $300 to the founding of the White Hand. *La Propaganda*, an Italian socialist weekly, also fueled criticism against the White Hand, arguing that the society benefited the rich at the expense of the poor. The newspaper wrote numerous attacks on the White Hand and expressed sympathy with the Black Hand as an organization composed of poor and wronged people. Additionally, it was argued that the organization, by its existence and use of the name "White Hand," validated the existence of the Black Hand, casting suspicion and discredit upon the Italian name.[35]

The White Hand Society failed just when police arrested a man who some hoped could reveal the inner workings of the Black Hand gangs operating in Chicago. Detectives Longobardi and Bernacchi arrested Vincent Crapa for the attempted extortion of Benedetto Cairo, a grocer on South Greenwood Avenue.[36] Cairo had received two threatening letters purporting to be from the Black Hand directing him to pay $1,000 under penalty of death. He ignored the first letter but took the second to the Chicago police. The letter instructed Cairo to take the money to a corn patch at Eighteenth Street and Cottage Grove Avenue. There a man with a red handkerchief would signal him to place the money in a cigar box under the wooden sidewalk. Longobardi and Bernacchi arrived half an hour before the appointed time and discovered Crapa concealed in a thicket with a loaded revolver in hand. Crapa, who the press described as a forty-four-year-old Sicilian with the "moustache of a brigand," asked the detectives to kill him because the Black Hand would take his life when they discovered that he had failed to collect the money.

Once safely locked away in the county jail, Crapa changed his story, denying any connection to the Black Hand.[37] Crapa, who had recently arrived in Chicago from New Orleans, said he knew nothing about the Black Hand and had been sleeping under a bush when arrested. Crapa's change of heart did not trouble the detectives, who doubted Crapa's connection to a Black Hand gang. After failing to identify Crapa's alleged confederates, they determined that he had worked alone. They also concluded that any individual with an extortion plan might use the Black Hand name because of the fear that it engendered.

Although Detectives Longobardi and Bernacchi were often successful in their efforts against Black Hand crime, the people of Chicago were generally unhappy with the way that the police department was handling the problem. An editorial in the *Chicago Record-Herald* argued that the city needed to take drastic measures to curb the menace of the Black Hand and that a large part of the problem was the inadequacy of police efforts against Black Hand criminals. The *Chicago Daily Tribune* expanded on this theme, arguing that police forces in the United States were far smaller than would be required in Europe to control the large body of Italian immigrants. In Chicago and other American cities, the newspaper argued, police were accustomed to leaving Italians to their own devices owing to their ignorance of the customs of the Italian people and the Italians' habit of segregating themselves from other nationalities.

In fact, the police often left the supervision of Italians in the big cities of the United States to a few officers of Italian birth. In spite of this lack of supervision, the number of crimes committed by the Italian immigrant was relatively small, and the crimes that did occur were largely restricted to offenses against people of their own nationality. Considering that Italian crime, especially crime against non-Italians, was extremely rare and considering the part that Italians had played in the economic development of the United States, the *Tribune* concluded that Italians did not deserve the criticism heaped upon them in sensational news stories in connection with fanciful Black Hand crime.[38]

Less than a month after its demise, there was an attempt to revive the White Hand Society. In September 1908, Black Hand criminals kidnapped seven-year-old Giuseppe Guinta after his father, Antonio, did not react to several extortion demands. Six weeks earlier, the senior Guinta had received three letters in quick succession demanding that he place $500 under a railroad crossing near Little Sicily. After he reported the threats to the police, detectives secreted themselves at the viaduct but found no trace of the blackmailers. Then Giuseppe mysteriously disappeared from the front of his home where he was playing. Aroused by the return of Dr. Volini from Montana, the members of the White Hand met to confront this latest outrage.[39]

One week after the boy's disappearance, his father received a letter demanding a ransom of $10,000. The father was to give the money to his best friend and, when delivered, Black Hand criminals would release the boy. The blackmailers signed the letter with three crosses and suggested that harm would come to Giuseppe if his father did not pay the money. Unable to raise such a large sum and in spite of the efforts of the White Hand Society, the family had given the boy up for dead. After an absence of nearly four weeks, police found Giuseppe wandering about a railroad station in downtown Chicago.[40] The thongs used to bind his hands had left his right wrist and two of his fingers badly bruised, but he was otherwise unharmed. Police questioned the boy at a local police station and again later at home, but nothing of value could be determined about his abduction. Police believed that the kidnappers concluded that they had little chance of getting the ransom and finally released the child.

Although he had returned, Dr. Volini refused the presidency of the White Hand, stating that business and professional reasons prevented him from giving the society the time required for the leadership of the organization. The membership elected another physician, Dr. Joseph Damiani, to take his place. Their next order of business was to draft a letter demanding increased police protection for the Italian residents of

Chicago. There were only three Italians on the police force at the time, in spite of the fact that there were over 200,000 Italians living in the city. The White Hand hoped to convince Mayor Fred Busse and the city council to hire more Italian American police officers and to form a "Black Hand Squad" of Italian officers to fight Black Hand crime. The White Hand also organized a committee to visit Chicago's mayor and urge him to appoint the new police force. The committee included Camillo Volini, Joseph Damiani, Godfrey Trivisonno, and Stephen Malato, who had recently returned from Italy. The group believed that the typical police officer, usually of Irish birth or extraction, was powerless to handle the situation; in order to suppress Black Hand crime, the city needed to hire police officers who spoke and understood the Italian language.[41]

Even the press, which was often critical of Italians in general, supported the White Hand's proposal to hire Italian American police officers.[42] In an editorial appearing in September 1908, the *Chicago Daily Tribune* argued that the respectable Italians of Chicago were justified when they asked for more men of their nationality on the police force. Not only did the *Tribune* agree that there should be more Italian police officers, but thought the officers should be of Sicilian or Neapolitan descent, because it was from the south of Italy that many of the blackmailers came. The *Tribune* added, however, that the value of a detective was often lost when his identity became known. In New York, Black Hand Squad detectives were the best-known Italian police officers in the city, making it impossible for them to spy on Black Hand criminals. To solve the problem, Chicago needed undercover auxiliary officers who could slip quietly into Black Hand circles and get the evidence needed to break up the various gangs of criminals. In short, Chicago needed a small "secret service" squad of Italian operatives, such as those enlisted by the White Hand, as well as Italian police officers and detectives.

The idea of hiring undercover agents to work among Black Hand criminals was not unusual. Police detectives during this time typically worked among the criminal element. Police believed that investigative work was a clandestine activity and that the identities of detectives should remain unknown. Detectives often wore disguises and "shadowed" suspects in the hope of catching them in the act of committing a crime. In fact, Chicago detectives sold a trunk of disguises to the Denver Police in 1879 because the crooks in Chicago were "on to them." Unlike detectives of today who investigate reported crimes, detectives at that time in history were primarily concerned with looking for suspicious behavior and monitoring known criminals.[43]

One of the reasons repeatedly cited by the city for failing to hire Italian American police officers was that Italians generally could not meet the police department's height requirement. Frustrated by this obstacle, Dr. Volini responded that Black Hand crime had created a crisis in the Italian community and that the size of the man had nothing to do with his skill in ferreting out criminals. He believed that a dozen intelligent Italian police officers, even though short in stature, were worth a thousand ordinary American police officers when it came to discovering Black Hand criminals.[44]

Some believed that local authorities were slow to react to Black Hand crime because Black Hand criminals confined their activities to the Italian community. Although there is ample evidence that some members of the force were concerned about Black Hand crime, there are examples of the police doing less than a professional job when it came to investigating Italian crime. Take the example of Tony Tavolocci, a grocer in the Near North Side. Tavolocci received a blackmail letter demanding $500 in July 1909. Having no enemies, he immediately suspected Black Hand extortion and reported the incident to the Chicago police. When a second letter came, followed by two gunshots through the front window of his store, he again reported the extortion attempt to the police department. The blackmailers signed the second letter "La Mano Nera" (the Black Hand), which left no doubt in Tavolocci's mind that Black Hand criminals were involved. However, the police never investigated his complaint. An inquiry by the *Chicago Record-Herald* failed to identify anyone at the police department who was familiar with the case. Because of the press inquiry, police finally assigned a number of detectives to the investigation. The blackmailers then exploded a bomb in front of Tavolocci's store, wrecking the display windows. Even after the explosion, police were slow to respond, taking over half an hour to get an officer to the scene. Police eventually arrested several suspects but failed to charge anyone with the crime.[45]

The fact that the White Hand enjoyed prominent influence in the Italian community, both nationally and internationally, yet had difficulty accomplishing its agenda at the local government level, supports the argument that city officials paid little attention to crime in the Italian community. The king of Italy made Volini a chevalier (the lowest order of nobility) for his efforts in forming the White Hand Society, but Volini had little access to Chicago's city hall. Part of the reason for the failure of the White Hand Society was the absence of political power within the Italian community. Although there had been three Italian city council members before 1913, the Italian community in Chicago did not have a powerful representative. In fact, as late as 1921, Irish machine politicians controlled all three of the large Italian communities on the north, west, and south sides of Chicago.[46]

Stephen Malato further demonstrated the apathy of city government: he placed Black Hand crime on the agenda of a conference on Italian immigration that was to meet in Italy in October 1908, but he could not gain access to Chicago officials to talk about the Black Hand problem. When asked about the White Hand Society by the press, Mayor Busse responded that he did not know much about the White Hand movement, but he was sure the police would give them whatever assistance they needed.[47]

Since its inception, the White Hand Society had been preparing a study of Black Hand crime in Chicago. Published in September 1908 and written in English and Italian, the study was the first authoritative attempt to explain Black Hand crime. Titled *Studies, Action and Results*, this twenty-seven-page document had six sections:

1. *Black Hand*
   The Black Hand was a "signature" or method of extortion that often involved the use of threatening letters.
2. *Is the Black Hand Really an Organized Society of Malefactors?*
   The Black Hand was not a vast criminal organization; small groups of independent criminals committed Black Hand crime, and some of these groups were composed of offenders who had left Italy to escape the Italian police.
3. *Favorable Conditions and Environment*
   Black Hand crime occurred only in communities that exhibited certain social conditions.
4. *The Criminals' Methods*
   Black Hand letters escalated in their threats in order to intimidate the victim, and someone known to the victim, a "friend," was often involved in the extortion scheme. Additionally, Black Hand criminals used acts of violence such as breaking a window, firing a revolver in the dark, or placing a small bomb under a stairway to demonstrate the seriousness of the threat.
5. *Effects*
   Black Hand crime had a detrimental effect on the Italian community. Not only had it led to widespread fear, which kindled feelings of hatred and vengeance, it also led to a profound distrust of the American government because of the failure to control it.
6. *The White Hand*
   The White Hand Society argued that the press's unfair portrayal of Black Hand crime caused native Americans to discriminate against Italian immigrants.[48]

The White Hand Society's belief that the press's portrayal of Black Hand crime caused prejudice against Italian immigrants was demon-

strated when a young American man in Evanston, Illinois, began sending extortion demands to prominent men in Chicago. The members of
the press immediately attributed the crimes to Italian criminals and the
Black Hand. Further investigation revealed, however, that Italian criminals were not involved in the scheme. The Italian-language newspaper *La
Lotta* used the occasion to point out that "ignorance, narrow-mindedness,
and race prejudice" characterized the relationship between the American
press and the Italian community.[49]

The incident came to the attention of postal authorities in 1908
when an undisclosed citizen brought a mysterious package to the post
office.[50] The citizen at first believed that the package contained a bomb
and stood at a respectful distance as postal inspectors opened the parcel. The contents proved to be a quantity of small bones, some pieces
of iron, and a note worded similarly to recent Black Hand missives.
It was signed, "Knights of the White Death." City physicians declared
that the bones came from the foot of a body that had been interred for
several years. As a result, Postal Inspector Stuart put his staff on watch
for similar parcels. The next day, postal authorities intercepted a package addressed in the same hand to Assistant Police Chief Schuettler. It
was found to contain an assortment of human finger joints, hardware,
and an extortion demand illustrated with crude drawings of a skull and
crossbones, daggers, and bombs. William O. Waters, rector of the Grace
Episcopal Church, received a similar package. It also contained bones,
old metal, and an extortion letter. The letter was written in red ink and
had the crossbones and dagger decorations. When he learned that postal
authorities had intercepted a package directed to him, Chief Schuettler
responded that there was no need to hold up his mail and that he could
take care of himself better than post office officials.

The investigation of the Knights of the White Death conducted by
Inspector Stuart and his agents was remarkable. One of the first clues
observed by Stuart was the fact that the would-be extortionist made no
effort to disguise his handwriting.[51] It was a peculiar, vertical style and
had the characteristics of a child's penmanship, which led the inspector
to conclude that a school pupil had written the letters. Inspector Stuart
found that the same vertical writing style had been taught in local schools
until five years earlier. With this clue in hand, investigators visited more
than 100 public and parochial schools and inspected the examination
papers of pupils from that period. Finally, one paper was uncovered with
handwriting that was almost identical to the Knights of the White Death
letters. The paper belonged to Evanston resident William Pollard, now
twenty-two years of age.

Pollard was arrested, at the direction of Stuart, by Evanston detective Arthur Johnson on charges of violating quarantine.[52] Two of Pollard's sisters were ill with scarlet fever, and Pollard had persisted in appearing in public instead of remaining at home as required by law. At the station, Evanston police asked Pollard to provide a written statement that he was never notified by the health department of the quarantine regulation. Inspector Stuart then compared the statement to the blackmail letters. The handwriting was identical. When confronted with the letters, Pollard admitted their authorship. He confessed to having written to Reverend Waters and Chief Schuettler as well as Reverend A. C. Dixon of the Moody Church, Reverend D. F. Roberts of Quinn Chapel, and Dr. Adolph Ghermann.

Pollard expressed an unusual motive for his crimes. Scoffing at the Sherlock Holmes variety of detective stories, Pollard said that he wrote the letters in order to demonstrate that all the logic in the world would not reveal a criminal who never talked about his crimes.[53] The detectives would not be able solve the mystery if he kept still, he told investigators. Pollard had read some of the stories written by Arthur Conan Doyle and believed that if a man worked alone and did not tell anyone what he had done, no detective could catch him. He never expected to get any money out of his scheme and never went near the places where he had ordered the money left. He collected the newspaper reports of the crimes and laughed when he read how the police worked. Pollard obtained the bones and coffin handles that accompanied some of the letters at Calvary Cemetery in Evanston, where Pollard's deceased father had been the sexton for nearly twenty-five years. Pollard said that he had found the bones and coffin handles in the scattered sand where new graves had been dug. They had been thrown there by the grave diggers and left lying on the ground. Pollard was completely surprised when the police arrested him and did not understand how they had discovered his identity.

Four months after the Knights of the White Death episode, Dr. Peter Cutrera of the White Hand Society became the target of Black Hand extortion. After sending Cutrera a number of extortion letters, Vincenzo Geraci called on Cutera at his office and demanded that the physician pay him $3,000.[54] Cutrera immediately notified Assistant Chief Schuettler, who assigned Longobardi and Bernacchi to the case. The next morning, Geraci called again and told Emanuel Cutrera, Peter's brother, that the money would have to be paid or he would kill the doctor. Again he was put off, but he loitered in the neighborhood until he saw Dr. Cutrera return. Brandishing a razor, Geraci confronted Cutrera and renewed his demand for $3,000. Geraci told Cutrera that he had been targeted because he was a member of the White Hand Society and that any effort at deceit would end badly. Trying to delay the blackmailer, Cutrera asked Geraci to accompany him to a bank to withdraw the requested sum. On their way down Milwaukee Avenue, they met Detectives Longobardi and Bernacchi, who took Geraci into custody. Cutrera believed that Geraci was a leading Black Hand criminal and that the Black Hand had sent Geraci on a special mission to kill him because of his involvement with the White Hand Society. Police did not agree. Although they believed that Geraci meant to kill Cutrera if the money was not paid, they were not convinced that he was a leader of the Black Hand. Cutrera had known Geraci in Sicily thirteen years earlier. As a result, the Italian detectives were more inclined to believe that Geraci was down-and-out and had attempted to bluff his old acquaintance into giving him the money.

The same month as the Geraci incident, Detectives Longobardi and Bernacchi arrested Isadore Carlino for attempting to extort $6,000 from Joseph Macaluso, a steamship and labor agent on South Clark Street. Macaluso had been receiving Black Hand letters for several months advising him to pay different sums of money to different strangers. The letters threatened death and destruction unless the money was forthcoming. Macaluso refused to be intimidated and informed the police of the extortion attempts. After he disregarded the Black Hand demands, a bomb was exploded in the hallway of his home. One of the Black Hand letters named Isadore Carlino, a friend of Macaluso, as a "mutual friend" who could intercede with the Black Hand on behalf of the hapless victim.[55]

Macaluso sent for Carlino on the advice of Detectives Longobardi and Bernacchi. Carlino advised Macaluso to pay the money and agreed to accept it on behalf of the Black Hand. Macaluso received a telephone message instructing him to go to his bank, withdraw $6,000, and stand in the front door until a stranger approached and requested the money. Following police instructions, Macaluso went to the bank as directed but only withdrew $360 in small bills. No one appeared to claim the money. When Macaluso returned to his office, however, he found Carlino waiting. Carlino accepted the money on behalf of the extortionists and walked north on Clark Street, where he was arrested by Longobardi and Bernacchi. The Macaluso case again highlighted the fact that the "mutual friend" was part of the blackmailing scheme.[56]

The next day, banker Pasquale Schiavone was again the victim of an extortion attempt. Schiavone was a member of the White Hand's executive committee and was one of the businessmen whose victimization had led to the establishment of the White Hand Society. In fact, the original extortion attempt against Schiavone led to one of the White Hand Society's earliest victories. Police arrested Salvatore Dellacav for attempting to extort $5,000 from Schiavone based upon evidence provided by the White Hand Society. The newest extortion attempt involved a demand for $2,000. After consulting with the police, Schiavone agreed to put $2,000 in bogus money in a window of the Goodrich school as instructed by the extortionists. Two Jewish men were arrested as they retrieved the money: Samuel Berkson, a forty-year-old peddler, and seventeen-year-old Jacob Robinowitz. Both were released by Maxwell Street police after Schiavone refused to prosecute the case.[57]

The growing number of Black Hand crimes led to increased action on the part of the Chicago police. Chief Schuettler, determined to put an end to the crime wave, announced that he would assign every man in the police department, if necessary, to investigate Black Hand crime. He cautioned, however, that not all Black Hand crimes were bona fide attempts at extortion. In fact, he believed that the victims themselves sometimes wrote the letters in an effort to gain notoriety or place some acquaintance in an embarrassing position. Although the number of fraudulent Black Hand cases was probably very small, Italian attorney Bernard Barasa provided a notable example of a fake Black Hand case. An Italian merchant doing business in one of the outlying sections of the city was not prospering and he could not afford to advertise. One day he received a Black Hand letter. Upon investigation, it was found that the businessman had written the letter and gone to another part of the city and mailed it to himself. The next day he was at police headquarters telling a terrible story of extortion. He received several thousand dollars' worth of free advertising when his story was published in the newspapers.[58]

Chief Schuettler, in spite of his doubts about the authenticity of some Black Hand crimes, believed that heavy terms of imprisonment would discourage Black Hand criminals. He also traced the recent increase in Black Hand crime to a December 1908 earthquake in Sicily and southern Italy, which he believed had caused a number of Italian criminals to migrate to the United States. Chicago police were openly wondering whether the Italians who had fled to the United States caused the recent wave of extortions. Accompanying Chief Schuettler's statement was an editorial in the *Chicago Daily Tribune* attributing Black Hand crime to the desire of one or more Italian criminals to extort money from prosperous, law abiding fellow countrymen. The editorial warned that although in the past the blackmailers had preyed on their own kind, it was only a matter of time before they extended their operations to others unless the police adopted the appropriate measures to stop them. What Chicago needed, the newspaper argued, were detectives who understood Italian criminals and could spy on them, gain their confidence, and inform on them after their plans had matured but before they carried them out. The city needed preventive detective work, no matter the cost.[59]

The seriousness of Black Hand crime was highlighted in May 1909 when Black Hand criminals attacked Detective Longobardi in the doorway of his home at 116 Bunker Street. Longobardi, who the press referred to as the "Petrosino of Chicago," after famed New York Black Hand Squad officer Joseph Petrosino, had gained a reputation for his effectiveness against Black Hand criminals. Looking out of his kitchen window, Longobardi saw two men prowling around the alley at the rear of his home. When Longobardi confronted the men, one of them attacked Longobardi with a stiletto knife, striking him on the left wrist. Longobardi wrestled the knife from the offender and was about to overpower him when the second offender landed a hard blow behind the detective's ear, rendering him unconscious. Longobardi was found by neighbors some minutes later in the doorway of his home, still clutching the knife that he had he taken from one of the assailants. Dr. Peter Cutrera of the White Hand Society was summoned to attend to Detective Longobardi's wounds. Ignoring Cutrera's advice, Longobardi immediately set out in search of the offenders.[60]

The attack on Longobardi was no doubt related to his efforts against Black Hand criminals. Longobardi and his partner, Julian Bernachi, had been extremely active in investigating Black Hand crime in the Italian community. Assistant Chief Schuettler personally supervised the investigation of the attack on Longobardi. The March 14 murder of Lieutenant Petrosino was fresh in his memory. More than a score of detectives searched for Longobardi's assailants. Detective Longobardi, with his head and chest swathed in bandages, aided in the search. Schuettler announced that the attack would inaugurate a campaign to drive every Black Hand criminal out of Chicago and that he would take no chance of having the Petrosino murder duplicated in his city.[61]

It later came out that Longobardi had been under sentence of death by Black Hand extortionists because of his arrest of Giuseppe Bertucci for the murder of John Umbrello. Vincenzo Geraci provided the information regarding the plot against Longobardi. Geraci had been in the same cell as Bertucci while Geraci was awaiting trial in the Cook County Jail for having attempted to extort $3,000 from Dr. Peter Cutrera. The plot against Longobardi's life was outlined in two letters written by Geraci to the detective. In his first letter, Geraci stated that Bertucci had told him that his friends were plotting to help him escape from the jail, and that he planned to kill Longobardi as soon as he regained his freedom. Bertucci also told Geraci that he had concealed a knife and a bottle of acid to aid his planned escape. A search of his cell, however, failed to uncover any trace of the knife or the acid. In his second letter, Geraci told Longobardi that a "secret society" had ordered his death and he warned him to be on his guard. Whether the information furnished by Geraci was true or he was merely making a play for leniency was never determined. Police viewed the warning with some concern, however, in light of the recent assault on Detective Longobardi.[62]

One month later, Longobardi received another letter from a county jail inmate concerning Black Hand extortion. Nineteen-year-old Antonio Baffa wrote Longobardi asking for his help. Police had arrested Baffa in April 1909 for the murder of grocer Giuseppe Fillipelli. Baffa killed Fillipelli in the presence of his wife and baby boy in front of their grocery at 7737 South Greenwood Avenue. Fillipelli had left his store with his two-year-old son in his arms and was crossing the street to his residence when two men ran out from behind a fence. One of them knocked the baby from Fillipelli's arms and then attempted to stab him. The assailant, whom police later identified as Antonio Baffa, knocked Fillipelli to the ground and, while the two men were rolling around on the pavement, fired two shots into Fillipelli. In spite of his wounds, Fillipelli was able to hold on to his attacker until the police arrived. He died later that night at St. Bernard's Hospital. Police took Baffa to the Grand Crossing Station where witnesses identified him as the assailant. The second man escaped, but police arrested him the next day. He was Pasquale Nudo, a known associate of Baffa.[63]

Baffa was part of a Black Hand gang called *Loguisto*, which ironically translates as "The Society of Justice."[64] He decided to cooperate with Detective Longobardi because the other members of the *Loguisto* gang refused to come to his aid. It seems that the activities of Longobardi in the Fillipelli investigation had prevented the members of *Loguisto* from hiring an attorney for Baffa and from visiting him in jail for fear that the police would identify them. Baffa identified Antonio Nudo, Raffaele Nudo, Pasquale Nudo, Giuseppe Cara, and a man named Ernesto as members of the gang. The Nudos, whom he worked with on the Illinois Central Railroad, recruited Baffa into the gang with the promise of marriage to one of their sisters.

The police knew Raffaele Nudo. They had arrested him the previous October for assaulting Samuel Lento, also of South Greenwood Avenue. Police believed that Nudo assaulted Lento because of Lento's failure to heed a Black Hand letter demanding that he leave the Grand Crossing area. The Lento letter did not contain a demand for money. Police believed that the gang was also trying to drive out the more prosperous of their fellow countrymen in the hope of obtaining good locations for stores and saloons in the district.[65]

Baffa's confession led to the arrest of three more suspects: Giuseppe Cara, Antonio Nudo, and Ernesto Serrese.[66] The fourth, Raffaele Nudo, was still being sought. Police believed that he had fled to Pittsburgh or another eastern city. All but Baffa claimed that they were innocent of Black Hand crimes. Detectives Longobardi and Bernacchi were also looking at other crimes suspected of being perpetrated by the *Loguisto* gang. Police believed that the gang authored a letter sent to John Aiello, a saloonkeeper at 7700 South Greenwood, warning him to move from the neighborhood on fear of death. The letter followed an attempt to shoot Aiello in his place of business the previous January. Detective Longobardi believed that a member of *Loguisto* undoubtedly wrote the letter.

The detectives also believed that the group had sent a letter to Benedetto Cairo, warning him that they would kill him if he failed to pay the amount demanded by the blackmailers.[67] Cairo, the brother-in-law of Fillipelli, was the target of a Black Hand extortion attempt in August 1908 when the blackmailers demanded $1,000 from him on threat of death. The letter sent to Cairo referred to the recent attack made on Detective Longobardi and declared that the next attempt on Longobardi's life would be successful. At the *Loguisto* trial, Raffaele Fillipelli, the twelve-year-old son of the murdered man, testified that he had hit Baffa with a lantern after Baffa had attacked his father. Raffaele also told the prosecuting attorney that he would avenge his father's death by killing the offenders if the state did not send them to prison.

The letter written by Antonio Baffa to Detective Longobardi confessing his involvement in the Fillipelli murder provides an informative look into the workings of a Black Hand gang. Baffa wrote:

> I came to this country three years ago and worked as a laborer on the Illinois Central Railroad. I first met these men, Antonio Nudo, Rafaela Nudo and Pasquale Nudo, Joseph Cara and a man of the name Ernesto— his first name I do not know, who is a brother-in-law of Cara—about three years ago.
>
> They wanted me to belong to their gang a long time ago and they promised to give me a sister of the Nudo's to marry. They had a kind of a private name for the gang and when they were asked about it by outsiders they called it the Loguisto. The gang was formed for the purpose of extorting money from people who were supposed to be well off by sending letters and telling the person to bring the money to a certain place.

The letters were usually written by Giuseppe Cara and Rafaela Nudo. I know of their writing two letters to a man by the name of Beneditto Cairo and another one to John Aiello. They sent a letter to Beneditto Cairo and Fillipelli, the deceased.

They were in business together in one store and this Rafaela Nudo told me that they sent a letter to Beneditto Cairo and told him that they were going to kill a man by the name of Pisello and two others if they did not send the money. They said that Cairo and his brother-in-law Fillipelli had too much mouth and was talking and calling us Black Hands, and so we decided to cut their faces.

Then we were laying for Fillipelli for about three months and we have no chance to get him because he always had his wife with him or a baby in his arms.

On the day that Giuseppe Fillipelli was killed I met Pasquale Nudo at his brother's house. We were careful about anybody seeing us, and the three Nudo brothers Joseph, Cara, Ernesto, and myself were in the shanty talking. Rafaela Nudo said "Well nobody can see us to-night and we will go there."

Then we went there and laid for him until he came out. We were on the corner of Seventy-eight street.

I saw Fillipelli come out of his store carrying a baby in his arms; I also saw four or five children, and one of the boys was carrying a lantern. We passed Fillipelli's house and two colored men were standing near the vacant lot.

We wanted to get around Fillipelli; we wanted to spy and see when he came out and get him between the five or six of us.

I didn't see these other fellows after Fillipelli came out of the house, but Pasquale and I walked down where the fence is near the vacant lot, and we turned around and Pasquale hit Fillipelli with his club, but missed him.

Fillipellli turned around, grabbed me by the throat and was choking me and knocked me down and I saw nobody helping me, and I pulled a revolver and shot two times.

I don't know where I shot him. I was lying on the ground and had a lot of blood in my eyes from where he had been scratching me. The boy hit me on the shoulder with the lantern. He was standing by the gate when we passed by. We also passed his mother when she was carrying a baby. Fillipelli was carrying a baby, too, in his arms.

Pasquale Nudo had the hammer. He got it from the railroad shops. Rafaela Nudo, the brother of Pasquale, owned the knife and Pasquale had the umbrella. This was all done about 9 o'clock or a little after and it was dark and raining.

The boy hit me here on the shoulder and the marks on my face I got from the father scratching me. He had me down and then kicked me and was choking me and then I pulled the revolver and fired the shots.

Then they took Fillipelli to his house and they all began to beat me.

The police Came and took me away and afterward brought me to the hospital.

Joe Pisello grabbed me and held me until the police took me from Fillipelli's house. I saw Fillipelli afterward at the hospital and he said to me: "What did you shoot me for?" And I said I never shot you.

The police asked me if I was the man that shot him and I said "No." but Fillipelli declared I was. Then the police took me to the station. Since then I have been in jail.

I have seen Pasquale Nudo and his brother and they said: "Don't say anything. We will pay your lawyer and expenses."

Antonio Nudo, Rafaela Nudo, and Cara told me that. They hired George Barrett and they said they were going to defend me. I saw him two or three times. I don't know if the Italian lawyer Borrelli is going to take care of me or not.

I have talked to Borelli, but did not tell him I wanted to make any statement. I told only the guard and a fellow prisoner. My father came over last Friday. He told me to tell the truth about the matter. I want to tell the truth now. But I did not want to tell the truth at the corner's inquest. I did not see Fillipelli after he died, but the police told me the man died.

These men did other jobs besides this. Pasquale Nudo and Cara cut a man's face who works at the Burnside shops. I think his name was Dominick. They also cut a man named Saveria Lendo. I was not with them at that time, but the three brothers told me about it.

They wrote two or three letters. Rafaela Nudo and Joe Cara did the writing. This Lendo was cut in the face and he skipped away from here because they sent him a letter telling him if he didn't get away they would kill him.

They wrote Fillipelli letters demanding money, and because he did not pay it and was calling them Black Hands they were angry. I owed Fillipelli $27. He never said anything about that, but Pasquale owed him money, and tied his wages up at the railroad and that was one of the reasons why they wanted to kill him before this.

Pasquale Nudo claimed Fillipelli had lots of money because his wife gave money to the priest. He says: "We can make a couple of thousand, and we can be all right then."

I don't know what became of the revolver after I shot Fillipelli. It fell out of my hand. Pasquale had the hammer and the umbrella and his brother Rafaela had the stiletto. I saw the stiletto and club at the corner's inquest and they were the same ones that they had with them when they started out on that night.

Antonio Baffa[68]

Baffa's letter provides a number of interesting insights into Black Hand extortion. He was not a Black Hand member before he came to the United States, and there is no mention in his confession of the Mafia,

Camorra, or any other Italian criminal society. In fact, the killers became upset when Fillipelli accused them of being Black Hand members. Nor does the confession provide a description of a highly organized criminal group but rather a small gang of violent opportunists, much like a robbery gang. Baffa's confession also supports the position presented by Detective Bernacchi and the White Hand Society that Black Hand criminals often personally knew their victims. Both Pasquale Nudo and Antonio Baffa owed money to the victim.

In the midst of the Baffa investigation, postal authorities announced that they had broken up a Black Hand gang in Cincinnati, Ohio, named the "Society of the Banana."[69] The press reported that the Society of the Banana was organized along the lines of the "old Mafia" and that it had branches in Pittsburgh, Chicago, Cincinnati, Cleveland, Columbus, and even South Dakota. Postal authorities arrested the members of the Society of the Banana for extorting money from three fruit merchants in Columbus, Ohio. Chief postal inspector Holmes stated that the group was a well-organized society with secret "grips and passwords" and that the incidents were not simply sporadic cases of individual extortion. The members of the gang sent letters, in the same handwriting and written on the same watermarked paper, to victims in Cincinnati and Columbus, but they always mailed them from different cities in order to conceal the identities of the offenders. A book found in the safe of Salvatore Lima, the principal defendant, at the time of his arrest contained the bylaws and regulations of the society. The regulations, which prosecutors read into the court record, described horrible penalties for disobedience of its mandates and probably had an impact on sentencing. Lima received fourteen years for his part in the extortion racket.

Postal authorities also linked the activities of the Society of the Banana to Chicago.[70] Salvatore Rizzo, a Cincinnati fruit merchant, received a Black Hand letter from Chicago telling him to pay an earlier $5,000 demand. A few days later, he received a third letter that was sent from a little town in South Dakota, warning him to obey Black Hand demands. The third letter instructed Rizzo to take $2,500 to Pittsburgh, where he was to walk across a bridge over the Allegheny River at midnight on the appointed day carrying a live chicken in one hand and the money in the other. A man would then meet him and collect the money, but leave him in possession of the chicken.

The fact that the Society of the Banana operated in more than one location added fuel to the belief that the Black Hand was a nationwide cartel of criminals. Both the government and the press used the Society of the Banana arrests to support this position. Postal authorities announced that the evidence uncovered during the investigation convinced them that they had uncovered the national headquarters of the Black Hand. The *Literary Digest*, a nationwide news magazine, reported that the arrests in Ohio proved that Black Hand criminals worked together and maintained much closer connections than did criminals of other nationalities.[71]

One of the most unfortunate incidents of Black Hand crime to come to the attention of the Chicago police involved fourteen-year-old Rudolph Berendt. Police killed Berendt when he attempted to extort $15,000 from a wholesale grocer named S. E. Grossfeld. Berendt and his fifteen-year-old cousin, Alfred Haase, were attempting to raise money to go to the West and become "outlaws." Together, they created a menacing extortion letter in which they identified themselves as the world-famous "Black Hand Death League." The missive was signed "Black Hand Gang. Capt. Giovanni." One week after receiving the extortion letter and turning it over to Chicago police, Grossfeld received several telephone calls from the offenders. One directed him to deliver the money to the intersection of Des Plaines Street and Grand Avenue at 8 o'clock that evening. Under the watchful eye of police detectives dressed as laborers, Grossfeld proceeded as instructed. Upon arriving at the appointed location, he was approached by Berendt, who produced a revolver, which was later found to be empty of bullets, and demanded the extortion money. As soon as he obtained the money, Berendt attempted to run, but he was shot down by police. Detective Phillip Weinrich of the Sheffield Avenue Station fired the shot that killed Berendt. The boy died later at Passavant Hospital after having given a full confession to police officials, including Assistant Chief Schuettler. A search of Berendt revealed two masks, one black and the other red, and a picture of a cowboy mounted on a pony. Just before he died, Berendt begged forgiveness of Grossfeld and pleaded with the grocer to give him a "dying kiss."[72]

Berendt's accomplice, Alfred Hasse, admitted that he was present at the scene of the shooting but claimed that he was there only to see what would happen.[73] Hasse claimed that he knew nothing of the extortion attempt. Police believed otherwise. In an effort to establish Hasse's participation in the extortion scheme, the police had him telephone the victim in order to determine if Hasse was the person who had repeatedly telephoned the Grossfeld home as part of the extortion scheme. Mrs. Grossfeld, who had received the extortion calls, stated that young Hasse's voice sounded like the person who had given her the threatening messages.

At the coroner's inquest, it came out that Berendt was an avid reader of cheap novels dealing with the Wild West and Black Hand plots, which is where he got the idea of holding up wealthy citizens to obtain money. A disagreement between the mothers of the two boys marked the inquest. Louisa Berendt, the mother of the deceased boy, told Ida Hasse that police would not have killed Rudolph if she had kept Alfred away from "5 cent theaters." Hasse replied that her son was not to blame and that it was better for him to spend his time at the movies than reading cheap novels as Rudolph did.[74]

The tragedy of the Berendt slaying was the subject of a *Chicago Daily Tribune* editorial.[75] The newspaper recognized that the stories of alleged Black Hand crimes, as outlined in the newspapers, had influenced these imaginative young boys. Unable to distinguish between the romanticism of adventure and the realities of crime, the boys had succumbed to the allure of crime. The *Tribune* used the occasion of the Berendt killing to direct public attention to the problem of delinquency in Chicago. Crime among gangs of boys and young men was a serious problem, a problem that was related to the manner in which Black Hand and other crimes were reported to the reading public. The *Tribune* recognized that press accounts of the Black Hand influenced the minds of these imaginative boys and that inaccurate but sensational reporting led to the construction of a mysterious and even romantic image of the Black Hand in Chicago— one that was not true.

Two weeks later, police arrested seventeen-year-old Robert Zabel, a schoolmate of Berendt, after he attempted to extort $1,000 from the drug store where he had formerly worked. The druggists, who had received two extortion letters, remembered finding Zabel reading *The Kidnappers of New York* or *In the Hands of the Black Circle*. This information led police to suspect Zabel, who later confessed that he wrote the Black Hand letters. One month later, yet another "boy" Black Hand incident occurred. Fourteen-year-old Lawrence Salerno told police that Black Hand criminals had kidnapped his sixteen-year-old friend Scori De Rose. Mary De Rose, the mother of Scori, then received several letters demanding a $1,000 ransom. One of the letters directed Mrs. De Rose to place the money under the sewer cover at Taylor and Halsted streets. It was signed the Black Hand and contained the usual crude drawings of a skull and crossbones. When police detectives went to the appointed place, they saw young Scori walk up to the corner, where he was seized by the detectives. Police believed that the two boys wrote the letters in the hope of getting money from Mrs. De Rose and that her son went into hiding to await the ransom money.[76]

In November 1909, Chicago's chief of police, Leroy Steward, made the startling announcement that he had "discovered" that the Italian residents of the Near North Side (Little Sicily) were in constant fear of death or injury and that many were paying tribute to the Black Hand.[77] This discovery had come to his attention during the course of what police described as the "gambling bomb" investigation. A war had been going on since 1907 between the various factions of Chicago's underworld for control of illicit gambling in the city. Whether the revelation at this time was the result of a lack of attention by the police department or increased Black Hand activity in the Near North Side is not certain, but Chief Steward proclaimed that he was concerned and he was formulating a plan to drive Black Hand criminals from the city.

The information uncovered by Steward revealed that a gang of blackmailers had developed an elaborate system to levy tribute from wealthy Italians.[78] Police believed that the gang selected its victims by watching real estate transfers in the city. As soon as they discovered that a man had paid several thousand dollars to purchase property, they sent him a letter threatening injury or death unless he paid the gang. Although Steward announced that the police had already arrested three members of the gang, he refused to divulge his plan of action except to say that he was thinking of hiring several Italian detectives to work in the Near North Side.

In an effort to control the rising number of Black Hand crimes in Little Sicily, Chicago police raided six saloons believed to be centers of Black Hand activity in January 1910. Little Sicily had become a refuge for Black Hand criminals, and police blamed local saloons and saloonkeepers for the epidemic of Black Hand crime. Police assigned eight patrol wagons, every detective in the Chicago Avenue Station, and a squad of uniformed officers to the raid. The sweep began at 4 o'clock in the afternoon and continued until 6 p.m. It provided a great spectacle for the children at the Jenner School, who were leaving their classrooms just as the raids began. The dragnet resulted in the arrest of 194 suspects. Police believed these men to be the group from which Black Hand gangs recruited members. Rounding up the "usual suspects" was a common police practice during this period. Of the 194 persons arrested, 187 were fined one dollar and court costs, and seven were discharged. Police brought the arrestees before Judge Crowe, who called for the deportation of all those who had been in the country for less than three years and did not intend to become naturalized citizens.[79]

Some speculated that the raid was the result of a need for the police to respond to the death of Benedetto Cinene, who had been murdered a few days earlier, reportedly by Black Hand criminals, as he slept in the rear of his cigar store in Little Sicily.[80] There were a number of explanations for his murder. Foremost was that Cinene had cooperated with the police in rescuing a young boy named Joseph Junta from Black Hand kidnappers. Police, however, doubted this theory. They suspected that Cinene might have known something about the boy's disappearance from the beginning because he had never explained how he knew the whereabouts of the child, raising suspicions that Cinene was involved in the crime. Others speculated that Cinene was a victim of Black Hand extortion. Stephen Malato, the attorney for the White Hand Society, provided evidence that Cinene had received four letters from Black Hand criminals demanding $5,000. Others speculated that Cinene, who was also a fortuneteller, was the victim of a customer who had sought revenge because the fortune that Cinene predicted proved to be the recipient's misfortune. Whatever the motive for the crime, it caused an immediate uproar. Over twenty Italian business and professional men met in the offices of the White Hand Society to map a new strategy to deal with Black Hand crime.[81]

Police officials announced that the Little Sicily raids were only the start of a new effort to eradicate Black Hand crime and that the raids would continue as long as the crimes occurred. Inspector O'Brien, who had been in charge of the raiding party, told the press that the raid was to "instill the fear of the law in their [the Italians] hearts." Others thought that the dragnet approach to fighting Black Hand crime had limited use. Stephen Malato commented, "The work of raiding saloons and billiard halls is all right, but evidence can only be collected secretly." Malato's comments were an obvious reference to the widely held belief that the police department in Chicago needed to hire undercover operatives to work in secret among Black Hand criminals. Detective Longobardi, commenting on the saloon raids, said that arrests under such conditions only angered the Italians and caused them to seal their lips. He thought that the show of force had reduced his chances of gaining information from local Italians. Longobardi believed that not all of the men arrested in the dragnet were Black Hand criminals. Guido Sabetta, the Italian consul, told the press that at first he was concerned about the raids, but when he found out that the police had only raided saloons, he approved.[82]

The sensational Little Sicily raid apparently had little effect on Black Hand crime. Only twelve hours after the mass arrests, Joseph Noto, a friend of Cinene, received a Black Hand demand for $500. Noto did not report the matter to the police for fear that the blackmailers would kill him just as they had Cinene. He knew that Black Hand criminals believed the police were ineffective against them. While Noto remained frightened in his shop, funeral services were being held for Cinene at St. Philip Benizi's Church, less than two blocks away. The extortion letter received by Noto seemed to be in defiance of police efforts against Black Hand crime. In fact, Noto believed that one of the men arrested in the recent police dragnet had written the letter. Black Hand criminals further demonstrated their contempt for the police when there was another attempt on the life of Detective Longobardi. Two men attacked him as he was passing an alley, but they fled when he drew his revolver.[83]

A few weeks later, Joseph Loverde, a neighbor of Benedetto Cinene, was found murdered near his home in Little Sicily. The killer fired two shoots at the unsuspecting victim, one striking him in the heart. A police dragnet sweeping through the Near North Side searching for the killer arrested Samuel Licatao for carrying a concealed weapon. An examination of Licatao's revolver revealed that it had been shot twice. Headlines in the *Chicago American* named Licatao as the "Black Hand" slayer of Loverde. In spite of newspaper accounts of Black Hand involvement, Inspector Revere of the East Chicago Avenue police thought that romance was the real motive. Loverde's widow, Maria, told Revere that she believed the murder to be the closing chapter in a love affair that had started three years earlier in Palermo, Sicily, when two different men had sought her hand. She believed the murderer of her husband was the unsuccessful rival. Police then began a search for Felix Orsino, the jilted suitor.[84]

Although the Loverde killing had nothing to do with Black Hand crime, it renewed demands for more police officers of Italian descent. Stephen Malato announced that the merchants of the Near North Side were formulating plans to bring the matter to the attention of the Italian consul in Chicago. Then in February 1910, police arrested Christopher Ebbole for the murder of Charles Wiltshire, a North Halsted Street merchant.[85]

The press described Ebbole as a former "special investigator" assigned to the office of Assistant Chief Schuettler. He reportedly worked with Schuettler's regular Italian sleuths on Black Hand crimes. He may have even been a former White Hand Society investigator. Ebbole had applied to become a member of the force but feared that he would not pass the civil service exam because of the height requirement. Whether Ebbole was an example of the type of secret service operative that many believed was necessary to work among Black Hand criminals or simply a police informant is uncertain. The incident, however, highlights the difficulty of working with persons who themselves may have been part of the criminal element. It may also explain why the City of Chicago was reluctant to hire undercover officers to work among Italian criminals.

No one who lived in the Near North Side in the area of Little Sicily seemed immune from Black Hand extortion, not even elected officials.

In February 1910, State Representative P. J. Sullivan received a $5,000 extortion demand directing him to take the money to the bridge at Chicago and Halsted streets.[86] This location was commonly used as a drop by Black Hand offenders. The bridge spanned the Chicago River and provided a number of hiding places as well as locations to observe the area from a point of safety. The letter was mailed to a saloon at 507 West Chicago Avenue that was formerly owned by Sullivan's brother. Sullivan told the press that he thought the letter was a joke and did not intend to report the matter to the police. Sullivan was involved in a heated race for alderman in the area and was vigorously opposed by the Municipal Voters League and other civic bodies, which may have had something to do with the threat.

On March 4, 1910, three men shot two Chicago police detectives near Chicago and Townsend streets. Patrick Quinn and John Wren, assigned to the East Chicago Avenue police station, were walking in Little Sicily when they saw three suspicious-looking men peering into the window of a barbershop. The officers, crouching in a doorway across the street, observed the men for nearly ten minutes before deciding to approach them. When they confronted the suspects and showed their police stars, there was a flash and loud report when one of the men fired a revolver through his coat pocket, striking Detective Wren. As the detective staggered back, the gunman fired again, striking Wren a second time. The assailants then dashed into the street, firing as they ran. Although mortally wounded, Wren raised himself on one elbow and continued to fire his revolver until it was empty. Detective Quinn, wounded and knocked to the ground by a bullet wound to his foot, also returned fire. One of the more than forty bullets fired during the exchange hit one of the offenders.[87]

The assailants were described as thirty years of age, of medium weight, with dark complexions and black moustaches.[88] Police found an overcoat nearby, apparently dropped by the offenders, containing an "Italian" stiletto, revolver cartridges, and a handkerchief with the initials "PC" or "PG." Police also recovered a suit of clothes near the scene of the shooting containing an identification card issued by the Hod Carrier's Union bearing the name James Grady.

Because Quinn described his assailants as Italians and because of the location of the gun battle, the shooting of the two officers was immediately described as the work of the Black Hand. More than twenty suspects were arrested for the shooting in the usual manner. All but four were released after being questioned by the police.[89] One of the suspects, Girolamo Morici, arrested by Detective Longabardi, was believed to be one of the assailants. The clue that pointed toward Morici was the old black overcoat that was found near the scene of the gun battle. The overcoat fit Morici, and when brought before Detective Quinn, the officer twice declared that he thought that Morici was one of the men who did the shooting, but he could not be absolutely sure.

The failure to identify Girolamo Morici as one of the assailants did not deter Detective Longobardi. Searching the crime scene, he found a button that he believed was made in Italy because of its peculiar material and pattern. Further investigation revealed that a local Italian of suspicious character wore a coat with similar buttons. It was said that he also traveled with two friends, and they were missing from their usual haunts on the night of the shooting.

The next day, Detectives Parodi and Loftus traced the button to a house on North Milton Avenue, where it was learned that a man with similar buttons on his coat had resided until two days before. A search of the man's room revealed a collar with the laundry mark "PG," which police believed to be the same as the initials found on the handkerchief in the overcoat recovered near the scene of shooting. From the initials, the detectives were able to learn the names of the suspects, which they did not release to the press.[90]

Three weeks later, Barrato Cornico, of North Townsend Street, was arrested for robbery and taken to the East Chicago Avenue police station.[91] The facts that Cornico lived near the corner where the two officers were shot and possessed an old peak cap similar to the hat worn by one of the assailants led officers to believe that they may have arrested one of the attackers of Detectives Wren and Quinn. After being summoned to the station, Detective Quinn stated that he was almost certain that Cornico was one of the men who had shot him and killed Detective Wren. He also identified the old peak cap that was found in Cornico's home. But like the mysterious "PG," police never charged Cornico with the attack on the officers.

There is another theory that the shooting of detectives Quinn and Wren had nothing to do with Black Hand crime at all and the assailants were not even Italian. Inspector Revere believed that the men who attacked the officers were not Italian because Italians were more likely to fight with knives than revolvers. Thieves fought with revolvers. Revere believed that old-time robbers had shot the detectives. Information received later supported his belief. Police discovered more information that Detectives Quinn and Wren had confronted the notorious robbery gang led by Irishman Mike McKevitt.[92]

The shooting of the detectives was apparently the catalyst that caused the Chicago Police Department to move forward with the establishment of a "foreign detective bureau" as suggested by the press. The new foreign service was to be composed of twenty Italians as well as a number of other nationalities and was to work apart from the regular police force. Chief of police Leroy Steward argued that the foreign service officers were necessary because civil service requirements prevented him from hiring Sicilians as regular police officers. Sicilians generally lacked in regulation height and weight, and were unable to pass the entrance exam because it was given in English. The establishment of this new arm of the department would circumvent civil service requirements and yet provide men to the department who had a thorough knowledge of the language, habits, and environment of the city's foreign population. Chief Steward introduced the ordinance to the city council on March 9, 1910. Each of the foreign operators was to be paid $1,200 a year. It took the Chicago City Council nearly one year to pass the ordinance.[93]

Whether the result of the Wren murder or continued Black Hand activity, the *Chicago Daily Tribune* ran a two-page story in March 1910 titled "100 Black Hand Brigands Terrorize 100,000 Italians and Sneer at the Chicago Police."[94] The article described the Black Hand as one of the greatest problems facing the people of Chicago and said the police were unable to stop Black Hand criminals. Of the 100,000 Italians living in the city, the newspaper estimated that 30,000 had paid tribute to the Black Hand and 8,000 were making weekly or monthly payments. Criticizing Chief Schuettler's opinion that Black Hand crimes were committed by individual offenders and there was no Black Hand organization in Chicago, the *Tribune* argued that the magnitude of Black Hand crime suggested a careful organization with a headquarters for the reviewing of information, issuing of demands, and sentencing of traitors. Although there was no source given for the information provided by the newspaper, it is highly unlikely that each of Chicago's 100 alleged Black Hand criminals had successfully blackmailed 300 local Italians.

In June 1910, there was an attempt to create a successor to the White Hand Society. The problems encountered by the White Hand apparently had taken their toll. Named the Twentieth Century Italian-American Independent Club, the Italian community formed the new group to ferret out crime and turn the information over to the police.[95] The Eli Bates settlement house, in the heart of Little Sicily, organized the group. The new club elected Antonio Bellavia, a local banker, as president. In a speech before the group, Ballavia announced that the many murders committed in the Near North Side gave the wrong impression of the Italian people and that his group would change that impression by cooperating with the police. The organization also intended to bring wholesome amusement and recreation to the poorer Italian people of the area. The Italian community heard little of the organization after the initial fanfare.

On September 22, 1910, the press reported that someone had detonated a "Black Hand bomb" near the general store of Cosimo Geraci at 2240 South Wentworth Avenue, less than a block from the Twenty-second Street police station.[96] Although reported as a Black Hand bomb, the police announced that the blast was the result of a "feud among the Italians." Unable to find traces of the bomb after the explosion, police concluded that the device was common black powder contained in a glass bottle. The bombing incident was reported as the forty-second in a recent string of bombings, most of which were related to a gambling war that was occurring in Chicago. The fact that the headline of the article did not correspond with the facts of the case was common. Of the forty-two alleged Black Hand bombings identified in this volume, only ten of the news reports provided any evidence of extortion.

There was a call for the renewed efforts of the White Hand Society in December 1910 when banker Modestino Mastrogiovanni became the victim of a Black Hand attack.[97] Five sticks of dynamite were set to explode at his bank. Only one of the sticks exploded, however, because of a defect in the fuse. Mastrogiovanni had received three demands for money from Black Hand criminals. Just as others before him, Mastrogiovanni blamed the continued success of Black Hand criminals on the inability of the Chicago police to control the Black Hand problem. Mastrogiovanni, a former White Hand Society member, believed that they had been successful in their efforts against Black Hand criminals because they had turned the Black Hand's weapons against them, unmercifully hunting down the blackmailers. Mastrogiovanni also stressed that there was no such organization as the Black Hand, but blamed Black Hand extortion on bands of youth who loafed around neighborhood saloons.

Local authorities handled most Black Hand investigations. Black Hand crime, however, also came under federal jurisdiction because Black Hand criminals often used the U.S. mail to send their extortion letters. As a result, the federal government pursued an occasional Black Hand case. For instance, the Justice Department indicted George Pavlick, a fifteen-year-old Russian boy, in December 1910 for sending Black Hand letters to grocer Max Maas. Pavlick had become incensed with Maas when he received only thirty cents pay for working an entire day in the grocery. Determined to scare his employer, he sent Mass two Black Hand letters. Mass turned the letters over to police at the Cottage Grove Station. Detectives were waiting for Pavlick when he arrived to claim the money. At the station house, Pavlick confessed that he got the idea of sending Black Hand letters from cheap novels.[98]

By the time of the Pavlick arrest, the White Hand Society was virtually nonexistent. Four years from its founding, Black Hand criminals either had attacked its leading members or had threatened them with extortion. The drug store of Joseph Damiani had been bombed.[99] Police believed that he was a special target because of his leadership of the organization. Camillo Volini, the White Hand's first president, had property damaged and received numerous threatening letters. Stephen Malato was threatened and he barely escaped death, on two separate occasions, after being assaulted by Black Hand criminals.

In spite of the demise of the White Hand Society, Volini continued in public life. He worked with Mother Francis X. Cabrini, the first American saint of the Catholic Church, to establish Columbus Hospital in Chicago and was himself one of the founders of the hospital's Near West Side Cabrini branch.[100] He served as an attending physician at the Cook County Hospital for ten years and was an assistant city health commissioner in Chicago. Illinois governor Charles Deneen appointed Volini to lead the Italian earthquake relief drive in 1909, and he was the head of the Italian Red Cross in America. The Italian government made him a Knight of the Crown of Italy because of his many charitable efforts. He died in 1927 at the age of sixty-four.

After leaving the White Hand Society, Stephan Malato continued to pursue crime in the Italian community. After failing to be elected to the bench, he took a job at the Cook County State's Attorneys' Office. His experience in investigating Black Hand crime made him a formidable prosecutor. In one case, a private investigator named Frank De Maria accused Malatto of putting him through the "third degree" for seven hours in an effort to make him admit that he had induced another man to commit perjury. The third degree was a common police practice during this time in history. The first degree was the arrest, the second the ride to the police station. The third degree was also referred to as "sweating" and often involved intimidation and rough treatment. It was so common that mentioning it the context of a forced admission is probably more notable than the fact that it had occurred.[101]

Malato was involved in a number of important prosecutions. One of his most notable cases included being the first prosecutor in the United States to win a conviction for reckless homicide—the unintentional killing of another with a motor vehicle. He also became an expert in the insanity plea, calling for the creation of a state commission to determine the ability of a defendant to stand trial rather than relying on the legal opinion of paid experts. Malato was highly critical of the executive pardons granted by the governor of Illinois, no doubt a result of his experience with the White Hand Society. It was his opinion that those who were pardoned and released after serving only a portion of their sentences often went on to commit other crimes.[102]

The White Hand Society challenged a number of important beliefs about Black Hand crime. While the White Hand argued that the Black Hand was not a powerful criminal organization, it did recognize that Black Hand criminals might have been members of the Camorra or Mafiosi in Italy. They even provided evidence of the use of blackmailing letters in Palermo, Sicily. Their position, however, was clear; there was no Black Hand organization in Italy or the United States. The White Hand considered immigrant Italian Black Hand criminals to be Italian brigands and highwaymen and not members of any secret criminal organization. Although immigrant Italian criminals may have corrupted local Italians, the White Hand Society argued that they themselves often became better criminals from contact with Black Hand crime in the United States, and eventually returned to Italy bringing the "evil seed" of the Black Hand with them.[103]

3   The Black Hand Squad

The end of the White Hand Society placed responsibility for Black Hand enforcement squarely on the shoulders of the Chicago police. Until this time, Gabriel Longobardi and his partner Julian Bernacchi had spearheaded the police department's efforts against Black Hand crime. Personnel records indicate that the Chicago Police Department assigned four new officers to work with Detectives Longobardi and Bernacchi in the spring of 1911. Police officer Paul Riccio was transferred to Assistant Chief Schuettler's office in May and Officer George De Mar the following June. Officer Riccio, a native of Italy, had been on the force since 1906 and, like Longobardi, had gained experience investigating Black Hand crime while assigned to the Maxwell Street Station. Officer De Mar had been a police officer since 1909. Michael De Vito joined the department in April 1911 and was immediately assigned to Chief Schuettler. Officer Phillip Parodi transferred to the squad a short time later. This was the beginning of the Chicago Police Black Hand Squad. Also referred to as the Italian Squad, Black Hand officers worked directly on cases of Black Hand extortion and assisted local detectives in solving murders and other crimes in the Italian community. Unlike its New York counterpart, little is known about the Chicago Police Black Hand Squad. The only published account of the squad's activities, outside of newspaper sources, is a brief mention of some of the officers by John Landesco in his 1929 book, *Organized Crime in Chicago*.[1]

Whether it was the demise of the White Hand Society or the increased boldness of Black Hand criminals, 1911 proved to be the most eventful year in the history of Black Hand crime in Chicago. The year began with an outbreak of Black Hand bombings in Little Sicily. On January 9, Paul Figaro, the proprietor of a small store at 1025 Larrabee, became the first target.[2] Someone placed a bomb in the entranceway to the basement of his store and residence. The force of the explosion shook the entire building, breaking all the basement windows. Figaro had recently received a threat that Black Hand criminals would kill him and the other members of his family unless he paid a $3,000 demand. He also admitted that he had been receiving an average of one threatening letter a week for the last three months.

Two weeks later, nine people were hurt when a stick of dynamite exploded in the stairway of the butcher shop of Carmelo Marsala at 834 Gault Court. Marsala had been the target of Black Hand extortionists for nearly three years. He had received a long series of letters, each demanding $500. Refusing to pay, he reported the extortion demands to the police and purchased a revolver to await the attack that he was sure would come. The eventual explosion destroyed a staircase, caused the side wall of his building to cave in, and threw everyone in the building onto the floor. Upon regaining his senses, Marsala seized a revolver, shouting, "It's the Black Hand." He rushed for the door, but when he swung it open, he found himself in a slatted chicken coop that the offenders had placed against the door to prevent him from leaving. By the time he had freed himself, the offenders had vanished into the crowd that had gathered around the damaged building. Within an hour, police from the East Chicago Avenue Station had arrested a young Italian, Gianni Alongi, whom they ultimately charged with the Marsala bombing. The arrest of Alongi followed a comparison of the letters received by Marsala with the suspect's handwriting. Alongi denied sending the letters, arguing that he could not write, but witnesses placed him within 100 feet of the Marsala meat market when the bombing occurred. Police eventually matched his handwriting with nineteen Black Hand letters sent to residents of the Near North Side.[3]

Just when police believed they had solved the rash of Black Hand bombings occurring in Little Sicily with the arrest of Gianni Alongi, someone exploded another bomb in the front vestibule of Artizo Stiano's drugstore at 1001 North Larrabee.[4] The explosion occurred in the heart of Little Sicily, the district that Black Hand criminals had selected as their major target. Everyone known or thought to have a savings account had received threatening letters. In every instance, the letter was the same, demanding sums ranging from $500 to $1,000 before a certain date or dire consequences would result.

The arrest of Alongi for the bombing of the Marsala butcher shop had convinced the police that they were making progress in their efforts against Black Hand crime. The bombing of the Stiano drug store proved otherwise. Within a few hours of the bombing, the Chicago police turned Alongi, who they believed possessed extensive knowledge of earlier Black Hand crimes, over to federal authorities for prosecution.[5]

The Alongi case proved to be more than the typical Black Hand extortion. Police tied Alongi to a feud between warring Black Hand gangs that had resulted in the death of five Black Hand criminals.[6] Giuseppe Abitta, Philip Frataloni, Charles Gagliona, and Carmelo Tumminala had all been murdered because of a deadly fight between the "old Chicago gang" and an "eastern gang." The old Chicago gang had been operating in the city for five years, while the eastern gang had recently settled in Chicago after police in New York City ran them out following the murder, in Sicily, of police lieutenant Joseph Petrosino. Police believed that the division of territory and Black Hand spoils that followed the demise of the White Hand Society caused the feud. The deaths of the suspects saved the police the necessity of arresting them in connection with the recent scourge of Black Hand bombings.

The demise of the White Hand Society may have led to an increase in Black Hand crime, but police suspected that it also caused other Italians to seek vengeance on Black Hand criminals.[7] Police cited four murders that they could not solve as evidence that Black Hand victims were hunting down the blackmailers. Reportedly in retaliation, Black Hand criminals had exploded a bomb in front of Giuseppe Matalone's produce store on North Austin Avenue. The gunpowder bomb wrecked the front of the store and hurled Matalone, his family, and some of their neighbors from their beds at 6 o'clock in the morning. Detectives had been guarding the store for two weeks but had departed only a short time before the bomb was exploded.

In February, Regina Marco received a letter demanding $1,200.[8] Marco also received telephone calls threatening to blow up her house and kill her two children unless she paid money to the Black Hand. Police first thought that Marco's divorced husband had sent the letters but later learned that he had moved to El Paso, Texas. Responding to the Marco incident, the U.S. attorney in Chicago announced that he would confer with the postal inspector to determine if the case required federal attention. In addition, the U.S. attorney indicated that he might open an investigation and call all those who had received Black Hand demands before a federal grand jury to force them to tell what they knew about the authorship of the letters. One of the difficulties encountered by local police investigating Black Hand crimes was the reluctance of victims and witnesses to provide information. Guido Sabetta, the Italian consul in Chicago, Stephen Malato, and several Italian merchants who were victims of Black Hand crime welcomed the announcement that a federal grand jury might take up the investigation of the Black Hand. All agreed that such an action would force those who had refused to cooperate with the authorities to tell all they knew of the origins of the extortion letters.

According to postal inspector Stuart, Black Hand criminals had sent nearly 1,000 threatening letters within the previous months to people in the Chicago area.[9] He believed, however, that many were written simply to frighten the recipients and were not the beginnings of full-fledged extortion plots. He also believed that the police did not capture the writers because they looked for the offenders in the wrong places. Stuart argued that many of the offenders could be found in first-class hotels in fashionable neighborhoods and not in the Italian district where police concentrated their efforts. Although he only investigated the matters referred to him, Stuart thought that his investigators could find the writers of the letters that had caused so much excitement if only given the chance.

The surge in Black Hand crimes in 1911 forced the city of Chicago to revive its efforts to hire a squad of secret service agents to work among Black Hand criminals. There had been little discussion of the proposal since June 10, 1910. The civil service commission finally gave an examination for the squad on February 2, 1911.[10] The exam for what newspapers described as the "White Hand Squad" was given in secret in order to protect the identity of the candidates. Several Italian scholars administered the test. Even the names of the test examiners were kept secret in order to protect the identities of the newly recruited secret police. Forty-seven men took the exam. Eight were to be chosen from the eligibility list. The candidates were tested on their ability to translate Italian into English and their fluency in three Italian dialects: Sicilian, Neapolitan, and Calabrian. These were the dialects used extensively by Black Hand criminals. Fluency in Italian was not enough—Italians themselves had difficulty understanding people who were not from their own district in Italy. In addition, the criminal jargon used by Black Hand criminals included Greek and Arabic words that were only familiar to southern Italian dialects.

Much to the surprise of the Chicago police, the list of candidates who had successfully completed the civil service examination and were eligible for assignment to the new Black Hand Squad contained the names of known Black Hand criminals.[11] As a result, the city of Chicago appealed to Romano Lodi, the new Italian consul in Chicago, for assistance in weeding out the supposed spies from the eligibility list. There were also charges of fraud in the examination process. It was alleged that some candidates had been "primed" before taking the test, resulting in a call for a new exam by the Chicago Civil Service Commission. Although the city finance committee approved the plan for a foreign service bureau, the unit was never organized. Police officials decided that regular members of the police department should do the work. The police leadership feared that unless the Black Hand operatives were regular police officers, they would not do their work properly or be of any value to the city.

Among the most famous crimes ever committed by Black Hand criminals in Chicago were the four shootings attributed to the so-called Shotgun Man. Three of the shootings occurred at or near what the press described as "Death Corner," Oak Street and Milton Avenue (now Cleveland). Only one of the victims lived to talk about the crimes. There was a fourth man killed within the same period whose death is often attributed to the Shotgun Man, but he was murdered entering his home in the Near West Side Italian community and not in Little Sicily where Death Corner was located.[12]

Two of the murders at Oak and Milton occurred at the same time. Antonio Dugo and Phillip Maniscalsco were killed on March 14, 1911. The police developed a number of theories to explain the murders. The first theory argued that Maniscalsco, who was a member of a Black Hand gang and an expert bomb maker, lured Anthony Dugo to the murder scene after Dugo refused to meet Black Hand demands. When he arrived, an accomplice shot Dugo with a shotgun blast, but the bullet passed through the intended victim and also struck Maniscalsco. The second theory, favored by Detective Longobardi, proposed that Black Hand criminals had killed Maniscalsco and Dugo, both Black Hand criminals themselves, because they had kept $200 taken from an earlier blackmail victim. Police also suspected that Black Hand criminals had killed Maniscalsco because he had attempted to secure an appointment as an agent of the proposed foreign service bureau of the police department. Maniscalsco had made inquiries about the date of the examination and even told his friends that he intended to join the squad. Lastly, police speculated that a trio of wealthy Italian businessmen, determined to wipe out the Black Hand, had killed both men.[13]

Tony Getios was the third man shot near Death Corner by the so-called Black Hand Shotgun Man. His roommate, Frank Ambro, told the police that he thought the gunman had meant to shoot him and not Getios. Getios had lived in the area for only a short time and did not have any enemies. Ambro attributed the shooting to Joseph Rusto. Ambro had quarreled with Rusto because Rusto had insulted his sister. Police made an arrest in the Getios investigation two days after the shooting. The shooting was, in fact, over a young woman, as Ambro had theorized. Additionally, Getios was not wounded by a shotgun blast as reported. Upon examination at Chicago's Passavant Hospital, it was determined that someone had shot Getios with a .38 caliber revolver. Attributing Getios's shooting to the Shotgun Man was the work of the Chicago press.[14]

Police arrested two men for the murders of Maniscalco and Dugo. First, they arrested Tony Scardina on information received from Joseph Dugo, the brother of one of the murder victims. When the police went to Scardina's home, they recovered two boxes of shotguns shells and a freshly cleaned shotgun. One of the boxes contained shells similar to those used to kill the two men. The second arrest was that of Lorenzo Maniscalsco, a witness to the shooting.[15]

Commenting on the murders, Dr. Camillo Volini said that the killers did not appear to be Black Hand assassins because there was no attempt to extort money. Volini believed that the double shooting of Dugo and Maniscalco was a vendetta crime, a private feud. Whatever the cause of the Shotgun Man murders, the killings left Little Sicily in a state of terror. According to the press, the succession of murders and bombings left the community in a state of fear "reminiscent of the dark ages." In an area covering little more than twenty blocks, the press reported that nearly twenty persons had been killed in the last year.[16]

Another significant fact about the murders was that the family of one of the victims was cooperating with the police in the investigation. Until this time, police had received little cooperation from Black Hand victims and Italians in general. This lack of cooperation did not go unnoticed by the leaders of the Italian community. Reacting to the Black Hand bombing of an Italian saloon at 1901 South Clark Street, L'Italia chastised the Italian community for not cooperating with authorities. The newspaper argued that the Italians themselves were responsible for the Black Hand situation because, when questioned by the police, "They become dumb as fish and answer with the usual shrug of the shoulders." Black Hand crimes flourished, L'Italia argued, because this indifference occurred citywide.[17]

There were several good reasons why local Italians were reluctant to cooperate in Black Hand investigations. First, Black Hand crimes were difficult to solve and the police had a poor success rate with them. The victim often preferred to pay the money rather than to take a chance on telling the police. The reason was that there was generally a go-between, the "friend," who knew the victim's secrets and who warned the plotters when the victim notified the police. There was also the belief that the police could not be trusted. Black Hand victims knew that local ward heelers often protected Black Hand criminals. Lastly, southern Italians and Sicilians traditionally did not go to the police when wronged, believing that revenge was their personal responsibility—*sangu lava sangu* (only blood washes blood).[18]

Less than one week after the Shotgun Man murders, police developed a new lead in the shootings. The home of Frank Balzano, the secretary of Local 233 of the Hod Carrier's Union, was bombed after he had ignored several Black Hand letters demanding that he resign from his union post. (A hod is a wooden box attached to a pole used to carry bricks and mortar.) The family expected their eight-month-old son to die from the wounds received in the explosion. John Gagliardo, the business agent for the union, was the chief suspect in the case. At the time of his arrest, police recovered several slug-loaded shotgun shells such as those used to kill Maniscalsco and Dugo, but they were not able to charge Gagliardo with the shootings; the shotgun shells found in Gagliardo's possession were too common to be important evidence. The following month, federal officials announced that they knew the identity of the Shotgun Man, but he was never arrested.[19]

The growing number of Black Hand crimes in Chicago was not confined to Little Sicily or the Italian community. Sabath Munyer, a Syrian rug merchant living in the Near West Side, had received a constant stream of Black Hand letters for almost a year. Munyer was so frightened that he mortgaged his home to hire a private detective to guard it at night so that his family could sleep in safety. In spite of the detective, someone placed newspaper clippings in his hallway that told of Black Hand crimes. Dr. Theodore Munchowski, of North Noble Street, also received threatening letters. Five Black Hand missives were mailed to him and a crude drawing of skull and crossbones was pasted to the front door of his residence. Each letter demanded that he place $2,000 in an old wagon parked in a vacant lot at Ogden and Fulton streets. In still another case, police arrested Ralph Palmer for sending a Black Hand letter to Ann Williams, the wife of his employer.[20]

Until now, federal involvement in the investigation of Black Hand crime had been sporadic at best. Then in March 1911, federal district judge Kenesaw Mountain Landis received a letter threatening to take his life if he did not discharge Black Hand extortionist Gianni Alongi, who was on trial in his court. The letter, written in a crude scrawl, read, "Judge Landis Federal Building Chicago: You discharge John Alongi or we will kill you as we did the others. Black Hand." During the trial, Judge Landis received a number of telephone messages in which all manner of threats were made. There was also a would-be bomb left near the door of the judge's chamber. The phony bomb was believed to be a reminder that Black Hand criminals could carry out their threats. The sinister-looking device was cylindrical in shape and filled with a substance that looked like hardened mucilage. Although government officials knew it was not an actual bomb, there was an undercurrent of apprehension. If a phony bomb could be placed in the federal building, so could a real one.[21]

It is doubtful that Black Hand criminals actually believed that the threatening note would divert Judge Landis from his duty. The letter may have been part of a calculated plot to prejudice the case. Lawyers for Alongi argued that the threat had biased the judge, thus preventing him from passing impartial judgment on the case. Judge Landis was not the only target. W. P. Dannenberg, a special investigator brought to Chicago by the federal government to investigate Black Hand crime, received a threatening letter warning him, "We know every move you make. If you don't get out of town and let the Black Hand alone we will put you where you never will do us any harm." In addition, a friend of Gianni Alongi threatened Postal Inspector Stuart. While waiting for an elevator in the federal building, someone whispered through the grating of the closed door, "You be careful what you say about Alongi or you will go to your death, as others have."[22]

The members of the Alongi jury were also subject to Black Hand threats. As a result, the jury was not able to reach a verdict. They stood eleven to one for conviction, and the case collapsed. The one man who held out against a guilty verdict was reportedly in a state of fear that prevented him from properly weighing the evidence. Suspecting foul play, the government assigned U.S. secret service agents to investigate whether Black Hand criminals had threatened any of the jurors. Ultimately, the suspected jury tampering resulted in a mistrial, and the government retried the case one week later after Italian federal agents from New York gathered additional evidence in the case. The new jury was chosen from a group of forty potential jurors who were summoned to appear in federal district court. On April 8, 1911, a newly impaneled jury in Judge Landis's court convicted twenty-six-year-old Black Hand extortionist Gianni Alongi. Described as the government's first victory against the Black Hand, Judge Landis sentenced Alongi to five years imprisonment in the federal penitentiary at Fort Leavenworth, Kansas. Fearing an escape attempt, Secret Service agents assisted U.S. marshals in guarding Alongi on his way to the prison.[23]

The boldness of the threat against the life of a federal judge caused a sharp turn in the attitude of federal officials who until now had viewed Black Hand extortion as a local problem. Charles De Woody, superintendent of the Justice Department's Bureau of Investigation, immediately assigned agents to investigate Black Hand crime. So did Inspector Stuart of the Chicago post office. The government also announced that it would send additional Secret Service agents to Chicago to bolster federal efforts against Black Hand criminals. Postal authorities were probably the most active in trying to counter Black Hand efforts. For example, the Kinzie postal substation, from which many Black Hand letters were sent, was placed under surveillance in order to identify suspect Black Hand offenders. Postal authorities, however, had experienced the same frustration as Chicago police. Inspector Stuart, in spite of his earlier boasts, announced there was little he could do about the volume of Black Hand crimes.[24]

The intervention of the federal government could not have come sooner. Prominent Italians were terror stricken by the rising number of extortion demands. Many did not know where to turn for protection from Black Hand criminals since they believed that the local police were incapable of coping with the Black Hand threat.[25] Dr. Joseph Damiani, former head of the White Hand Society, complained that in spite of all their efforts, they had obtained little cooperation from the police department. Police Chief Stewart admitted that there was difficulty and that there might even be Black Hand criminals in the police department. Alarmed by Chief Stewart's statement, Elton Lower, president of the civil service commission, responded that his office conducted a rigorous investigation of the character and reputation of all applicants and that it was not likely that Black Hand criminals could obtain appointment to the police force.

The case of Antonio Bodini highlights the distrust that local Italians felt for the Chicago Police Department. Bodini, who lived on West Van Buren Street, reported that he had received a Black Hand letter in March 1911. He did not report the matter to the police because he knew from the experiences of several of his friends that the authorities were incapable of affording any degree of protection for the intended victim. Disregarding the rule of silence that generally surrounded Black Hand victims, he added that many of his friends had received threatening letters and most of them had paid the amounts demanded. It was the only way they had of protecting their lives and their families. An editorial in the *Chicago Record-Herald* argued that the only way to change the attitude of the Italian community was for the national government to

take responsibility for the campaign against Black Hand crime. Once local Italians felt secure, their cooperation would be forthcoming.[26]

Whatever the problems with the Chicago police, it was clear that
some members of the department were making progress against Black
Hand criminals. Detective Longobardi was apparently so effective that
he received a letter threatening his life for his efforts against Black Hand
crime. The address on the letter was spelled out in large printed letters in
a disguised hand. The letter said that the Black Hand would kill Longobardi if he persisted in his efforts to uproot the organization in Chicago.
Police suspected that Joseph De Salbo was the writer of the letters. Their
belief was strengthened when they arrested De Salbo in a house within
100 feet of the Longobardi home. De Salbo was being sought for attempting to extort $1,500 from Frank Zapullo, a grocer on South Morgan Street.
De Salbo and three other men, Francesco Scrico and brothers Salvatore
and Rocco Basso, came into the Zapullo store and demanded money.
They were all armed. One of the men drew a revolver and placed it at
the head of Mrs. Zapullo, stating that if she did not produce the money
in ten days, she, her husband, and their five children would all die. After
the men left, the Zapullos contacted the police department and Detectives Longobardi and Bernacchi were assigned to the case. A raid of the
De Salbo home resulted in the arrest of the three men and the recovery
of a number of stilettos, revolvers, shotguns, and photographs of dead
men in coffins.[27]

Detective Bernacchi told the press that he expected an increase in
the type of crime practiced by the Zapullos. Many Italian immigrants
had jobs building railroads throughout the Midwest, but the railroads
had adopted a tighter screening policy that drove men like De Salbo
back into the city for lack of work.[28] Bernacchi believed that those who
could not find employment idled their time away in local saloons and
were sometimes recruited into criminal activity. The detective argued
that lax parole laws and the opportunity for Black Hand criminals to post
bail made his work almost impossible. Black Hand victims knew that
the courts would release their tormentors before trial. As a result, they
were afraid to testify against them.

The trial of thirty-five alleged Camorra members in Viterbo, Italy,
may have also contributed to the increase in Black Hand crime in Chicago. Enrico Cantolloni, an alleged Camorra agent, was under investigation for collecting money in Little Sicily and another Italian community
on the South Side of Chicago.[29] Soliciting amounts ranging from $10 to
$500, he told those that he obtained money from that the funds were for
the defense of the Camorrists on trial in Viterbo. Cantolloni had been in

Chicago for three months, and after obtaining a room on Gault Court, he began collecting the money. Those who would not pay received letters signed the Black Hand. Cantolloni told one of his victims that he needed to collect $250,000. A check of the records of the central post office indicated that the amount of money sent to Italy in postal money orders had increased $3,000 during the previous two months as compared to the same months the year before. Whether the increase was due to Cantollini's sending money to Italy is uncertain. A more likely explanation is that Cantollini was using the Viterbo trial as an excuse to extort money from vulnerable countrymen.

The trial in Viterbo stemmed from the 1907 murder of Gennaro Cuoccolo and his wife Maria.[30] Cuoccolo was a singer and a thief. He would use his position as an entertainer to assist fellow Camorrists in planning burglaries. Unhappy with the division of the spoils, he betrayed his accomplices to the police. In retaliation, his former partners brutally murdered Cuccolo and his wife. The chief suspect, Enrico Alfano, the reputed leader of the Cammorra, fled to New York City. He was later arrested by Lieutenant Joseph Petrosino of the New York Black Hand Squad and subsequently deported back to Italy to stand trial. The brutal manner in which the Cuoccolos were killed stirred the Italian police into action. Over the next four years, the Italian *Carabinieri* (national police) detained more than 900 people during the course of their investigation. Forty-seven people eventually stood trial.

The Viterbo trial and the continued occurrence of Black Hand crime filled the newspapers right up to the last day of March, when Phillip Purpurpa, a wholesale fruit merchant on East Ninetieth Street, was arrested in a Black Hand plot to extort $1,000 from Max Rice.[31] Rice had received four Black Hand letters. The final letter instructed him to place $1,000 in a package on the platform of the Illinois Central Railroad Station on South Chicago Avenue and to mark the hiding place with chalk. Rice had reported the letters to the police, who instructed him to place a dummy parcel as directed. Rice hid the package at 1 o'clock in the afternoon. At 4 o'clock, detectives hiding on the train platform observed a man sneak up and furtively look about. He then boarded a northbound train and left, followed by one of the detectives. At Seventy-ninth Street, the stranger changed to a southbound train and, with the officer still shadowing him, rode back to South Chicago Avenue. When he left the train, the suspect waited for the platform to clear and picked up the hidden package. The detectives then arrested him before he could leave the station.

At the South Chicago Avenue police station, Purpurpa, "after many hours of sweating," confessed to Captain Plunkett that he had written at least twenty-five extortion letters to South Chicago business owners, all signed the Black Hand. The victims included theater owner Peter Lapina, clothier Theodore Rasch, bar supplier Morris Lippert, saloonkeeper Frank Medosh, a grocer named Geometti, and Dr. H. Stedman. Purpurpa also said that he worked alone. Purpurpa was turned over to federal authorities for prosecution. In court, Purpurpa admitted writing the letters but said that three Italians had forced him to write the demands while they pointed revolvers at him. Judge Landis, who was no stranger to Black Hand crime, heard the case. At the trial, Landis called Purpurpa's defense "a grotesquely absurd lie" and sentenced him to five years in the Leavenworth penitentiary, the maximum federal penalty.[32]

What was significant about the Purpurpa case was that it firmly established that many of the crimes attributed to the Black Hand were really the work of individuals or small bands of offenders who took advantage of the dramatic and mysterious stories surrounding these crimes. Commenting on the Purpurpa affair, the *Chicago Record-Herald* wrote in an editorial that "mystery, panic and fiction hamper the police and enable the alien criminals to operate with far greater safety than they could if all so-called 'Black Hand' outrages were treated as ordinary affairs and everyone concerned did his obvious duty without conjuring up dreadful possibilities."[33] In other words, sensational newspaper reporting contributed to the power of Black Hand criminals. Two weeks later, a letter written to the editor of the *Chicago Record-Herald* protested that the indiscriminate use of the term *Black Hand* gave both the crime and the criminal a larger importance than would arise if the press treated the crimes as separate incidents.

The same day that the Purpurpa editorial appeared in the *Chicago Record-Herald*, another editorial in *L'Italia* called for the resumption of the activities of the White Hand Society.[34] *L'Italia* argued that until recently crimes in the Italian community were almost all restricted to crimes of passion or crimes to avenge the honor of a wife, sister, or daughter. They were now, however, often committed in the name of the Black Hand and motivated by money. The editorial went on to say that these frequently atrocious crimes were creating an unfavorable impression of the Italian people that the Italian people must correct themselves, particularly in light of the failure of the Chicago police to cope with the Black Hand problem. The inability of the police to bring Black Hand offenders to justice, the newspaper argued, did not escape the attention of the criminals themselves who, almost secure from punishment, were becoming more audacious every day.

The failure of the police in Chicago to cope with Black Hand crime and other crimes of violence was the subject of an ongoing newspaper debate. Critics had routinely blamed the police department for their failure to convict those persons accused of murder and manslaughter. The police, however, argued that it was the prosecutor, not they, who had failed to convict those brought before him. Of 547 persons arrested for homicide between 1906 and 1910, police pointed out that the prosecutor's office obtained only 132 convictions. State's attorney Wayman responded to police criticism by arguing that the blame for the large number of dismissals rested with lax police investigations and police use of the dragnet method, which often resulted in the release of those arrested for lack of evidence.[35]

A report of the murder of one of its investigators followed the call for the renewed efforts of the White Hand Society. A man tentatively identified as Frank Temerno was found shot to death, with five bullets in his body, in the rear of 865 Gault Court. The story arose that three mysterious Italians had arrived in Little Sicily the day of the shooting. Some believed that they were special detectives employed by the White Hand Society. They allegedly spent several hours that evening with federal agents from the Justice Department's Bureau of Investigation. Despite the denials of the former leaders of the White Hand, it was believed that the society was attempting to renew its activities in Little Sicily and other sections of the city. Inspector John Revere of the East Chicago Avenue Station was in charge of the case. Revere, himself an Italian, believed that the victim was slain for revenge, which supported the theory that the man was a White Hand detective. When police viewed the body, they identified the man as Frank Enero. They believed Enero to be a former Mafia member who may have deserted the underworld to work for the White Hand Society.[36]

Further investigation revealed that Enero, also known as Frank Fernero, had quarreled with another man in a saloon near Oak and Milton.[37] Witnesses claimed that they had never seen either of the men, but all believed that they were quarreling over money. Police believed that they may have quarreled over the division of proceeds from some Black Hand extortion that they had engineered. Another theory was that jealousy caused the shooting. In fact, police were seeking a woman with whom Fernero was especially friendly. After angry words passed between the disputants, they reportedly started for the alley door. Once in the alley, five shots were fired and Enero fell dead. No one in the saloon would admit to having seen the shooting, and like most murders in Little Sicily, it remained unsolved.

Two months later, someone killed Giuseppe Giglio, a witness to the Enero murder.[38] The shooting occurred under the banners and strings of lights that lined Gault Court in honor of a religious celebration at Saint Philip Benizi's Church. Like Enero, police suspected that Giglio had been a member of the Mafia in Sicily. He had reportedly fled the old country after his activities had come to the attention of the Palermo police. Upon settling in the United States, Giglio opened a barbershop on West Harrison Street. Like Enero, he had become friendly with those investigating Black Hand activities. Although his assailant shot Giglio multiple times, he did not die until reaching Passavant Hospital. Nevertheless, he refused to provide police with any information about his assailants.

The renewal of the efforts of the White Hand Society was also called for after the explosion of a wholesale liquor store at 840 Grand Avenue in the Near Northwest Side.[39] The press charged the crime to the Mafia, and police Black Hand Squad officers were assigned to the investigation. The Italian detectives determined that Joseph Morici and Pietro Misuraci, the owners of the property, planned to destroy their store, point the finger at the Black Hand, and collect a tidy profit in insurance money. The stock in the liquor store was insured for $8,000, and Morici reported that he had received several threatening letters from the Mafia. Police began to focus their investigation on Morici and Misuraci after they learned that Morici had bought fifteen gallons of gasoline the morning of the explosion. The gasoline was stored in the basement of the liquor store.

Although Morici had told the police that he did not have a criminal record, their investigation revealed that he had been involved with the authorities on several previous occasions.[40] The Chicago police had arrested Morici ten years earlier for killing a man named Ganbarzello in a gunfight at Grand and Halsted streets, but he claimed self-defense and was acquitted in court. Following the shooting was a bombing of a saloon that Morici owned at 181 Sangamon Street, which he attributed to the Black Hand. Pietro Misuraci, Morici's partner, also figured in police and fire annals. He had been the victim of a fire several years earlier and had blamed the Black Hand for it, collecting the insurance money.

Misuraci then became the treasurer of a patent medicine company that he had established with several other men. An incendiary device destroyed a house belonging to one of his partners. A plot to burn another building was frustrated by the police investigation of the first fire, and Misuraci moved shortly thereafter to Danville, Illinois. While in Danville, Misuraci engaged in the fruit business with two other men. The business was insured for $12,000 by several companies. In November 1909, a nitroglycerin bomb wrecked the building. The fire insurance company refused to pay in full, settling for 50 cents on the dollar. Misuraci then returned to Chicago. A short time later, his former partners in Danville received a number of Black Hand letters demanding that they bring money to Chicago to pay an agent of the society. The victims reportedly came to Chicago and consulted with Misuraci, who arranged to pay the money. Misuraci next entered into the business with Morici at the Grand Avenue address.

The Morici/Misuraci case highlights a number of important issues about Black Hand crime.[41] Both men claimed to be victims of the Black Hand, but, in reality, they were using the name Black Hand to commit insurance fraud. How many other crimes were incorrectly attributed to the Black Hand and not discovered? Misuraci was almost certainly the perpetrator of the extortion attempt against the Mascari brothers, his former partners in Danville, which further supports the belief that Black Hand crime was a method of extortion carried out by individuals or small groups and not a highly organized criminal conspiracy. Anyone could commit Black Hand crime. One did not need to be part of the Mafia or the Black Hand. If the Black Hand was a hierarchical organization as often portrayed, how could a member like Mascari be a victim one day and the offender the next?

Just as Joseph Morici and Pietro Misuraci used the Black Hand name to disguise the arson of their liquor store, the Black Hand name was also used to divert police from solving the murder of contractor Joseph Vacek. Vacek was found slain in his home on South Hamlin Avenue in August 1911.[42] On his chest was a note from the killers addressed to his wife, Barbara Vacek. The note explained that her husband had originally hired them to kill her, but when they failed and demanded payment anyway, they killed him because he would not pay. The note was signed "B. H.," and decorated with crude drawings of daggers and other insignia of death. Police, however, believed that a member of the family might have killed Vacek. Their attention focused on sixteen-year-old Joseph Vacek Jr. when they discovered that he had been deceiving his father about going to work and feared punishment for failing to bring home his earnings. Police devised a scheme to get a handwriting sample from young Joseph by asking him to provide a statement of his whereabouts at the time of the shooting. A comparison of the statement with the alleged Black Hand letter left at the scene of the murder revealed that the same person had written both letters. Confronted with the discovery, Joseph Jr. confessed to killing his father because he had hated and feared him, and to writing the Black Hand letter to divert police attention.

The idea that Black Hand offenders enjoyed virtual immunity from punishment because of the self-imposed silence of their victims was shattered when Frances Sottosanto shot and captured Black Hand extortionist Joseph Vitetta.[43] Sottosanto and her husband, Ignacio, were the proprietors of a saloon at 2218 South Wentworth Avenue. The Sottosantos had received a Black Hand letter in March directing them to take $1,000 to the bridge at Archer Avenue and Clark Street. They were to give it to a man who would ask for a match. When the Sottosantos failed to heed the extortion demand, the blackmailers exploded a dynamite bomb in the front of their business. The Sottosantos then received a second letter, this time demanding $1,500. They turned the letter over to the police. The police made up a dummy package of money and accompanied Ignacio Sottosanto to the drop, but no one approached him. The next night another bomb exploded in the doorway of the saloon, further damaging the front of the building. The Sottosantos then received a third letter demanding $2,000 under penalty of death. On the same day that the letter was received, a man came into the saloon and asked Mrs. Sottosanto if she had received the Black Hand letter. When she replied that she had, the man admitted to having written the letters and that unless the money was paid, he would blow up the saloon and kill her and her husband. The man, later identified as Joseph Vitetta, warned her not to call the police and that he had two accomplices watching the saloon. Mrs. Sottosanto assured Vitetta that she would not contact the authorities and told him to invite his friends in for a drink. A plan was then worked out for the men to return later to pick up the money.

After the offenders left, the Sottosantos immediately contacted the police, who assigned Black Hand Squad detectives to the case.[44] Discouraged after a lengthy stakeout, the officers finally left at nine in the evening on the second day. After they had gone, Vitetta and his accomplices returned. Frances was tending bar. Vitetta went upstairs to the rooms above the bar to confront Ignacio. The saloonkeeper still had the phony roll of bills that the police had given him to give to the extortionists. After a while, the two waiting men became suspicious and ran out of the saloon whistling a warning to Vitetta as they left. Hearing Vitetta running down the stairs, Frances stepped from the barroom into the stairwell and grabbed him as he came down, shouting, "Here's your money, take it." Vitetta, however, broke away from her grasp. She shot Vitetta twice with a revolver that she had been holding in her hand. The first bullet struck Vitetta in the left shoulder. The second bullet stuck him in the nose. Police officer Hugh Joyce of the Twenty-Second district was nearby and heard the shots. When he arrived, he found Mrs. Sottosanto standing guard over the Black Hander, shouting, "Throw up your hands, or I shoot."

At the police station, Vitetta argued that he was not a Black Hand member but a member of a gang of blackmailers who had been trying to secure tribute from the Sottosantos under the pretense that they would in return disclose the identity of the persons who had blown up the Sottosanto saloon.[45] Vitetta implicated a relative of the Sottosantos as the leader of the gang. He also identified Antonio Graziano and Dominico Zavello as his accomplices. Both men were arrested in a raid of a boarding house on West Taylor Street. The police were inclined to believe Vitetta's story. They had recently received information that a gang of Italians was attempting to get money from Black Hand bombing victims by selling them the identities of those who were responsible for the explosions. This defense, however, did not exonerate them. Vitetta and his accomplices were indicted by a Cook County grand jury and eventually tried for the attempt extortion of the Sottosantos.

Probably the most important Black Hand case to come to the attention of the Chicago police was the kidnapping of six-year-old Angelo Mareno. The case was important because it provided a firsthand account of how official corruption worked to protect Black Hand criminals. Mareno was kidnapped in Little Sicily on August 6, 1911. Detectives learned from a playmate that the boy was last seen in the company of a man going west on Oak Street shortly after 10 a.m.[46] Police and neighbors searched every house, barn, and shed in the area for the missing boy. Even Angelo's kindergarten schoolmates at St. Phillip Benizi School were organized into a search party. Apparently unfazed by the searchers and the fact that the whole of Little Sicily was involved in the effort, one of the kidnappers was seen the next day leisurely walking through the neighborhood right past the location where the kidnappers had taken the boy. He was identified by a neighbor who saw Angelo in the company of the man on a Southport Avenue streetcar the day of the kidnapping.

At first, police believed that the kidnapping of Angelo was in retaliation for the murder of Modesto Barona, an alleged Black Hand chief.[47] Barona was shot down in March 1909 by Angelo's father, Antonio, in a gunfight in front of Barona's home on Gault Court in Little Sicily. The men had quarreled in a nearby saloon and had renewed the argument when they met on the street an hour later. Guns were drawn, bullets fired, and Barona fell to the ground dead. Mareno fled but was arrested two months later after a lengthy police investigation. Mareno was brought before the grand jury in May, but the jurors refused to indict him. The evidence showed that he had shot in self-defense. Mareno knew that the failed grand jury proceeding was not the end of the case, and he expected that Barona's family would try to avenge his death.

Baffled in their efforts to follow the trail of the abductors, police turned to questioning the friends of the father after a special delivery letter demanding $5,000 for the return of the boy arrived later that afternoon.[48] The letter informed Mareno to "look among friends" for the man to whom the money must be paid, and was signed the Black Hand. Police immediately made a list of all the acquaintances of the father. On the list were two men who had previously attracted the attention of detectives investigating Black Hand crime. Both were sought for questioning. The police department assigned Detectives Longobardi, Riccio, and Parodi of the Black Hand Squad to the investigation. Two days later, the Marenos received a second letter informing them that they had only four days left to buy back their child. The same night a mysterious fire was started directly across the street from the Mareno home. Neighbors instantly rushed into the street, discharging their revolvers, as was the custom, to summon firefighters.

Two days later, Inspector Revere announced that Antonio, his wife Bernarda, their son Phillip, and their daughter Stina were withholding information from the police. After "sweating" Phillip, Angelo's older brother, at police headquarters, Revere was convinced that the family knew more than they were letting on. He proved to be right. The Marenos had begun secret negotiations with the kidnappers the morning after the neighboring fire, which some believed had been set as a warning from the kidnappers.[49]

After having been missing for nearly five days, Angelo Mareno was returned to his family on August 11, 1911. He was found walking on Gault Court at 10 o'clock at night by detectives assigned to the kidnapping case. The boy told the officers that he had been held in a house on West Division Street. Police also discovered that Biagia Cutrona had told Antonio Mareno that he could find his son at a five-cent theater at Larrabee and Elm streets. Cutrona was the mother-in-law of Carmelo Nicolosi—saloonkeeper, associate of Gianni Alongi, and suspect Black Hand offender. Carmello Nicolosi and his brother Joseph (Giuseppe) owned a saloon at 134 Gault Court. Police had questioned both men in May 1909 regarding the murder of Joseph's father-in-law, Mariano Zagone.

The next day, police had eleven persons in custody in connection with the kidnapping of Angelo Mareno: Carmelo Nicolosi, his wife Paulina (Cologera), his brother Joseph, and mother-in-law Biagia Cutrona. The other seven people were being held as witnesses pending further investigation.[50] In a curious turn of events, a letter of apology was received at the Mareno home less than ten hours after the return of the boy. The letter, originally written in Italian, read:

We wish to inform you that we are sorry that we made a mistake. We were informed that you had $10,000 in bank. We have come to the conclusion that you are a laborer and have not so much money. That you are laborer and couldn't have so much. We ask you to excuse us this time. Your boy will be delivered to you on Friday. He will be dressed in white and be in front of one of the depots in Chicago. Yours with regards.[51]

The apology letter was not the only strange thing to occur. It seems that Joseph Nicolosi was the godfather of the kidnapped boy. Additionally, Antonio Moreno was the godfather of one of Joseph Nicolosi's children, as well as one of Carmello Nicolosi's children. The bitterness between the Mareno and Nicolosi families that led to the kidnapping was the result of a feud that began in Sicily years before. Joseph Nicolosi and Antonio Mareno had reportedly quarreled over the love of a woman, which resulted in a fight with a revolver. Inspector Revere's earlier suspicion that the Marenos knew the identities of their son's kidnappers was confirmed. There were also other complications. Antonio Mareno had paid Paulina Nicolosi $500 for the return of his son. None of the money had been recovered. More importantly, little Angelo Mareno was unable to identify any of the arrestees as his abductors. Determined to get some answers, Inspector Revere brought Antonio Mareno in for questioning. After five hours of interrogation, police still had not gotten to the bottom of the alleged kidnapping. In desperation, Inspector Revere sent for the Reverend Louis Giambastiani of Saint Philip Benizi's, the local parish church. Although new to the parish at the time, Giambastiani's reputation would grow to legendary proportions during the fifty years that he spent in Little Sicily.[52]

Giambastiani convinced Mareno to cooperate with the police. As a result of the priest's intervention, Mareno gave a twenty-five-page statement. He began by admitting that the Nicolosi brothers had blackmailed him three years earlier when he gave them $50 to protect him from Black Hand vengeance. In fact, Mareno admitted that the letters he received in relation to his son's kidnapping were written in the same hand as the earlier extortion demand. During the interview, it came to light that Mrs. Cutrona, on several occasions prior to the kidnapping, had discussed the possibility of Black Hand threats and the abduction of Angelo, as well as methods of affecting settlement with the blackmailers. Mareno told the police that after the kidnapping, an undisclosed person had advised him to obtain the ransom money and then walk around the neighborhood wearing a stiff hat as a signal that he was ready to pay. Mareno, working with police, did as instructed and paraded around the neighborhood wearing the hat. He then, unknown to the police, complied with a "mysterious" request to meet "somebody" in the Nicolosi saloon before going to the bank to withdraw the ransom money. At the saloon, Joseph Nicolosi informed Mareno that he believed the matter could be "fixed up" for $2,000 or $3,000. When Mareno explained that he did not have that much money, Joseph said that he would send his brother Carmelo over to speak with him. When Carmelo Nicolosi met with Antonio Mareno, they settled on $500 for the return of the kidnapped boy. Paulina Nicolosi came later that day to the Mareno home and collected the money.[53]

Joseph Nicolosi argued at his arrest that he was innocent and Mareno based his charge on a long-standing grudge, and that he was a respectable businessman. Surprisingly, some influential members of the Italian community may have agreed. Antonio Sbarbaro, an undertaker, and Joseph De Voney, a real estate agent and banker, provided the $10,000 that was needed to post Nicolosi's bail. Even Antonio Mareno thought that the Nicolosi brothers were only guilty of being go-betweens and the real persons responsible for kidnapping his son had not come to the attention of the police. Police, however, believed otherwise. They thought that the the feud had been disclosed for the sole purpose of throwing them off the track. Whoever the kidnappers, Antonio Mareno had become the target of retribution. A dozen men reportedly warned him that his assassin had already been selected and that before the Nicolosis were brought to trial, he would be killed. Even one of the detectives assigned to the case was threatened. Detective Anthony Gentile received a Black Hand letter warning him, upon penalty of death, to end his investigation of the Mareno kidnapping: "Dear Friend—We let you know that you must not go further in the investigation of the Mareno case. This is the first notice we will send you. If you go further you will receive harm from the Black Hand." Police reacted by closing the Nicolosi brothers' saloon.[54]

In spite of Joseph Nicolosi's protests, indictments were returned against him, his brother Carmelo, Paulina Nicolosi, and Biagia Cutrona. Besides the kidnapping charge, they were indicted for attempting to extort money from Antonio Mareno two years earlier. Indictments were also returned against two new defendants, Calogero Costandino and Leoluca Macaluso, who were with the actual kidnappers of the boy. Both were still at large. Angelo Mareno would later testify that Macaluso came to the street in front of his house with a big red wagon and took him for a ride around the block and to a big black house on Division Street.[55]

Three weeks later, Detectives Longobardi, Bernachi, Riccio, and De Vito raided a grocery store at 908 Sholto Street where they found explosives and a list of 150 persons who allegedly were contributing to a fund to defend Joseph and Carmello Nicolosi.[56] Anthony Loungora and another man were taken into custody. The large amount of evidence recovered included bombs, dynamite fuses, percussion caps, and other explosives. During the raid, police heard Loungora tell the other men not to resist the police because three of the bombs were ready to explode. Police hoped that the evidence would help them clear up a number of other ongoing Black Hand investigations.

Just one month after their indictments, Joseph and Carmello Nicolosi were found guilty and sentenced to life in prison for their crimes. Paulina Nicolosi was sentenced to seven years for her part in the blackmailing scheme. The severe sentences were meant to send a strong message to Black Hand criminals, especially those operating in Little Sicily. The sentences were never carried out, however. Judge Honore granted the Nicolosis a new trial on February 19, 1912, arguing that newspaper coverage of the case had influenced the jury. On February 24, the case was taken off the court call. It was put back on, postponed, and taken off again at least a half dozen times. It would be two years before the new trial began. The Marenos were mystified. The mystery was solved when court records revealed that Chicago alderman John Powers had posted bonds for both men after having arranged to reduce the defendants' bonds in the new trial from $25,000 to $10,000. John Powers was the alderman of the Nineteenth Ward, which was located in the Near West Side of Chicago. Its population consisted of Italian, Irish, and Jewish immigrants. He ran two saloons and a gambling house, and was known as the "Prince of Boodlers" because of his ability to push corrupt measures through the city council.[57]

Already under police protection because of the arrest of the Nicolosi clan, the knowledge of Alderman Powers' involvement in the rescheduling of the trial only heightened the Mareno family's fear.[58] Antonio and his two sons moved to what they thought was a safer location a few blocks from Little Sicily. Bernarda Nicolosi, the mother of the abducted boy, had died the previous November, ostensibly from the trauma related to the kidnapping of her son.

The involvement of Alderman Powers finally led to a public outcry. The Reverend Elmer L. Williams, pastor of the Grace Methodist Church, attacked the activities of Powers in the case, stating that Alderman Powers misrepresented the people of the Nineteenth Ward and "recognized the political value of a neat little organization like a Black Hand society."[59] He concluded that the "blackest hands" were not found in Little Italy but were those stretched out to sign bail bonds for characters such as the Nicolosis and to write continuance on the judge's call sheet.

Public sentiment and pressure from the *Chicago Daily Tribune* forced the court to set a new date for the retrial of the Nicolosi clan. Frederick Burnham, the prosecuting attorney, told the press that he had tried many times to have the case called, but there seemed to be a "hidden power" that balked at his efforts. The case finally was set for trial on May 5, 1914, the day after the *Tribune* article disclosing Alderman Powers's involvement in the case. Jury selection began the same day. On May 7, Antonio Mareno took the witness stand and told how he had been victimized by the blackmailing scheme. He also explained the "system" of blackmailing that existed in Little Sicily and challenged prosecutors to do something about what he described as the "saloonkeeper bosses" who held power there. As Mareno testified, two detectives sat in the courtroom to protect him. In fact, he had been under police protection for the past two years. Police had even accompanied him to work at his job as a street sweeper. As many as twelve officers had been assigned at one time to protect the Mareno family at a cost to the City of Chicago of $10,000.[60]

Whatever the system of Black Hand crime and whatever the connection to saloonkeeper bosses, Black Hand crime in Little Sicily and throughout Chicago plummeted in 1912. Black Hand criminals may have been down, but they were not out, however. Detective Anthony Gentile, who had headed the Mareno guard detail, was transferred to Hegewisch and ordered into uniform, allegedly because he watched Mareno "too diligently." While assigned to the East Chicago Avenue Station, Gentile had played a prominent role in a number of other Black Hand investigations. Being transferred to Hegewisch in the Chicago Police Department was the equivalent of being transferred to Siberia. The transfer of Gentile was not the end of the story. The new trial only lasted three days. Much to the astonishment of everyone involved, Judge McKinley acquitted the Nicolosis of all charges.[61]

Although direct evidence that Alderman Powers had a hand in dismissing the charges against the Nicolosis has not come to light, the fact that he was involved at all signaled that Black Hand criminals had some tie to elected officials. Powers's involvement also demonstrated the often-felt futility of testifying against Black Hand criminals. On the other hand, the Mareno case demonstrated the heroic efforts made by members of the Italian community and Chicago Police against Black Hand criminals. Former White Hand Society members, in spite of the demise of the organization, had provided financial support to the Nicolosi investigation, and any number of police officers risked their lives and careers to fight Black Hand extortion, as demonstrated by the action taken against Officer Gentile.[62]

An interesting article appeared in the business section of the *Chi-*

cago Daily Tribune on June 26, 1927. The article reported that Joseph and Carmelo Nicolosi had sold the Glengyle Apartment Hotel, one of the first tall buildings erected in the Edgewater community, for $450,000, a substantial sum of money in 1927.[63] The Glengyle contained sixty-four suites and had a bungalow on the eight-story roof. They used the proceeds of the sale to buy three other apartment buildings in Chicago: not bad for two neighborhood saloonkeepers.

There may be more to the corruption angle than Alderman Powers. The Chicago Civil Service Commission brought charges against police inspector John Revere, Captain Bernard Baer, and Lieutenant John Hanley in December 1911. The commission alleged that they had allowed vice to flourish in the East Chicago Avenue district. Two police lieutenants, John Dammann and Timothy Cullinan, testified that they had personally made written reports to Revere concerning saloons that had allowed unescorted women, "resorts" (houses of prostitution), and other shady hotels. On the witness stand, Baer testified that Revere had ordered him to ignore the twenty-six vice resorts that Dammann and Cullinan had identified. In his defense, Revere replied that he had taken the list of the illegal vice dens to police chief John McWeeney, who had told him not to move against the vice operators on the list.[64]

The motive for the charges against Revere is not certain. What is certain is that vice was common in the area. In fact, the Near North Side of Chicago was known as "Honky-Tonk USA."[65] North Clark Street in the East Chicago Avenue police district was one of the major vice districts in Chicago. Clark Street also ran through the Sands neighborhood, one of Chicago's original tenderloin districts. Saloons and cabarets marked every block on Clark Street from Grand Avenue to Division Street. Given Alderman Powers's involvement in the Nicolosi case, it is within the realm of possibility that Revere was replaced because of his efforts against Black Hand crime, not his failure to take action against vice.

History would prove that the Mareno case was the single most important case ever pursued against Black Hand crime in Chicago. Italian businessmen and attorneys appearing at his civil service trial testified that Revere was the one man in Chicago who was able to defeat Black Hand crime in Little Sicily.[66] C. A. Raggio, a local real estate developer, argued that even the efforts of the United States government could not compare to the accomplishments of Inspector Revere against Black Hand crime. Attorneys Stephen Malato and Bernard Barasa gave similar testimony. Undertaker Antonio Sbarbaro testified to the improved conditions in the North Side vice district since Revere became the commanding officer of the East Chicago Avenue Station, and so did former city council member John Minwagen. C. J. Appel, of the Illinois Tunnel Company, whose men worked in the area, testified that the "Black Hand section" (Little Sicily) was now as quiet as a graveyard.

One has to wonder why the Mareno case was not pursued in federal court where the chances of political interference were less likely. In fact, there was another federal Black Hand prosecution during the time of the Mareno investigation. Police from the New City Station had arrested Jacob Basta, a twenty-two-year-old Bohemian man, on the charge of sending a Black Hand letter demanding $500 to Jacob Steck, a grocer on West Fifty-first Street.[67] The letter instructed Steck to place the money in a hollow tree near Fifty-Fifth and Robey streets. Basta was arrested when he attempted to retrieve a decoy package left by the victim. When detectives, who had secreted themselves in the tall grass of a nearby vacant lot, attempted to arrest Basta, he tried to escape, firing three shots at the officers as he ran away. Police returned fire and apprehended Basta after a foot chase of several blocks. Under police interrogation, Basta admitted to having sent the Black Hand letter, stating that he needed the money because he was broke and soon to be married.

The Basta case was followed some months later by another federal indictment in which postal authorities charged Philip Sandberg and James Peterson with sending a series of Black Hand letters to a Northwest Side businessman named Olsen.[68] The letters demanded $10,000 under penalty of death. Sandberg and Peterson were arrested by the Pinkerton National Detective Agency after they picked up a decoy package that was placed by Olsen at the location designated in the extortion letter. During interrogation, Peterson confessed that he had worked for Olsen but had not received a "square deal." Both men admitted that they had blackmailed other area businessmen.

The year 1911 ended with the murder of Joe Rebella on New Year's Eve. A sawed-off shotgun blast struck Reballa as he walked past 457 Hein Place. He was attacked by two offenders who threw the gun away after the shooting. Police first believed that a rival Black Hand gang had slain Reballa, a known Black Hand criminal. They later determined, however, that he was the victim of his own plot to obtain money from the slayers. Police theorized that Reballa had made an appointment to meet his intended victims, who rebuked his demands and shot him. Rabella died in a police ambulance while being taken to Alexian Brothers Hospital. He passed away without making a statement. Detectives Longobardi and Bernacchi of the Black Hand Squad worked with district police in the search for the killers. The killers had shortened the barrel of the shotgun used in the slaying to sixteen inches in length. It was the same type of weapon that had been recently used in a number of other Black Hand shootings. Longobardi said that the shooters sawed off the barrels in order to conceal the weapons. The reduced size made it almost as portable as a revolver and at short range far more deadly.[69]

Black Hand crime declined dramatically in 1912. Police believed that the Mareno case had "annihilated" Black Hand crime.[70] Chicago would never again experience the number of Black Hand extortions that it did in the four years from 1908 through 1911. In fact, the Chicago Police reported on August 5, 1912, that they had not heard of any Black Hand letters since they had apprehended Angelo Mareno's kidnappers. The Mareno case also supported the argument of the White Hand Society that Black Hand crimes were the work of politically connected saloonkeepers.

Then there was the bombing of a two-story brick bakery on Milton Avenue in May 1912. It was described as the "greatest explosion that Little Italy had ever witnessed." The force of the explosion shook buildings and hurled frightened men and women from their beds for blocks around. The fire that followed the bombing burned six horses to death and damaged a number of neighboring buildings. The incident was the second bombing directed at Antonio Morici, the bakery's owner. Police received information that Black Hand extortionists had demanded that Morici pay $10,000 to safeguard his property. Police assigned detectives Longobardi and Gentile to the case. (The police department had apparently rescued Gentile from his exile in Hegewisch and assigned him to work with the Black Hand Squad.) The lack of evidence and the failure of Morici to cooperate with the detectives prevented the officers from solving the crime. Morici had continually denied that he was the victim of Black Hand extortion, arguing that the bombing was the result of a labor war. Morici believed that the attempt to wreck his place of business was the result of his refusal to discharge a number of nonunion bakers in his employ. Police became suspicious, however, when a witness reported that he had seen a fire in the building before the explosion occurred. Morici's reluctance to cooperate with the authorities was finally explained when police determined that Antonio Morici and his brothers Filippo and Agostino had deliberately set the fire in order to cash in on their property insurance.[71]

Police subsequently charged the three Morici brothers with arson and released them on $100,000 bonds.[72] Five months later, police arrested Charles Furthmann, a special investigator for State's Attorney Maclay Hoyne, for selling state's evidence to the defendants in the Morici case. Furthmann allegedly sold a copy of the confession of Ben Fink, a known "fire bug" who had been employed by the Morici brothers to set fire to their Milton Avenue warehouse. Stephen A. Malato, now an assistant state's attorney, was assigned to the case.

The Morici bombing led to the canceling of insurance policies in Little Sicily even though it was not a Black Hand crime.[73] The claims paid out because of the reign of terror caused by Black Hand crime had affected the profits of the insurance companies. Every barn that was burned and every store or house that was bombed by Black Hand criminals had been heavily insured, and despite the extra premiums demanded by the insurance companies, their losses were enormous. The policy cancellations strengthened fear of Black Hand crime. If Italian merchants could no longer insure their stores, a Black Hand strike would mean financial ruin. They would have to pay the blackmailers.

While Black Hand crimes had dramatically declined, shootings continued in Little Sicily. For example, in April 1912, Frank Tardio was murdered on Gault Court as he left a church meeting. Giovanni Manolla was found with his head "nearly severed" at Oak and Crosby streets, two blocks from Death Corner, in February 1913. Two months later, an unidentified man was shot seven times at Elm and Crosby streets. In February 1914, sawed-off shotgun blasts cut down Anthony Puccio and Rosario Dispenza. Puccio was the first to be murdered. He was shot as he exited his saloon at 1031 Milton Avenue. Dispenza was shot a short time later while examining the bloodstained street where Puccio had been killed. Police believed that Puccio was murdered in revenge for his part in the recent killing of Charles Catolina in Urbana, Illinois. Dispenza was no stranger to Black Hand crime. His saloon in Little Sicily was one of those believed by the White Hand Society to be a gathering place for Black Hand criminals.[74]

Victor Barone, an intimate friend of Puccio and Dispenza, was killed two days later.[75] Barone was no stranger to the police. They had frequently arrested and questioned him in connection with Black Hand activities. Police believed that the shooting was part of a continued campaign by Black Hand victims to rid themselves of local criminals. Police officer Michael Walsh, who was walking a nearby beat, heard the shotgun blast that struck Barone. As he turned down Cambridge Avenue (the new name for Gault Court), he saw two men carrying Barone into his place of business, a wine room at 1024 Cambridge Avenue. Upon entering the building, the family told the officer that they did not need him and that they had summoned a private ambulance. Officer Walsh told family members to send the ambulance back and that the victim was going with him to the hospital. At the hospital, Barone insisted that he did not know the identity of his assailant.

Three months later, Black Hand Squad detectives arrested brothers Paul and Pietro Mennite for extorting $300 from an Italian shoemaker named Anthony Petrone. Police had immediately suspected Pietro Mennite, a friend of the victim, because he had discontinued his visits to Petrone's shoe shop following the receipt of the first letter. The blackmailers instructed Petrone to take the extortion money to the corner of Elizabeth and Austin streets in Chicago. Black Hand Squad officers, assisted by federal agents, staked out the location where the money was to be delivered and waited. After the Mennite brothers arrived and retrieved a package of marked money, police arrested them. During interrogation, the Mennites confessed to having written the Black Hand letters and provided the names of others who they claimed had been involved in some of the worst Black Hand crimes committed in the Italian districts of Chicago. The Mennite case resulted in a renewed federal offensive against Black Hand crime. The confessions provided concrete information to work on, which postal authorities hoped would lead to immediate results. The U.S. District Court sentenced both men to five years in the federal penitentiary at Leavenworth, Kansas.[76]

The new federal effort may have been in response to pressure from Chicago's business leaders.[77] Black Hand crimes not only terrorized the community but also affected real estate values. The tenants of the buildings where Black Hand murders occurred often moved away within twenty-four hours of the incident. It then became almost impossible to rent the premises to other Italians, who feared meeting the same fate. Moving was a practical alternative to Black Hand violence. It must be remembered that bombings were a common method of enforcing Black Hand demands. Tenants feared living in the same building with Black Hand victims because of the possibility that the building would be fire-bombed.

In an address before the Women's Association of Commerce, Chicago Real Estate Board member Preston Nolan declared that property values had decreased and in some cases disappeared altogether because of Black Hand crimes, and that the murders in Chicago's Little Italy districts depreciated real estate values. Nolan provided the example of a building that had to be torn down because it was impossible to rent. In addition, some Italians were afraid to own property for fear of Black Hand extortion, and others would not buy property because they knew it was almost impossible to find tenants. Real estate broker and former city council member Bernard Clettenberg also believed that Black Hand crimes had affected real estate purchases in the Near North Side. He cited the example of a building that he had sold to an Italian for $9,500. Ten days after the sale, the purchaser asked Clettenberg to take the property back because he had received several Black Hand letters.[78]

An editorial in the *Literary Digest*, an influential early-twentieth-century magazine, applauded the renewed efforts of the federal government to fight Black Hand crime.[79] The editorial argued that the federal government had a "special obligation" to help local authorities for two reasons. First, the Black Hand problem resulted from the laxity or weakness of U.S. immigration laws, which allowed undesirable immigrants to enter the country. Second, the Black Hand criminal could hardly operate without sending his letters through the U.S. mail. There was also the added benefit of the "mysterious activity and reserve power" of the federal government that the proceedings of familiar local authorities usually lacked.

Two weeks after the Mennite arrests, another sensational murder occurred in Little Sicily. Pietro Catalanetto, the alleged leader of a gang of fifteen Black Hand criminals, was shot at 1228 North Sedgwick.[80] Black Hand Squad officers had been watching his activities for months. One of the most striking figures in the Near North Side, Catalanetto was a large man with a fringe of snowy white hair. People referred to him as "Don Pietro, king of the Black Hand" and the "Silver King." Time and time again he had been suspected in connection with some mysterious shooting, but he always escaped arrest. Catalanetto had no legitimate occupation but claimed that he was an olive oil vendor. Students at the nearby Lane Technical High School saw the Catalanetto slayer flee from the scene. Fireman Henry Hammerschlag, who had been receiving a shave in a local barbershop, heard the shots and, upon exiting the shop, saw the offender bend over Catalanetto's body and fire two more shots at the prostrate man. When a newspaper reporter informed Mrs. Catalanetto of the death of her husband, she and her daughters proceeded to the local morgue, where the daughters vowed vengeance on those that had killed their father.

The next day, police identified Michael Locascio as the slayer of Catalanetto.[81] The shooting brought to light the story of the extortion of Locascio and of the net with which the police had hoped to catch the Silver King. The week before the killing, Michael Locascio had paid $150 to one of the members of Catalanetto's Black Hand gang. Locascio had received a letter demanding $250 from the group. He took the letter to the police and agreed to work with them to ensnare Catalanetto. Black Hand Squad detectives marked the extortion money, and Locascio agreed to let the officers know when he was to meet with Catalanetto. Locascio, however, changed his mind and failed to let police know of the meeting. When confronted by the police, Angelina Locascio, Michael's fifty-one-year-old mother, promised to go to the coroner's inquest and tell all she knew. One hour before the proceeding, she was shot to death as she sat on the doorstep of her home. Two men walked up to her and her grandson and fired six bullets at her at point-blank range. The men then paused to fire two more shots at the little boy, but missed as he fled.

Detectives Longobardi and Bernacchi were on their way to the Catalanetto inquest when they heard the news of the shooting.[82] The detectives suspected Vietro Barone, Catalanetto's lieutenant, of the slaying. The detectives also suspected that Mrs. Locascio had been marked for death even before the slaying of Catalanetto, as she had cooperated with the police a year earlier when Black Hand extortionists had killed her son-in-law, Joseph Igno. Black Hand criminals targeted the Locascios because they believed that the Locasios owned considerable property in the area. In fact, Angelina Locascio had secretly moved out of the neighborhood in order to avoid the attention of Black Hand criminals but, after a considerable length of time, had returned to Little Sicily.

The killings of Catalanetto and Locascio so frustrated Captain James O'Toole of the East Chicago Avenue police that he announced that he was going to ask the city health department to depopulate Little Sicily.[83] O'Toole argued that fear of the "Mafia" resulted in the unwillingness of witnesses to testify in court. The only remedy was for the health department to stop the overcrowded housing that made it impossible to keep a census of the area. When a murder occurs, he argued, the killers enter almost any house where there are likely to be a dozen people in a room. They remove their coats and are playing cards with the residents by the time the police arrive. The people in the house, fearing retaliation, declare that the men are boarders, hindering the police investigation. In addition, O'Toole believed that political influence had a lot to do with the ability of Black Hand criminals to get their conspirators released even when high bails were posted.

As dramatic as it sounds, Captain O'Toole's recommendation may have had some merit. The Bureau of Immigration had established an Information Division for the purpose of providing immigrants with settlement information once they arrived in the United States.[84] The Information Division was to direct the newcomers to areas where they would find better housing and better living conditions than in the slums of congested cities. In a speech given in Chicago, Terrence Powderly, the chief of the Information Division, announced that had his division been in existence earlier, there would be no such thing as the Black Hand—an obvious reference to the fact that many Black Hand crimes occurred in the congested Italian ghettos of America's cities.

In November 1916, someone killed Pietro Catalanetto's son John on the Belmont Avenue streetcar.[85] Police suspected John Locascio, Michael's brother. This new killing brought out the fact that the Catalanetto and Locascio families were related by marriage. Joseph Locascio was married to Maria Catalanetto, the daughter of Pietro. Joseph, however, had died of poison thought to be the result of suicide. Pietro Catalanetto allegedly sent many letters topped with skull and crossbones and signed with the image of a hand crudely drawn in black ink to Joseph Locascio's mother Angelina. Fearing for her life and the lives of her children, Mrs. Locascio paid the extortion demands. Finally, she had to place a mortgage on her home to raise additional money. Police had discovered that John Locascio murdered Pietro Catalanetto rather than pay the final extortion amount and that Catalanetto's sons, John and Philip, were the killers of Angelina Locascio. John and Phillip were arrested and tried for the murder but found not guilty in a jury trial. As a result, Michael and John Locascio swore that they would avenge the killing of their mother. The murder of John Catalenetto by John Locascio fulfilled this oath.

In yet another shooting, an unknown assailant killed a private detective named Frank De Maria near Death Corner in June 1914. Police believed that De Maria was killed because he was attempting to solve the murder of Isaac Levin, a Chicago Heights produce merchant. A business rivalry with the Battaglia brothers, who were also in the produce business, prompted the murder. Pietro Siatta, an Italian laborer employed as a deliveryman by the Battaglias, claimed to have overheard a conversation in which August Battaglia and George Livreri plotted Levin's murder. Siatta reported the plot to Lee Hook, the mayor of Chicago Heights, and gave a written statement to Manuel Sultan, the local justice of the peace. Siatta later repudiated the affidavit, confessing that Frank De Maria had promised him $300 for making the false statement. The county prosecutor sought an indictment for perjury against Siatta, and Chicago Heights hired Frank De Maria to investigate the case. De Maria had developed a reputation as a "Sicilian investigator" because of his ability to speak Italian and familiarity with the Italian community.[86]

The Chicago Police Department dispatched Detectives Longobardi and Riccio to Chicago Heights to arrest Battaglia and Livreri once the plot became known.[87] While they were at the Chicago Heights police station, sheriff's deputies served them with a writ of habeas corpus ordering the release of the two men. A local Chicago Heights judge had issued the writ and set a $20,000 bond, which two local liquor merchants immediately met. Having had their prisoners taken away, Longobardi and Riccio returned to Chicago. Justice of the peace Manuel Sultan placed the blame for the murder of De Maria on State's Attorney Hoyne, whose office had not been aggressive in pursing the De Maria perjury case. Sultan argued that charging Siatta with perjury would have saved De Maria's life. Sultan also charged that the lack of effort on the part of the state's attorney was business as usual where Chicago Heights was concerned. The U.S. Secret Service, however, offered a different theory. They believed that counterfeiters killed De Maria because of his participation in another crime.

The police department responded to the increasing number of murders in Little Sicily by forming what they described as a "Mafia murder squad."[88] Chief of Detectives Jack Halpin assigned eight men to search saloons in Little Sicily for illegal firearms and to frisk hangers-on throughout the district. He ordered the men to go as far as necessary within the letter of the law to find Italian gunmen and disarm them. Officer De Mar of the Black Hand Squad was one of the officers assigned to the new traveling squad. Chief Halpin assigned the remaining Black Hand officers to assist the squad but ordered them to continue to work separately.

While there was no shortage of crime in Little Sicily, extortionists and pranksters in other parts of Chicago took advantage of the neighborhood's reputation to further their own criminal schemes. Take the case of Dorothea Skinner of 5129 Dorchester in the far South Side of Chicago.[89] It was formally announced that Dorothea and her sister Helen Skinner were each soon to be married. A short time after the announcement, they received an extortion demand. It stated that unless $500 was paid to the "B. H.," Dorothea would "never live to marry." In response, the Skinners placed an ad in the personal column of the *Tribune* that read "Personal—.H. WILL COME to Terms. Call. D.H.S." The Skinners received a second letter directing them to take the money to Oak and Milton streets and to deposit it there in a crack in the grating in front of a saloon.

Upon receipt of the letter, William Skinner, father of the girls and president of the International Livestock Exposition, contacted chief of police Charles Healey.[90] Healey referred the case to Herman Schuettler, who had risen to the rank of first deputy chief of police. Schuettler assigned detectives Longobardi, De Mar, and De Vito to the investigation. Schuettler then chose another squad of detectives to stake out Little Sicily and gave instructions to have a man appear at the appropriate time. The detectives moved into the district just before midnight and took up their assigned positions. The drop was made, but no one appeared to pick it up. Police concluded that the case was probably the work of a crank who had read of Miss Skinner's coming marriage in the newspaper.

In February 1916, Gabriel Longobardi, now a police sergeant, announced that he had received information about a new, highly organized Black Hand gang with plans for a blackmailing campaign that made the activities of the Silver King pale by comparison. The new gang had already sent scores of letters to Italian merchants demanding money.[91] Longobardi expected fifteen to twenty murders in Little Sicily during the following six months because of the efforts of this new group. At least nine murders, in fact, did occur in Little Sicily by the end of the year. Whether all the murders were related to Black Hand crime is doubtful.

One of the first victims of the new Black Hand menace was, luckily, a member of the gang. Gennaro Scrimmento was shot and stabbed near Oak and Milton while waiting for the dropoff of Black Hand extortion money. Police believed that Scrimmento was slain by the very men he had tried to blackmail. A search of Scrimmento's home revealed a loaded shotgun, a revolver, and letters from a man named Mariana, who had recently served five years in prison for the bombing of a butcher shop in the Near North Side. Scrimmento's murder was followed two weeks later by that of Michael Vaiana. Two men shot Vaiana as he walked home from a neighborhood meat market on North Larrabee Street. The *Chicago Daily Tribune* reported, "New Black Hand Murder, Eight since December," although police believed private vengeance to be the motive. A few days later, Helen Muscarello was shot down in front of a saloon at 445 West Division Street. She was estranged from her husband, who was suspected in the crime. Nevertheless, the headlines read, "Woman Shot Dead in Black Hand Murder Region." In April, George Medica was left for dead in the alley at 511 Oak Street. His murder was reported as the tenth to occur at Death Corner that year. A sawed-off shotgun blast had struck him in the neck. The *Tribune* reported that police believed Medica to be a member of the Black Hand because there were a number of "curious signs and marks" surrounding the killing.[92]

Antonio Militello, described as a former Black Hand chieftain, was the next to be killed.[93] Described as "Mafia Murder No. 11" by the press, the murder took place in an alley near his home. Militello was shot twice with a shotgun. A series of crimes was declared by Sergeant Longobardi to be responsible for Militello's death. Militello was believed to have sent Black Hand letters to his own brother. He was also suspected of killing his sister-in-law, Annie Nuccio. About a year earlier, Militello had had an affair with Catherine Nuccio, the niece of his wife. Annie Nuccio, Catherine's mother, was shot, and police suspected that Militello had pulled the trigger. As a result, police theorized that Charles Nuccio, Annie's husband and Catherine's father, had killed Militello to carry out a vendetta.

Two more men, Frank Di Leonardo and Tony Gariti, were then gunned down at Milton and Hobbie streets.[94] There was an attempt to associate these murders with the Catalanetto-Locascio feud. Sergeant Longobardi, however, thought the deaths were the result of a blackmail plot. A neighbor of the Di Leonardos alleged that both men had received Black Hand letters. Members of the immediate families of both victims, however, denied it, and a search of their homes failed to turn up the threatening letters.[95] Another angle to the mystery developed when it was found out that Di Leonardo was married to a niece of Marco Imburgio, who had recently been shot with seventeen slugs from a sawed-off shotgun. Imburgio had also resisted Black Hand demands. Police thought there might be some connection between the two shootings. The double murder occurred only a half hour after a flying squad of detectives had finished a sweep of Little Sicily. Police stopped and searched more than 400 citizens as they combed pool halls, saloons, and coffee houses searching for what they described as "gun fighting characters."

One month later, an unidentified Italian was killed at 1061 Polk on the West Side. The *Tribune* reported the incident as the twenty-sixth murder by the Mafia that year, although the suspects claimed that the shooting was the result of a fight over a card game. Black Hand Squad officers Parodi and De Vito knew one of the suspects, Lorenzo Ramondini, to be a former Black Hand criminal. Ramondini had been arrested three years earlier in an attempt to extort money from a local butcher and had recently been shot by an unidentified man. The Italian victim and Ramondini's past Black Hand experience apparently led the press to attribute the killing to the Mafia.[96]

The continued violence led to another series of sweeps by Chicago police. Deputy Chief Schuettler organized 120 detectives into thirty "flying squads" and sent them out into the city to round up local criminals and rid the city of known gunmen. In what the press described as "ironic defiance" of Chief Schuettler's efforts to stop the shootings, three men were murdered as police spread their dragnet throughout the city.[97] The victims included Joseph Diovardi, a grocer at 858 Milton Avenue, who was shot to death while standing in front of a saloon on Milton Avenue in the heart of Little Sicily. Police believed that the motive for the killing grew out of a quarrel over the division of Black Hand loot. Diovardi was shot four times, three times in the head and once in the left side near the heart. He had come to the attention of the police when Black

Hand Squad officers Riccio and De Vito had arrested him for carrying a revolver and a stiletto.

Schuettler's dogged determination to stamp out crime led to his appointment as Chicago's chief of police. City officials had considered him for the position before, but he had always refused it. When he finally accepted the office, it was with the understanding that he would close his police career when he relinquished his badge as chief. His appointment was described as one of the few good things that could be credited to the scandal-ridden administration of Mayor William Hale Thompson. Mayor Thompson's first assignment for his new police chief was to attack what the mayor described as the "crooked hand of whiskey," referring to the relationship between Chicago saloons and vice activity.[98]

Schuettler enjoyed the rare distinction of having risen through the ranks on merit alone, never having involved himself with the corrupt inner ring that controlled police promotions. This statement was more than speculation. In 1902, the Chicago Civil Service Commission mysteriously lost Schuettler's performance ratings, preventing his promotion to inspector. Rather than delay the promotions of the other officers, Schuettler declared that he would not go into court to fight his case.[99]

In what the press termed "Mafia Murder No. 28," Joseph Forelli was shot at Polk and Clinton in the Near West Side. As he lay in the street with a bullet wound in his head, a number of women who were waiting for a streetcar came over and tried to stanch his wounds. He died later at the Cook County Hospital. Police believed that the shooting was a Black Hand affair. Four days later, Peter Mandaella of Muskegon, Michigan, was shot to death in front of a saloon on South Wentworth Avenue, 200 feet from the Twenty-second Street police station. He was carrying a loaded revolver. Mandaella was being sought by the Muskegon police for shooting into a crowd of people, wounding two men. It was believed that he was killed by one of his intended victims. The *Chicago Daily Tribune* reported "Italian Slain; 29th on List of Black Hand." Reacting to the recent rash of murders in Chicago, the *Tribune* wrote in an editorial that the city had not taken a firm stand against crimes of violence and that there was a notorious indifference to murders in the Italian community.[100]

Of the ten murders that had occurred since Sergeant Longobardi's prediction, only two had evidence of extortion, yet the press attributed them all to the Black Hand or the Mafia. Whether these crimes were the work of Black Hand criminals or not, there were an inordinate number of murders in Little Sicily and in the Near West Side Italian community. A study of homicide in Chicago revealed that patterns of lethal violence among Italians paralleled that of other groups but occurred at a higher rate.[101] Before 1910, when Chicago's Italian population consisted primarily of single, young men, a large proportion of the homicides committed occurred in saloons and resulted from drunken brawls. Both killers and their victims were typically poor, unmarried, young males who resided in boarding houses in one of Chicago's Italian colonies. Beginning in 1910, the occurrence of drunken-brawl homicide plummeted. As with other Chicago newcomers, Italian immigrants were gradually settling into society. As more Italian women immigrated to Chicago, gender ratios evened and Italian men began to establish families, ending the bachelor lifestyle that included spending large amounts of leisure time in neighborhood saloons. However, despite the drop in drunken-brawl violence, the Italian homicide rate rose steeply after 1910. In fact, Italian immigrants became the single most homicidal group in Chicago.

Adler argues that the rise in Italian homicide, like that of other ethnic groups during this period, was the result of a surge in domestic homicide. Italians rarely murdered their spouses, however. Acting as heads of the family, Italian men committed homicide to protect their sisters' and daughters' reputations, and thus the reputation of the family. This responsibility was taken seriously, especially by Sicilian immigrants, which may explain the inordinate number of murders that occurred in Little Sicily. More than any other group of family killers, Italian men used violence to fulfill their role as the protector of women and as defenders of the family's honor. This code of honor extended beyond domestic relations to other forms of social conflict, as men avenged the wrongs committed against their kin. During the decade following 1910, Italian codes of personal vengeance added to the number of homicides as one Sicilian murder led to the next, igniting an explosion of killing that swept through the Italian immigrant community. The *Chicago Record-Herald* reported that twelve men were slain in a thirteen-month period in Chicago to satisfy the "barbaric code of the Sicilians which demands a life for a life."[102]

Many of these vendetta killings were attributed to the Mafia, Camorra, and Black Hand simply because of a lack of understanding on the part of the American public, who could not or would not differentiate between them. By 1920, the Italian homicide rate fell by 45 percent as a result of demographic, cultural, and institutional forces. Italian-born residents were older, better established, increasingly occupied with family life, and less wedded to Old World cultural ways. As Italian immigrants moved out of Chicago's immigrant colonies, they became better able to use legal forms of redress, were less dependent on aggressive self-help, and less invested in older notions of honor and personal vengeance.

New Year's Day 1917 began with the discovery of a "junior" Black Hand gang.[103] Three Italian youths were taken into custody by Detectives Riccio and De Vito after they sent a bomb threat to Joseph Schiff and Julius Morrison, the owners of the York Palace Theatre. The letter threatened the owners with death and the destruction of their theater unless $500 was delivered to Polk and South Jefferson streets. The detectives, suspecting an immature hand in the signature and crude drawings of caskets and skull and crossbones, believed the letter was the imaginative work of teenage boys. They subsequently arrested James Dimichle, nineteen years of age, who they found loitering at the corner designated in the note. The youth confessed to the Black Hand plot and gave the names of his two accomplices, Joseph Schilingo and Vito Carbonilli.

A few months later, Dr. Camillo Volini was back in the news when his home at 2929 West Washington Boulevard was damaged by a bomb.[104] The bomb was placed, or thrown, by a man who had jumped from a passing auto. The explosion destroyed the veranda, front hall, dining room, and living room of the house. The doctor did not suspect Black Hand activity in the bombing, however. Arguing that the White Hand had been inactive for a number of years and that he had not participated in White Hand activities in some time, he attributed the bombing to other sources. Although Volini had not received a Black Hand letter in a long time, he did receive a threatening letter demanding the hand of his daughter Cecelia in marriage and threatening death if he refused. Mrs. Volini theorized that the bombing might have been the work of pro-German fanatics, who opposed U.S. involvement in World War I and picked the Volini home because of the large Red Cross service flag that draped the front window.

Just as the breakup of the Nicolosi gang had a devastating effect on Black Hand crime, the public's perception of the invincibility of Black Hand criminals was forever challenged by the actions of Nicholas Abrino of 2603 Princeton Avenue. When Abrino came home from service in the U.S. Army during World War I, he found that Black Hand criminals had demanded $2,000 or the blood of his parents. Abrino was not intimidated. He told the blackmailers to come for $300 as a down payment and called the postal authorities. When the would-be extortionists came to collect the money, they were arrested. One night after the offenders were released on bond, two men in an automobile fired at Abrino as he was standing in front of his home with a baby in his arms. He then visited everybody in his neighborhood that had been subjected to Black Hand threats. He gained their confidence and obtained names, dates, documents, and other proof of Black Hand crime that he turned over to federal authorities. Soon eight alleged Black Hand offenders were in custody. Frank Russo, the leader of the gang, fled to New York where he was apprehended by federal authorities. Twelve people were eventually tried in what the press described as the "first government Black Hand prosecution in years." The trial resulted in the conviction of three of the defendants, including two women. The fact that three persons were convicted in a highly technical trial was viewed as a victory by government officials. Those convicted were Mrs. Philip Martello, Mrs. Lucia Naponiello, and Vito Petruzzi, who were all found guilty of mail fraud and conspiracy. Each received ten years in prison for their crimes.[105]

Herman F. Schuettler, the patron of the Black Hand Squad, died in August 1918 after thirty-five years of police service. The press described him as the greatest police chief that Chicago had ever known. Both his fellow officers and the criminal element respected and admired him because of his fairness and courage. The department held Schuettler up as a model for every rookie police officer coming on the force. He had been ill since January and had gone to Florida to try to regain his health. He returned in May only to suffer a relapse, and he finally died of pneumonia. At a time when police corruption was the norm, his integrity and honesty as a public official were never questioned. William Ludwig, superintendent of the Merchant's Special Police (a night watch service in the Near North Side), who had known him as a rookie officer, said that Schuettler was always attentive to duty and, no matter how stormy or cold the night, he was always at his post. Schuettler was born in 1861 in the Near North Side of Chicago, where he spent much of his police career. He was described as a giant of a man who was as kindly and thoughtful as a woman.[106]

Thousands of Chicagoans paid a final tribute to Schuettler. One hundred fifty mounted police officers, followed by 700 officers on foot and battalions of police reserves and firefighters, led his funeral procession.[107] The hearse was followed by a mounted officer leading a riderless horse draped in black. Two trucks were needed to carry the flowers from the church to the grave site. They had been sent by people from every walk of life. One unusual floral piece told the story of the great heart of Herman Schuettler better than the rest. It was from the mother of Harvey Van Dine, whom Schuettler had sent to the gallows. During her son's trial, Mrs. Van Dine was shown immeasurable understanding and kindness by the policeman.

Sometime after the death of Herman Schuettler, the Chicago Police Department transferred Black Hand Squad officers to the detective division. Although they continued to investigate crime in the Italian community, including Black Hand crime, they began to move about the police department as their careers progressed and they advanced to higher rank. Gabriel Longobardi, the Petrosino of Chicago, rose to the rank of sergeant and resigned from the police department in 1927. He died at his home at 326 South Francisco in October 1932. He was fifty-five years old. His partner, Julian Bernacchi, rose to the rank of captain, commanding the Des Plaines Avenue Station. His brother Peter was a Chicago police sergeant. Bernacchi retired from the police department in May 1940 after thirty-four years of service. He died at age eighty-three in February 1961.[108]

Police officer Michael De Vito of the Black Hand Squad died of mysterious causes on February 19, 1923. De Vito, who had been suffering from stomach problems, reported that he had contracted ptomaine poisoning after eating chop suey. Suspecting foul play, Michael Hughes, Chicago's chief of detectives, ordered a complete investigation of De Vito's death. Police feared that his death might have been the result of his efforts against Black Hand criminals. De Vito's partner, Paul Riccio, also believed that De Vito had died under suspicious circumstances. His official cause of death was listed as "acute indigestion."[109]

Paul Riccio rose to the rank of lieutenant and served at both the Brighton Park and Deering police stations. He died in January 1935 of a stomach ailment at age fifty-eight. Lieutenant George De Mar resigned from the police department in 1935 after twenty-six years of service. He had gained a reputation for honesty because of his work against bootlegging and illegal gambling in the East Chicago Avenue district. Anthony Gentile, a retired lieutenant, died in his home at 5513 Van Buren on August 23, 1944, at age sixty-seven. He suffered a heart attack. Much of his career was spent in the Maxwell Street District. He had also been assigned to the county prosecutor's office. Gentile had been a member of the force since 1911.[110]

Although the Black Hand crime wave had ended, it had made a lasting impression on the people of Chicago, one that would forever tie Black Hand crime to the Italian immigrant. Unfortunately, these lasting memories do not include the activities of the Chicago Police Black Hand Squad. Officers Gabriel Longobardi, Julian Bernacchi, Paul Riccio, George De Mar, Michael De Vito, Phillip Parodi, and Anthony Gentile, as well as their patron Herman Schuettler, deserve better. So does the memory of Inspector John Revere and all the other unnamed police officers who valiantly fought Black Hand crime.

Gas storage tank, similar to the one at Crosby and Hobbie streets in Little Sicily. Chicago Daily News *negatives collection DN-0000003, courtesy of the* Chicago History Museum.

Children playing in an empty lot in Little Sicily. Chicago Daily News *negatives collection DN-0000208, courtesy of the* Chicago History Museum.

*Rose Palma and child,
Black Hand victims.*
Chicago Daily News
*negatives collection DN-
0004618, courtesy of the
Chicago History Museum.*

Bride kidnapper Salvatore Forestiere and accomplices. Chicago Daily News
negatives collection DN-0006030, courtesy of the Chicago History Museum.

*Detective Gabriel
Longobardi, the
"Petrosino of Chicago."*
Chicago Daily News
*negatives collection
DN-0054624, courtesy
of the Chicago History
Museum.*

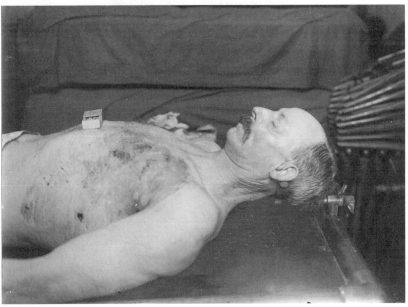

Murder victim Benedetto Cinene. Chicago Daily News *negatives collection
DN-0008062, courtesy of the Chicago History Museum.*

Detective Patrick J. Quinn, slain in a gun battle in Little Sicily. Chicago Daily News *negatives collection DN-0008177, courtesy of the Chicago History Museum.*

Detective Gabriel Longobardi and Black Hand suspect Girolamo Morici. Chicago Daily News *negatives collection DN-0055706, courtesy of the Chicago History Museum.*

Death Corner, scene of "Shotgun Man" murders. Chicago Daily News negatives collection DN-0056708, courtesy of the Chicago History Museum.

Black Hand criminal Gianni Alongi escorted by U. S. Marshals. Chicago Daily News *negatives collection DN-0056850, courtesy of the Chicago History Museum.*

Angelo Mareno, Black Hand kidnapping victim. Chicago Daily News *negatives collection DN-0057625, courtesy of the Chicago History Museum.*

Assistant Chief Herman Schuettler, Chicago police official who led the effort against Black Hand crime in Chicago. Chicago Daily News *negatives collection DN-0056626, courtesy of the Chicago Historical Society.*

Joseph Vacek killed his father and blamed the murder on the Black Hand.
Chicago Daily News *negatives collection DN-0057412, courtesy of the
Chicago* History Museum.

Black Hand victim Joseph Carsello and family. Chicago Daily News *negatives
collection DN-006399, courtesy of the Chicago History Museum.*

Angelo Petitti, kidnapper of ten-year-old "Billy" Ranieri. Chicago Daily News *negatives collection DN-0087182, courtesy of the Chicago History Museum.*

HON. CAMILLO VOLINI, M.D.

Dr. Camillo Vollini, leader of the White Hand Society. Courtesy of Vollini's grandson Michael Serritella.

4 *The Prohibition Years*

Black Hand crimes began to disappear after 1920. Evidence suggests that this was partly the result of Prohibition. The *Chicago Daily Tribune* reported that Al Capone, who came to dominate bootlegging in Chicago, helped rid the Italian community of the curse of the Black Hand that for years had extorted money from Italian American merchants. This theory flies in the face of the alien conspiracy theory. If the Black Hand was a transitional stage between the Mafia in Sicily and the Cosa Nostra in American society, why would Al Capone, the recognized leader of organized crime in Chicago, fight Black Hand crime?[1]

Interviews conducted in 1980 by the Italians in Chicago Oral History Project indicate that some Black Hand criminals, in fact, did turn to bootlegging after the outlawing of alcoholic beverages in the United States. Prohibition created a lucrative illegal market that was far less risky than bomb throwing and murder. People were needed to distribute illegal alcohol, and the existing criminal element provided a fertile recruiting ground for the new bootlegging gangs. Prohibition provided an opportunity for neighborhood criminals to leave their communities and participate in crime on a much larger scale.[2]

The Italians in Chicago Oral History Project also provides an interesting insight into the end of Black Hand activity in Little Sicily. Former residents of the area reported that the upward mobility and assimilation of the Sicilian community into American society contributed to the end of Black Hand extortion.[3] Once they left Little Sicily, Sicilian immigrants were no longer affected by the isolation of the community and the continued surveillance of the Black Hand gangs that sought potential victims.

No sooner had the Black Hand menace ended than the residents of Little Sicily were confronted by another crime problem. The public demand for alcohol was filled by various bootlegging gangs throughout Chicago. In Little Sicily, bootlegging was under the control of the Aiello brothers. The Aiellos owned a bakery at 473 West Division in the heart of the Near North Side.[4] They were a large family of nine brothers and numerous cousins. Joey Aiello was the kingpin of the group. The Aiellos were fiercely independent and spurned the advances of the Capone mob, who were attempting to consolidate all illegal liquor traffic in Chicago. War eventually broke out between the competing factions. Within a year, a dozen men had been killed in Little Sicily and $75,000 worth of property firebombed as the Aiello and Capone forces battled for control of the liquor business. The situation was so desperate that people began to abandon the neighborhood until the violence ceased. Some sought temporary refuge in Wisconsin and Michigan. Others moved away permanently. Father Luigi Giambastiani, troubled by the killings, posted a sign on the front door of St. Philip Benizi's Church that read, "Brothers! For the honor you owe to God, for the respect of your American Country and humanity; pray that this ferocious manslaughter, which disgraces the Italian name before the civilized world, may come to an end."[5]

Although Black Hand crime had waned in Little Sicily, other criminal groups throughout the city occasionally engaged in extortion. One of the most famous of these groups was the Cardinella gang. The Cardinellas were a robbery gang that participated in extortion as a sideline. The members of the gang included Nicola Viana, Tomaso Errico, Frank Campioni, Tony Sansoni, Leonardo Crapo, Salvatore Cardinella, Beniamino Tortorici, Giuseppe Dario, Frank Giuraputo, and Carlo Balasca. In November 1919, the Cook County grand jury indicted the members of the Cardinella gang on charges of murder, robbery, and assault with a deadly weapon. The gang had committed four murders; 100 saloon, poolroom, and street robberies; and 150 burglaries. The headquarters of the gang was a pool hall at 344 West Twenty-fourth Street where Salvatore "Sam" Cardinella, the leader of the gang, tutored neophytes in the art of crime. After his followers committed their crimes, he allegedly defrauded them of their criminal earnings in a crooked dice game. Of the four murders charged to the Cardinella gang, two were during a failed robbery of a saloon in which the proprietor and a customer were killed. The third was of a member of the gang who was slain for holding out robbery proceeds from his fellow members. The last was of a man named

Kurbalanzo, who was slain in the attempted robbery of a dice and card game on West Sixty-third Street. The proceeds of the robbery amounted to $27.30—less than seven dollars for each offender.[6]

One of those charged in the murders was nineteen-year-old Nicholas Viana, known as the "Choir Singer" because of his participation in a West Side church choir.[7] Attesting to the Fagin-like role played by Cardinella, Viana told officials, "When I entered Cardinella's poolroom, I was a boy in short trousers. Within a week, I was a criminal. After I was arrested, Cardinella threatened to kill my mother and three sisters if I talked to the police. He is the man that should be going to the gallows today." Much to his surprise, Cardinella was sentenced to the gallows under the Illinois felony murder rule. Even though he did not commit any of the murders, he was still responsible for them as a coconspirator and leader of the gang.

The execution of Cardinella, who was known as *Il Diavolo*—the Devil—is one of the strangest crime stories in Illinois history. While awaiting his death at the old Cook County Jail at Dearborn and Illinois streets in Chicago, Cardinella refused food and eventually lost forty pounds.[8] On the day of his execution, he refused to walk to the gallows, throwing himself on the floor at the feet of the two priests who had come to attend him. As a result, he was strapped to a chair and carried to the gallows, where he was hung while still strapped to the chair. After the execution, attendants took Cardinella's body to an ambulance that was waiting to receive the body on orders of the dead man's family. A jail attendant saw a woman in a nurse's uniform sitting inside the ambulance with two men, one of whom appeared to be a doctor. He also observed hot water bottles under a blanket at the bottom of the basket where Cardinella's body was placed. The attendant reported the unusual activity to the deputy warden, who ordered that the ambulance be delayed for nearly an hour. After the ambulance was released, a guard saw the nurse rub Cardinella's cheeks and wrists and observed one of the men prepare an injection. Officials believed that both were attempts to resuscitate Cardinella. A police car was ordered to overtake the ambulance and halt the efforts to bring Cardinella back to life. On inspection, the ambulance was found to contain a specially equipped bed with a rubber mattress filled with hot water, an oxygen tank, an electric battery, various hypodermic syringes, and other appliances that might be of use in the resuscitation.

There was another chapter to this macabre story that involved Nicholas Viana. After Viana's execution, the same set of circumstances was observed—the hot water bottles, the nurse, and doctor in the ambulance.[9] The body was delivered to them and they drove away. Viana was allegedly taken to a room two blocks from the jail, where an elaborate effort was made to revive him. Viana would be the test case for the resuscitation of Salvatore Cardinella. Legend has it that the efforts to revive Viana were successful, but he was not allowed to live because he had violated the underworld code and spoken out against the Cardinella gang.

The White Hand Society had argued that Black Hand letters often came from acquaintances of the victims, sometimes even from people who lived in the same building. An example of this was Samuel Saccio, who was arrested for extorting money from his downstairs neighbor, Antonio Potto. On January 7, 1920, Potto received a $2,000 extortion demand.[10] Although Potto and his wife lived in the West Side of Chicago, they were instructed to take the money to the corner of Chicago Avenue and Halsted Street, near Little Sicily. At the bottom of the extortion demand was the usual skull and crossbones and a heart pierced by a dripping dagger and the words *"moneto o morte"*—money or death. Potto became so frightened that he left home. One week later, Mrs. Potto received a second Black Hand letter telling her that unless the money was paid by January 19, her house would be bombed, and she would be killed. When Mrs. Potto told her upstairs neighbor, Samuel Saccio, about the threat, Saccio offered his assistance and that of his brother Joseph. In fact, Joseph offered to act as a go-between for Mrs. Potto and subsequently arranged to have the "black hand society" call her on the telephone to arrange payment. Becoming suspicious, Mrs. Potto called the Chicago police, and Sergeants Riccio and Parodi were assigned to the investigation. On the day that a Black Hand agent was to come to collect the money, the officers secreted themselves inside the Pottos' apartment. When the Saccios notified Mrs. Potto that the Black Hand agent was upstairs in their apartment, she gave them $400 in marked money, stating that it was all the money she could raise. Police moved in and found Joseph Saccio with the money. No one else was present in the apartment.

Popular literature often treats Black Hand crime as a stage in the evolution of organized crime in America. This position, however, was challenged by the attempts at Black Hand extortion directed at James Colosimo. Colosimo was Chicago's first Italian vice lord. Colosimo had risen to political importance by organizing fellow street sweepers into a voting block.[11] Known as the "White Wings" because of their distinctive white uniforms, the street sweepers in Chicago's First Ward were mostly Italian. As a Democratic precinct captain, Colosimo also controlled the vote in the Italian settlement centered at Polk and Clark streets. "Big Jim," as he was called, was additionally involved in prostitution. He had married Victoria Moresco, the operator of a Levee bordello. Soon Colosimo was operating three Levee houses of prostitution. He also served as the Levee bagman, carrying protection money from red-light district madams to First Ward Aldermen "Bathhouse" John Coughlin and "Hinky-Dink" Mike Kenna, which gave Colosimo considerable control over prostitution and other vice activity in the Levee district. The rates for "protection" included $300 a month for a three-story disorderly house, $200 a month for a two-story, and $100 for a one-story crib. Colosimo prospered. He wore so many diamonds that he was often referred to as "Diamond Jim." He opened a restaurant at 2126 South Wabash named Colosimo's Cafe. His restaurant became the center of social life in Chicago. Enrico Caruso and George M. Cohan frequented Colosimo's whenever they visited Chicago. If the Black Hand was truly a stage in the evolution of traditional organized crime in Chicago, Black Hand criminals could not have challenged the one man who is widely regarded as the first Italian crime boss in Chicago.

On May 11, 1920, Colosimo was murdered while working at his restaurant. Police have never officially solved the killing, but a number of theories have been offered explaining the crime. One theory attributes his murder to a New York Black Hand gang. Colosimo's slayers reportedly stole $150,000 from Big Jim's office at the time of his murder.[12] Colosimo, determined to retire in order to marry singer Dale Winter, had accumulated the money by selling securities and gems in order to purchase a new home on Chicago's fashionable Lake Shore Drive. The members of the Black Hand gang that carried out the killing allegedly took the money. Attorney Rocco De Stefano, the executor of Colosimo's estate, received a Black Hand letter shortly after Colosimo's slaying demanding additional money that Colosimo had entrusted to him. The letter, received on October 16, 1920, and written in Italian, accused De Stefano of misappropriating the money and demanded that he turn over half of the ill-gotten proceeds to the extortionists.

It was commonly believed that Colosimo had defied Black Hand extortionists in the past. His position as vice king of Chicago's First Ward protected him from Black Hand vengeance, but as Colosimo began to turn from crime and his old associates, Black Hand criminals grew bolder. Colosimo had confided in Detective Gentile that he had received several $10,000 demands from Black Hand criminals in the months prior to his murder.[13] Colosimo told Gentile that he was willing to pay the money if it ensured that he would be left alone. He knew, however, that paying would be seen as a sign of weakness and would lead to other demands. Colosimo told Gentile that once you gave in to these Black Hand fellows, they would "milk you to death." The second letter directed Colosimo to take the money to Twenty-second and State streets at midnight. Colosimo dropped the package as directed, but there was no money in it. He then stepped into a doorway, with revolver in hand, and waited for someone to claim the decoy package. The Black Hander, however, picked up the dummy package just as a streetcar passed and escaped before Colosimo could confront him.

Some of the threatening letters that reached Colosimo were traced to the Mike Carozzo gang. Carozzo was a known Black Hand criminal. On February 17, 1913, Black Hand Squad officers arrested Carozzo, commonly referred to as "Dago Mike," Frank Cozza, and Tony Pani for extorting $500 from Domenico Iaculli of 813 South Clinton Street. Assisted by postal inspectors, Detectives Longobardi and Bernacchi arrested the trio after they had come to the Iaculli home to collect the extortion money. Each of the offenders carried a revolver, and to the surprise of the officers, more than twenty poisoned bullets were recovered.[14]

Although police eventually dropped the charges against the Carozzo gang, Detectives Longobardi and Bernacchi suspected that Carozzo and Cozza were involved in a number of other Black Hand crimes. Tony Cirfaldo, another member of the band, murdered Cozza less than a year later for refusing to divide $500 with Carozzo. Police suspected Carozzo in the earlier Black Hand extortion of Nick Gironda, who conducted an ice business in the old Levee red-light district. His partner in the Gironda extortion attempt was believed to have been Vincenzo "Sunny Jim" Cusmano. Both Carozzo and Cusmano went on to become important labor leaders in Chicago. Carozzo became the head of the Street Sweepers Union and Cusmano the supervisor of street sweeping gangs in the city's First Ward.[15]

Colosimo reportedly incurred the enmity of Black Hand criminals some years earlier when, as the story went, he had three of their members shot and killed in the Archer Avenue subway under the Rock Island railroad tracks. Two of the men died instantly. The third lived a few hours to tell his friends that Colosimo had "jobbed" the three of them. The "jobbing" of the Black Handers was the result of an incident that began in Colosimo's saloon in the Levee district. A gang of Black Handers frequented the saloon, and Big Jim knew what their game was, but as long as they did not molest any of his friends, he did not interfere with their work. Then a friend of Colosimo's received a Black Hand letter demanding $2,000 from the gang. When appealed to for help, Colosimo told the extortionists to back off. They were insistent, however, and threatened to blow up the man's house. On the night they were supposed to collect the $2,000, a gang of men alleged to be Colosimo's waited for them in the pedestrian subway. Sawed-off shotguns did the rest. Two died instantly.[16] The third, still living, was rushed to a hospital where he asked to see Colosimo. Big Jim honored the dying man's request. When Colosimo arrived, the alleged Black Hander drew his fingers across his mouth and said in Italian "Jim Colosimo, traitor, traitor." From that point on, Colosimo was a marked man.

A newspaper account that appeared in the *Chicago Daily Tribune* on November 23, 1911, reported the shooting of the three alleged Black Hand offenders. The article describes the shooting of the three men in the Archer Avenue subway and the survivor's summoning of Colosimo to his deathbed. Additionally, police believed that the victims—Francisco Denello, Stefano Denello, and Pasquale Emico—were all members of a Black Hand gang that had been active in the Near South Side. Three weeks later, however, police reported that a love affair was probably responsible for the murders of the three men. The girl over whom the murders were committed was Mary Palaggi, the daughter of a saloonkeeper on South Armour Avenue. The Denello brothers and Pasquale Emico frequented the Palaggi saloon and were friends of Joseph Luki, Mary's fiancé. A man named Carmello La Rosa, however, also sought Mary's attention. As a result, Luki's friends shot him. La Rosa's friends responded by shooting the three men in the Archer Avenue subway. This account directly challenges the theory that Colosimo had the three men killed because they had attempted to kill a friend of his.[17]

Two thousand people including judges, municipal employees, lawyers, physicians, university professors, and ministers attended Big Jim Colosimo's funeral. His list of pallbearers and honorary pallbearers included three judges, nine city council members, and the leader of the Chicago opera ballet company—evidence of the extraordinary relationship between politics and crime that existed in Chicago at that time. It was originally planned that Colosimo would be buried in Mount Carmel Cemetery as were most Italians of the time. Chicago's Archbishop George Mundelein, however, issued an order preventing Colosimo's body from being buried in a Catholic cemetery or brought into a Catholic church. The archbishop pointed out that Colosimo had not abided by the dictates of the church in life, probably because of his pandering activities and divorce from his first wife, Vittoria Moresco.[18]

Occasional Black Hand crimes continued throughout the decade of the 1920s. In October 1921, police shot Anthony Seno at the climax of an attempt to extort $2,000 from Nicoli De Gennaro.[19] Black Hand criminals had demanded $2,000 from De Gennaro in a letter sent the previous January. De Gennaro told Seno, who was his cousin, about the extortion attempt. Seno agreed to "square the Black Hand" for $5 and an overcoat, but no more was heard about the incident until another letter was received the following August, when a new demand was made. This time the missive threatened the death of De Gennarro, his wife, and their five children. Ten days later, a third letter was received warning De Gennaro "his time was up." A fourth letter notified De Gennaro that his house was to be bombed. De Gennaro finally called the police. Detective Sergeant Riccio accompanied by Sergeant Patrick Alcock and Detectives Carroll and Dunn were assigned to the investigation.

Police suspected Seno from the start because of his willingness to settle De Gennaro's Black Hand problems, and they set a trap to apprehend him. On October 24, 1921, De Gennaro sent his children to a movie theater while Sergeants Riccio and Alcock hid in the De Gennaro home. When Seno arrived, he informed his cousin that the Black Hand would not take a cent less than $600. De Gennaro threw $300 on the floor, stating it was every cent he had. When Seno picked up the extortion money and put it in his pocket, Sergeant Alcock stepped from behind a closed door. Seno then drew a revolver and fired one shot at the officer. The bullet passed through the sleeve of Alcock's coat. Alcock and Riccio returned fire, striking Seno in the legs. Police found what they believed to be poison on the five bullets remaining in Seno's revolver. Once again, the go-between proved to be part of the Black Hand plot.

Postal inspectors were back in the news in June 1923 when they helped break up a Black Hand ring on the far South Side of Chicago. The investigation began when Giorgio Arquilla, a wealthy coal dealer at 9348 Cottage Grove Avenue, and his family were threatened with death if he failed to pay $10,000.[20] Arquilla and three relatives lured a member of the Black Hand gang to his home on the pretext of paying the money and gave the would-be extortionist a severe beating. They then called postal authorities. Those eventually arrested included Vincenzo and Frank Calabresi, Fred Maso, Dan Luczo, and Luigi Rega.

Chicago police scored another victory against Black Hand crime in September 1923 when they arrested Arrico Monaco and Dominick Lario. Both were shot and in critical condition after a gunfight with Sergeants Riccio, Maher, and Downey.[21] The shooting occurred in the home of Guiseppe Albano, a successful foreman for the Metropolitan Elevated Company and the owner of two apartment buildings. In August, Albano received a Black Hand letter marked with the usual skull and crossbones demanding $5,000, but he did nothing. Then in September, he received another letter saying that his name had been entered into the "dead book." Albano and his family were terrified. The letters also instructed Albano to seek a "good friend" to straighten out the matter. Several days later, the "good friend," Arrico Monaco, called and agreed to "fix" the case with the Black Hand. Albano, however, had called the police, who devised a scheme to catch the offenders. When he next visited Albano, Monaco was accompanied by Dominick Lario. The men informed Albano that the Black Hand would settle for $1,000. Unknown to Monaco and Lario, Sergeant Riccio and two other officers were hiding in Albano's apartment. After Albano passed the money to the Black Handers, the police officers leaped out and arrested the offenders after a short exchange of gunfire.

One month after the arrests of Monaco and Lario, Sergeant Riccio and company set up another trap for two Black Hand offenders who were attempting to extort money from Katy Antonucci of South Lincoln Avenue.[22] Shortly after separation from her husband, a local undertaker, Peter Maruca, proposed to marry her once she obtained her divorce. Antonucci, who was thought to be wealthy by neighbors, then received a series of Black Hand letters demanding $5,000. Hearing of her troubles, Maruca volunteered to intercede with the Black Hand for her. Fearing for her life and the lives of her three children, Antonucci arranged with Maruca to pay the money to the Black Hand; however, the blackmailers failed to keep the rendezvous and pick up the money. A second meeting was scheduled, and when the offenders asked to pick up the money at her residence, Antonucci called police. At the designated time, Joseph Zanghi arrived accompanied by Maruca. Zanghi remained at the back door while Maruca stepped inside the house. As he grasped the extortion money, the policemen burst out from their hiding places. Sergeant Riccio shot Maruca as he reached for his gun. Zanghi fled, but police later arrested him at Maruca's residence on West Grand Avenue.

Little again was heard of the Black Hand until May 1928 when Gaetano Acci of 1066 Polk Street was murdered.[23] Variously known as "The Wolf," "The King of the Black Handers," and "The Muscle," police found Acci's body in Harvard, Illinois, with two bullet wounds in his head and two in his body. Paul Riccio, now a police lieutenant, traveled to McHenry, the county seat, to make the identification. Only a week before, Riccio had laid a trap for Acci after he had written a letter to Mrs. Joseph Tita of 4948 West Washington Boulevard demanding $5,000. In the pockets of the slain man, police recovered six Black Hand letters, each addressed to a different person and ready to be mailed. Most of the victims were poor men and women who lived in Little Italy in the Near West Side of Chicago. One letter was addressed to Frank Tita, the brother-in-law of Mrs. Joseph Tita, from whom Acci had demanded $250. When Tita was unable to raise the money, Acci reportedly agreed to accept installments of $30 each month. It was said that Acci had severely beaten several men who would not or could not pay. Witnesses reported that four men in an automobile had called on Acci early Saturday morning. He was last seen alive in Rockford, Illinois, with the men at 4:30 that afternoon. Police believed that he was killed by one of his intended victims.

In September 1928, several men, driving in an automobile, kidnapped ten-year-old William Ranieri on his way home from school. The men stopped and asked the boy some questions, and then reached out and pulled him into their car. Billy, as the child was known, screamed, and one of the men struck him on the head and bruised his eye. He was driven to the home of Andrew Cappellano in Bourbonnais, Illinois. Shortly after returning home from work and discovering his son missing, Frank Ranieri received a telephone call from one of the kidnappers. Suspecting that the caller was Angelo Petitti, Frank Ranieri reported the boy's disappearance to the police. He then went looking for Petitti. Petitti denied any knowledge of the matter and promised to look into it. The next day Petitti contacted Ranieri and asked him to come to his soft drink parlor at 1737 Garibaldi Place in the Near West Side. At the meeting, Petitti told Ranieri to go home and wait for a telephone call from the kidnappers. Twenty minutes after arriving home, Ranieri received a call telling him that he would have to pay $60,000 for the return of his son. The next day Ranieri again went to see Petitti. Petitti told Ranieri to get the $60,000 and the two of them would then walk around the neighborhood until an agent of the kidnappers approached them. The father told Petitti that he could not raise $60,000 but would pay $5,000 for the return of his son. That night Petitti was arrested. When in court the next day, Judge Comerford told Petitti that he would not be released until little Billy Ranieri was found. That night Andrew Cappellano and his son Tony took Billy Ranieri for a long drive and finally dropped him off on a country road near Lockport, Illinois. Billy walked to a gas station where the attendant called the Joliet police.[24]

The Ranieri case is illustrative of the manner in which the press and public interchangeably grouped Italian crime. The press labeled the Ranieri kidnapping as the work of the Mafia. Although the offenders had been known to engage in Black Hand extortion, the Ranieri case was not described as the work of the Black Hand, nor did the family receive a Black Hand letter.

Angelo Petitti reportedly led a group of Black Hand extortionists who specialized in preying upon sewer contractors and former residents of Ambrosia, Italy.[25] Guilio Sausstro, one of the Ranieri kidnappers, worked as a cook and a waiter at a restaurant at 1421 West Taylor. There, he listened to the conversations of the contractors and learned the financial status of the diners, which he reported to Petitti. One of Petitti's victims,

Ole Scully, was a second cousin and the godfather of Billy Ranieri. Scully was a wealthy Italian sewer contractor who resided at 7658 South Laflin Avenue. Scully, whose real name was Scalzetti, had paid Petitti's extortion ring $800 on an earlier occasion. Outraged by the kidnapping of his godson, Scully agreed to cooperate with the authorities and provided a list of Petitti's other victims to the police. On the day that the Petitti trial began, Scully was killed in the same West Taylor Street restaurant where Sausstro had worked. Five men carrying baseball bats entered the restaurant and shot Scully twice before beating him. They also beat four other patrons, apparently to deter them from providing evidence to the police. That same day, Frank Ranieri received a special delivery letter threatening his life if he testified against Petitti.

It later came out that Angelo Petitti and a man named Pasquale "Hardhead" Capotosti were involved in a second extortion ring involving Italian contractors.[26] His friends called Capotosti Hardhead because that was the English translation of his surname. The press described Capotosti as the "secretary of Chicago's Camorrists" because police believed that he had written several hundred extortion letters. He had worked as a labor agent obtaining workers for Italian builders. When working for a contractor, Capotosti would determine how much the contractor was worth and whether he would scare easily or whether he was tough enough to resist an extortion demand. He would also estimate how much the intended victim was able to pay. Capotosti would then write a series of Black Hand letters that he would send in quick succession. At a certain point in the scheme, he would meet the contractor, learn of the extortion plot, and offer to assist the victim—a common Black Hand tactic. Capotosti would then tell the contractor that he believed he knew a man who could find out who the extortionists were, and he would be glad to put him in touch with that person. That man was Angelo Petitti. Petitti would then offer his services as a go-between and arrange to settle the matter for a smaller sum.

Lieutenant Riccio discovered that Capotosti was also using fake mediums to further his extortion plots.[27] Sometimes Capotosti would refer his victims to a spiritualist who had an unusual knowledge of their predicament, which usually made a deep impression on the unfortunate person. The medium's advice helped the extortion scheme along and usually added about $50 to the money obtained. The medium, besides charging for his advice, invariably told the frightened victim to do exactly what the extortionists demanded. Frank Ranieri had visited one of Capotosti's mediums after his son Billy had been kidnapped.

One of the last reported Black Hand crimes to occur in Chicago involved Attillo Scalditti, the nephew of Ole Scully, whom Black Hand kidnappers had beaten to death to prevent his appearance as a witness in the Billy Ranieri kidnapping trial. Three members of the notorious Forty-Two Gang demanded that Scaldetti pay them $2,500 to save his life because he was "on the list" of intended victims. The Forty-Two Gang derived its name from the legend of Ali Baba and the Forty Thieves. This gang had forty plus two members, hence the name. Their headquarters was Mary's Restaurant on the corner of Taylor and Bishop streets in Chicago's Near West Side. The gang specialized in truck hijacking and auto theft. There is no evidence, however, that the Forty-Twos were a Black Hand gang, and no Black Hand letter was involved in this extortion attempt. Scaldetti reported the attempt to the state's attorney, who provided detectives to work on the case. Shortly after noon on the appointed day, Joseph Muscato, Albert Woodrick, and Dominick De Palma, all members of the Forty-Two Gang, appeared at the Scully Monument Company on West Madison Street. De Palma was in fact a relative of Scaldetti, which is how the gang learned of Scaldetti's wealth. Immediately after the arrest, Muscato broke away from police and ran. Both the police officers and Scadetti fired at Muscato, striking him dead. Headlines read, "Slain by Victim as Black Hand Plot Is Foiled."[28]

The Ranieri kidnapping added to the growing concern in Chicago about the increase in crime resulting from the advent of Prohibition as bootlegging gangs throughout the city fought for control of the illegal liquor industry. The feud between the Capone forces, led by Antonio Lombardo, and the Aiello brothers in the Near North Side's Little Sicily neighborhood had dominated the news for some time. The fact that both groups were Italian contributed to existing beliefs about the Mafia and Camorra as the source of organized crime, in spite of the fact that there were also numerous Irish gangs violating Prohibition laws. There was also ample evidence that Chicago's machine politicians were protecting bootleggers, just as they had protected Black Hand criminals. In fact, Frank Loesch, special grand jury prosecutor and president of the Chicago Crime Commission, issued a special report on the "family tree" of Chicago crime reaching from "Crowe and Thompson through others to the chieftains and hirelings of the Mafia," clearly outlining the alliance of crime and politics in Chicago[29] (Robert Crowe had been the county prosecutor and William H. Thompson the mayor of Chicago). Just like Black Hand extortion, bootlegging was increasingly being viewed as an Italian problem. Sinister views of the Mafia and Camorra overshadowed evidence of official complacency and official corruption as the true causes of organized crime.

5 The Causes of Black Hand Extortion

Chicagoans and people in other cities labeled Black Hand crime as the work of the Mafia, and to a lesser extent, the Camorra. The common belief was that the Black Hand was a direct descendant of these Italian groups. This belief was apparent in news reports of the day. For example, headlines in the March 27, 1911, edition of the *Chicago Record-Herald* read, "Two More Dead; Mafia Tentacles Spread over City." The newspaper reported that two Black Hand murders were added to the "two score others committed by the Mafia during the last fourteen months." One month later, the *Chicago Daily Tribune* announced that the Chicago police were ready to lay the blame for Black Hand extortion on the Mafia as the result of yet another extortion attempt. The following year, the *Chicago Record-Herald* reported, "In Chicago, the [Mafia] organization has been active, but has been known as the Black Hand." The *Record-Herald* added that the Black Hand was a murderous Sicilian society that had gained a foothold in the United States. The newspaper described it as a union of persons who had developed blackmailing to the degree of an art, extorted Sicilian business owners and tradesmen, and even unduly influenced municipal elections.[1]

The Italian immigrant community did not share this view of the Black Hand. Bernard Barasa, former attorney for the Italian consul in Chicago and probably the best-known Italian lawyer in the city, scoffed at newspaper accounts of Black Hand crime. He argued that the Black

Hand Society was a myth and that no such organization had ever existed. Barasa believed that the term *Black Hand* originated in New York when a small group of blackmailers sent extortion letters to a banker under that name. Guido Sabetta, the Italian consul in Chicago, also argued that there was no such thing as the Black Hand. Blackmailers in America used the Black Hand symbol to inspire terror. Sabetta based his opinion on his own experience in Sicily, the alleged origin of Black Hand crime. He had never heard of the organization while posted there by the Italian government.[2]

Which of these two divergent opinions of the source of Black Hand crime is correct? Was the Black Hand an extension of a foreign criminal organization or was there an alternative explanation? An early account of the origin of the Mafia, published in 1895, said it formed circa 1266 to liberate Sicily from French despotism and tyranny.[3] The Mafia reportedly began in a stone quarry near Naples owned by a man named Mafoo. The quarry was called *Mafile*. The Mafia was an outgrowth of a feudal organization in Sicily known as the Camorra. Because open rebellion against the French was not possible, Sicilian peasants organized in secret to kill their leading oppressors one by one. Because immorality and vice were common during the reign of the French, the Camorra imposed a tax on gamblers in order to raise money to help expel their French oppressors. These activities were reportedly passed through the centuries to the Mafia of today. Although started with a noble purpose, the Mafia degenerated into a band of blackmailers, robbers, cutthroats, and counterfeiters.

These views of the origins of the Mafia remained dominant for more than fifty years. Although somewhat romantic, they are not true. The Mafia did not begin in Naples in mainland Italy; it is a phenomenon associated with the island of Sicily. Additionally, the Mafia did not exist at the time of the Sicilian revolt against the French. Little is known about the Camorra before 1820, and the term *mafioso*, from which the word *Mafia* is derived, first appeared in the 1863 play *The Mafosi of the Vicariate of Palermo*.[4] Nor were the members of the Mafia social bandits robbing foreign oppressors and sharing their proceeds with the poor. In fact, the Mafia may have worked with civil authorities to prevent unrest and maintain the ruling social order. What then was the Mafia in the south of Italy and what was its relationship to Black Hand crime? In order to answer this question, we must first understand the true nature of the Mafia and the Camorra. Both will be reviewed here in order to explicate their relationship to Black Hand crime.

The Mafia

There are several explanations for the origin of the word *mafia*. Among the most popular is the acronym M.A.F.I.A., which stands for *Morte Alla Francia Italia Anela*—"death to the French is Italy's cry." It was allegedly the battle cry of a revolt that began in Palermo on Easter Sunday, 1282.[5] Also called the "Night of the Sicilian Vespers," the incident started when a French officer killed a Sicilian woman. As the story goes, a beautiful young woman and her betrothed approached the Church of the Holy Ghost to be united in marriage. While the young man searched for the priest at the rear of the church, his bride-to-be waited for him at the front door. As she waited, a drunken sergeant of the French garrison named Druet walked up, threw his arm around her waist, and thrust his other hand into her bosom. As the woman tore herself from the attacker, her foot caught the coping of a stone in the pavement and she fell, striking her head on the corner of the church. When her betrothed returned, he found the young woman lying dead in a pool of blood. He pulled out his dagger and killed the French soldier. For the next seventy-two hours, armed bands led by the father and betrothed of the unfortunate bride hunted down and murdered French officials wherever they could be found, and the Mafia was born to fight French oppression. Forming themselves into a secret organization, the Sicilian people adopted the initial letters of the words of their death cry as the name of the organization. As lasting as this explanation has become, it is simply not true. In reality, the word *mafia* did not come into existence until six hundred years later.

The acronym M.A.F.I.A. has also been claimed to stand for *Mazzini Autorizza Furti, Incendi, e Avvelenamenti*—"Mazzini authorizes theft, arson, and poisoning"—the oath of a secret society began in 1860 to sabotage Bourbon rule. This secret society was named after Joseph Mazzini, founder of the Young Italy movement, which sought to establish an Italian republic.[6]

Several authors derive the word *mafia* from Arabic, either from *mahias*, meaning a bold man or braggart, or from *Ma afir*, the name of an Arab tribe that ruled Palermo. Another theory of Arab origin relates the word *mafia* to *maha*, a quarry or cave. Fugitive Arabs were said to have used the caves near Marsla as hiding places. Because the word denotes a method of social organization that is prevalent within the Sicilian culture, it is more likely that term was derived from the Arabic word *mu*, meaning safety, and the verb *afah*, meaning to protect. When spoken together, the words *mu afah* denote a clan offering protection to its members.[7]

Whatever the origins of the word, modern research suggests that the Mafia was not a secret criminal organization but a form of social organization that developed in Sicily and the south of Italy under very specific social and cultural conditions. In fact, Pino Arlacchi—professor of applied sociology at the University of Florence, former member of the Italian Chamber of Deputies and Senate, and executive director of the United Nations Office of Drug Control and Crime Prevention—has concluded that social research into the question of the Mafia has reached the point where we can say that the Mafia as the term is commonly understood did not exist.[8]

What then was the Mafia? So much has been written that it is sometimes difficult even for scholars to answer this question. My study of the available literature suggests that to understand the true nature of the Mafia, one must examine the Mafia in three different but related settings: the Mafia of the Sicilian village, the Mafia of the *latifundi* (plantations) of western Sicily, and the Mafia of the agricultural region, the *Conca d'Oro* (golden shell) that surrounds the city of Palermo.

The Mafia of the Sicilian village exploited the gap in Sicilian society left by an ineffective state government. It arose mainly in the areas where the state failed to affirm its traditional monopoly over the use of legitimate violence. The main function of the Mafia was to impose some form of rudimentary order on the anarchy of Sicilian life. It developed as a method of social control in an area where the official political structure was unable to impose its will on the populace.

The word *mafia* denotes a form of behavior and a kind of power, not a formal organization. Mafia was an attitude characterized by a proud awareness of one's self and the ability to defend one's dignity at any price. The typical mafioso was an *"uomo di respetto"* (man of respect) who did not tolerate injuries and avenged insults and injustices by recourse to private violence. Honor was important because people had nothing else. Poverty was the norm and there was little upward mobility. Those who were willing to use violence to protect their honor, and the honor of their family, were sought out by others who were less capable of protecting themselves from the hardships of Sicilian life.[9]

The eventual competition among the various mafiosi in each village led to conflict and finally dominance by one individual, who eventually brought the entire area under his patronage. Because of their position and willingness to use violence, such *"un'uomo d'onore"* (men of honor) were entrusted with a series of important functions that were normally the prerogative of the state. These included protection, repression of nonconformist behavior, and the mediation of disputes. The central characteristic of Mafia behavior was the private use of violence as a means of social control. The mafiosi also attracted a small group of associates who worked with them to attain their goals. This group, made of family members, friends, and clientele, was referred to as the *cosca* (artichoke). Each *cosca* controlled its own territory—a rural village or town, or an urban neighborhood. The size of these groups varied from half a dozen to over fifty members.[10]

Sicilians faced a closed social system in which upward mobility was virtually nonexistent.[11] They learned early that success depended upon their ability to develop relationships with those who held power. As a result, a system of patron-client relationships developed between family and kinship groups and local mafiosi that extended throughout Sicilian life. Such patronage systems are not unique to Sicily and can be found, even today, in electoral politics in some parts of the United States. The Mafia was nothing more than a system of patron-client relationships within a larger social system of patron-client relationships.

The Sicilian economy is largely agricultural. For centuries, Sicilian peasants worked the farms of the landed aristocracy. These farms *(latifundi)* were no different from the *hacienda* or the plantations found in other corners of the world where peasant populations labored under the watchful eye of the ruling gentry. The abolition of feudalism in 1812 relieved the Sicilian barons of the responsibility for governing their lands. This allowed many to rent out their estates and move to Palermo, Naples, and Rome, where the surroundings were more sophisticated. Absenteeism became a symbol of wealth. Land was the main source of material prosperity in Sicily. The further away a man was from his land and its demand of labor, the wealthier he must be. Landowners placed responsibility for their property in the hands of hired intermediaries, the *gabellotti*.[12]

The *gabellotti* (managers of the estate) held great power because they controlled access to farm labor and acted as mediators between the landowners and the peasantry. Their position allowed them to develop patron-client relationships with the laborers they employed. Not surprisingly, the *gabellotti* often hired kinsmen and friends from their hometown. Because the *gabellotti* were often the only people to have ready cash, they also became moneylenders, further increasing the dependency of the local peasantry on their good will. Money was lent to pay for weddings, funerals, medical care, and even emigration.[13]

One of the factors that gave rise to this type of Mafia was the estate owners' need to protect their property, especially land that was vulnerable to acts of banditry. Bandits not only stole from the *latifundi* but preyed upon farm workers who often had to travel four to five miles each day to reach their work in the fields. Traveling great distances in a country without police protection left the workers vulnerable to assault and dependent upon those capable of providing protection. Obviously, one of the ways to confront banditry was with violence. Because of the lack of government-sponsored mechanisms of social control, landowners hired well-known toughs to deter attack.[14]

The phenomenon of the Mafia grew in power when landowners hired the strongest *mafiosi* as *gabellotti* to manage their estates. Hiring men who were able "to make themselves respected" not only deterred bandits but helped to control peasant labor. Each estate also employed armed guards, the *campieri*, who were under the supervision of the *gabellotti*. In 1610, Philip III of Spain granted the Sicilian barons the right to administer justice in their areas.[15] This power was passed on to the *gabellotti* as the managers of the barons' estates. The *gabellotti* were called upon to settle disputes among the workers and, through the *campieri*, maintain order over the countryside.

These *mafiosi-gabellotti* eventually turned against the landowners by fixing the compensation they received for their services, the rents and prices charged for the use of the land, and the price of the crops entrusted to their protection. Their influence spread to nearby towns, making it practically impossible for grain and other farm commodities to be sold at open auction. *Mafiosi* charged tolls for the use of roads and water, monopolized access to fruit and vegetable markets, and hindered the construction of irrigation canals. They also accumulated wealth through the rustling of cattle and sheep. The chosen victims were often those who refused to come to terms with the *mafiosi* who controlled the local area.[16]

The Mafia exploited not only the relationship between the peasant and the landowner but the gap in communication between the peasant village and the wider society. For example, the *gabellotti* took advantage of their position and organized their employees into voting blocks, thus acting as mediators between the candidate and the electorate. The control of peasant votes allowed the *mafiosi* to develop patron-client relationships with political leaders who, in return, provided political protection for the *mafiosi's* illegal doings. The *mafiosi* also sought to establish beneficial relationships with local government functionaries and bureaucrats. The association between mafiosi and people of authority was referred to as the *partito*.[17]

There has been a tendency in the literature to locate the origins of the Mafia in the *latifundi* of western Sicily and to identify the prototypical *mafioso* with the *gabellotti*. The necessity of domestic and foreign commerce, however, also caused Mafia power to emerge in the relationship between the large estates and the city of Palermo. Palermo was the center of commerce for the entire island of Sicily. Grain was sold in Palermo, capital was found, the central government was located there, and produce was processed in the area that surrounded the city. The need to transport produce, which must be processed and sold in urban markets, allowed the *mafiosi* to travel and forge new bonds that extended as far as the city. The journey from the estates to Palermo was rife with difficulties in a society where regulation was not left to market forces. Allocation questions arose that demanded resolution: Who bought at auction? Who had access to water? Who had the right of way? Who got the right to pasturage? Who got the threshing contract? Who represented the producers at the city market? The failure of the Sicilian government to ensure that market regulation became the prerogative of the state allowed it to become the prerogative of kin and friendship networks whose collective activities came to be known as the Mafia. There were cattle and pasture Mafia, citrus grove Mafia, water Mafia (who controlled wells), building Mafia, commerce Mafia, public works Mafia, fish market Mafia, and wholesale fruit, vegetable, and flower Mafia. They all functioned to establish order in a society where government control did not exist. The Mafia prevented pilfering and provided protection from all kinds of threats including competitors, criminals, legal authorities, and rival Mafia groups. They also fixed prices and arranged contracts. People who transgressed against those under the protection of the Mafia were violently punished. Mafia influence extended to the citrus groves that were located in the *Conca d'Oro*, where property owners were forced to hire local *mafiosi* to protect their land and ensure the security and sale of their produce.[18]

The unification of Italy in 1860, and the establishment of government authority, did not end the influence of the Mafia. (Sicily and the south of Italy were united as the Kingdom of the Two Sicilies in 1734 but had not been united with the north of Italy since the Roman Empire). Locally, the incorporation of Sicily into the Kingdom of Italy was viewed as an invasion by a foreign power.[19] The moral absorption of state norms not only failed but resulted in the development of a dual morality. The norms of the family and the extended in-group—ritual relatives, friends, patrons, and clients—were observed with conscious conviction, while the norms of the state were ignored. This dual system of state and popular morality helped protect the role of the mafiosi in local society.

The Mafia also became a political force after the unification of Italy. The ability to deliver elections placed the Mafia in tacit partnership with the government in Rome and resulted in their control over government patronage. By 1900, a loose confederation of Mafia groups had developed that governed much of Sicilian life. The Mafia settled disputes, dispensed patronage, extorted protection, and controlled violence in Sicily until the 1920s when its members were forcibly removed from power by the Fascist government of Benito Mussolini. In one series of trials, more than 150 mafiosi were brought before the courts in Palermo. Some received life sentences for their crimes.[20]

The establishment of the Sicilian Mafia was in direct response to the "Hobbesian problem of order." In a society in which means are scarce relative to wants, there is a tendency for actors not to reciprocate in kind for the satisfaction of their own wants by others. Such negative reciprocity relations often end in violence and war. The Hobbesian question—how can one establish a society in which force and fraud are not routinely used in satisfying wants?—is satisfied through the establishment of normative solutions (law). In the absence of formal mechanisms of social control, groups often resolve problems of order through the use of force. In nineteenth-century Sicily, the motivation to avoid violence led to the creation of a specific set of norms and the establishment of the Mafia as a de facto method of social control.[21]

Up to the time of the Sicilian immigration to the United States, the island of Sicily never had any single criminal organization called the Mafia. There were, however, real *mafiosi*—men who exercised power through the systematic use of violence. The sum of these actions made up the phenomenon called the Mafia. It was not until after World War II that the Mafia evolved into a criminal organization similar to traditional Italian American organized crime. This *nuova Mafia* (new Mafia) developed because of the American occupation of Sicily, which brought many antifascist *mafiosi* back to power.[22] In addition, postwar Sicily was the scene of intensive economic development. The Italian state poured huge sums of money into Sicily in order to modernize agriculture and to improve roads, harbors, airports, and dams. Because of their *partito* connections to the Christian Democratic Party, the *nuova mafiosi* entered construction, transport, and other businesses in order to receive preferential treatment in the awarding of public contracts.

As this review has shown, the rural nature and social functions of the Mafia in Sicily made it an unlikely source of criminal activity in the United States. This is not to say that criminals did not practice blackmail and extortion in Sicily and the south of Italy. Italian police extradited Giuseppe Macaluso from Chicago for kidnapping a boy in Palermo, Sicily. Macaluso allegedly murdered the boy after his ransom demands were not met. There is even evidence that robbery and extortion occurred in Sicily at a higher rate than in other parts of Italy at the beginning of the twentieth century. However, threatening blackmail letters were more typical of bandits and highwaymen than *mafioso*. A man may have practiced extortion as a brigand before becoming a *mafioso*, but the role of the mafioso in instances of extortion was that of mediation. The mafioso, as an agent of social control, often represented the victim and negotiated the sums demanded. No evidence whatsoever has been uncovered that Black Hand activity was the work of the Sicilian Mafia or that former Mafia members masterminded a Black Hand campaign in the United States.[23]

The Camorra

The Camorra is a criminal group centered in the city of Naples. The origins of the Camorra, like the Mafia, are unclear. It is believed that the Camorra is a descendant of a group in fifteenth-century Spain that found its way to Italy during the Bourbon occupation. (The Spanish Bourbon dynasty ruled Naples from 1734 to 1860.) This group, known as the *Garduna*, was a fellowship of thieves and malefactors who, working with the Inquisition, targeted Moors and Jews, dividing their profits with the police and the clergy.[24]

Like the word *mafia*, there are many explanations for the origin of the word *Camorra*. One explanation is that the word is derived from the name of the organization's founder, a Spaniard named *Gamurra*. Another explanation reports that the name is derived from the Spanish word *gamurra*, a cloak worn by thieves and bullies. There is also a Spanish word *Camorra* meaning "a quarrel with fists" or *hacer Camorra* "to look for trouble." Yet another explanation suggests that the word *Camorra* is derived from the Arabic word *Kumar*, meaning a dice game, or *gamara*, the place where such gaming takes place. *Camorra* could have been derived from the game *morra* in which two players open their fists, varying the number of fingers displayed. The player who guesses the right number, which they must shout out as the fists are opened, is the winner.[25]

The word *guappo* is used to refer to a Camorra member, or *Camorrist* as they are commonly called. It is derived from the Spanish word meaning beautiful or impressive because of courage. The *guappi* were people who may have gotten their money by criminal means but were honorable, fair, and generous. Today the word *guappo* is generally used to denote a senior member of a criminal gang who is prepared to use violence. Being a Camorrist was a matter of pride among the criminal classes. In fact, during the period 1820 to 1860, *Camorristi* often wore a peculiar unofficial uniform that included a red necktie, a parti-colored sash, and a cane with brass rings, which distinguished them as members of the group.[26]

One explanation for the development of the Camorra is that it began in the sixteenth century as a society to suppress robbers and bandits.[27] Members hired themselves out to protect travelers and commerce from the highwaymen who had infested the roads between Naples and other cities. Known as the Honorable Society of the Camorra, the organization became a notable power as merchants and travelers alike sought their protection. Realizing a fertile opportunity for profit, the Camorra soon fell into league with the highwaymen that they were hired to guard against. Those travelers and merchants who did not meet their demands for protection money were betrayed to local bandits. In the end, the Camorra degenerated into a society of extortionists, blackmailers, and thieves.

A more likely explanation for the development of the Camorra is that it began in the prisons of Naples and spread to the city via former prisoners who had served their sentences. There are two theories about the emergence of the Camorra in Italy's prisons. The first argues that the Camorra was established for the protection of inmates who were treated poorly by their Spanish Bourbon jailers. The second maintains that the Camorra was established by senior inmates who demanded tribute from weaker prisoners ostensibly to pay for oil to light a religious lamp devoted to the Madonna. This tribute was reportedly shared with the Bourbon jailers, who welcomed the assistance of the Camorra in maintaining order.[28]

The harsh treatment of the Neapolitan population by the Bourbon government was not confined to the local prisons. Bourbon rule was marked by wholesale persecution. In eleven days in 1793, the hangman in Naples executed one hundred and twenty professors, physicians, and priests. During the reign of Ferdinand II (1830–1859), over twenty thousand people were held as political prisoners. Ferdinand II was known as "King Bomba" because he had ordered the bombardment of two of his own cities, Palermo and Messina, during the revolution of 1848. Although much of the tyranny of the Bourbon dynasty was directed at the middle class, the poor had little influence and were the subject of capricious treatment. As a result, many people gathered in secret organizations, including the Camorra, to protect themselves from public officials.[29]

The business of the Camorra was organized extortion. The Camorra extorted money from gamblers, prostitutes, counterfeiters, thieves, and smugglers as well as liveries, waiters, fruit peddlers, and small tradesman. This money bought protection against theft and annoyance. The Camorra shared the money it collected with the police, public officials, members in jail, families of deceased members, and finally the members themselves.[30]

In 1860, during the Italian revolution, order broke down in the city of Naples. The Bourbon government organized a national guard to maintain order and enlisted many members of the Camorra into its ranks. The Camorra had already established a relationship with the police, providing them with information on criminal activity, in exchange for immunity from arrest. This new police power included the collection of customs duties at the port of Naples and the city's gates, which gave the Camorra greater freedom to further its criminal interests. The Camorra took advantage of its new position by extorting money from those already involved in smuggling as well as forcing shopkeepers and merchants to purchase contraband goods.[31]

Not only were criminal opportunities expanded by the revolution, but an alliance was established between politics and crime. The original Camorra *Basso* (lower) continued its criminal activity, while the new Camorra *Alto* (high) participated in more sophisticated forms of crime and acted as the organization's contact with elected officials.[32] The Camorra's entrance into law enforcement, however, was short lived. In 1862, 300 of the most notorious *Camorristi* in Naples were arrested. Although its police powers had been broken, the Camorra's position within Neapolitan society had been established. Many people continued to call upon them to police and settle disputes. In fact, the *guappi* became a sort of informal justice of the peace in many inner-city areas. The Camorra was particularly effective at mediation because of its ability to enforce its decisions through violence.

Just as for the Mafia, the advent of Fascism ended the Camorra, though some members were invited to join Mussolini's Fascist Party. After World War II, the Sicilian Mafia began operating in Naples. The Mafia, working with local Neapolitan criminals, engaged in the large-scale theft of war materials and contraband smuggling. Then in 1970 a new Camorra was born. Unlike its predecessor, the modern Camorra consisted of a number of different gangs. The most prominent was the *Nuova Camorra Organizata*, who, like its predecessor, recruited members from Neapolitan prisons. Today, a number of different Camorra gangs operate in the Naples area. They continue to be involved in extortion in addition to cigarette smuggling and narcotics distribution.[33]

Although the main purpose of the Camorra was crime, no evidence has been uncovered linking the Camorra with Black Hand extortion in Italy, nor has any evidence been uncovered linking the Camorra to Black Hand extortion in the United States. In fact, there is no evidence linking the Camorra to the Mafia prior to the end of World War II, which casts doubt on the belief that the Camorra and Mafia were the same or somehow related criminal organizations.

Historically, the Camorra was more organized as a crime group than the Mafia, but for some reason it was the idea of the Mafia that caught hold of the American imagination.

THE REAL CAUSES OF BLACK HAND EXTORTION

While the American public believed that the Black Hand was a foreign criminal organization that had migrated to Chicago and other American cities from the south of Italy, the White Hand Society argued that the Black Hand was not an organization of Italian criminals but a method of crime, a method used by a special class of criminals who operated everywhere in the same way.[34] The White Hand Society also argued that Black Hand extortion was the outcome of conditions existing within American society and that it only occurred in places where these special conditions existed. The White Hand identified these conditions as the isolation of the Italian community, the Italian immigrant's distrust of formal authority, the presence of saloons and saloonkeepers with powerful political connections, and a criminal justice system that was ineffective in repressing crime.

What is so important about the White Hand's explanation is that it was the first attempt to explain the underlying social causes of Black Hand crime. Up to this point, all that Chicagoans knew about Black Hand activity was what they read in the local newspapers, the majority of which reported that Black Hand crimes were the work of a sinister foreign group. Although supposedly unbiased, news reporting has often been found to reflect the dominant views of society.[35] It is evident from newspaper reports of the day that the American public refused to acknowledge that social conditions in American society could be the cause of Black Hand crime. Just as in the case of organized crime in later years, the American public sought a foreign source for this new threatening form of criminality.

Isolation of the Italian Community

When the White Hand Society spoke of the isolation of the Italian community, it was largely addressing conditions in Chicago's Little Sicily neighborhood. Of the 261 locations of Black Hand crime identified in this study, over one-third (90) occurred in and around Little Sicily. Harvey

Zorbaugh described Little Sicily as the greatest concentration of poverty in Chicago. One Chicago newspaper described it as "the world's most desperate spot." A 1914 survey of housing in Chicago reported that 80 percent of the residents of a four-block area in the heart of the district were recently arrived Italian immigrants.[36]

The Local Community Research Committee of the University of Chicago reported that the people of Little Sicily were isolated from all other ethnic groups except Chicago's "colored" population. They also found that the neighborhood was "tough" and that the only recreational facilities available to Sicilians were the street and the poolroom. The area was physically conducive to lawlessness. Dilapidated buildings, dark and dirty alleys, streets in need of repair, and disorganized living conditions all contributed to crime in the area. Poor transportation and the barrier of the Chicago River also added to the isolation of the community.[37]

The White Hand Society also argued that the physical condition of the area contributed to Black Hand crime. People were crowded together in narrow quarters and out-of-the way streets with little light and no police protection. Such an atmosphere created the opportunity for Black Hand criminals to lie in wait, disappear after an attack, procure a safe hiding place, and find witnesses to provide an alibi and friends to aid in escape. Larrabee Street was so dark that women carried revolvers to protect themselves. A committee of citizens had petitioned city hall for better street lighting, but the city took no action.[38] The *Chicago Daily Tribune* described the area in 1910:

> The streets are narrow and the lights are few. At night, the stranger who turns north from Chicago Avenue into one of these streets is amply justified in drawing back and hesitating before he plunges farther into the doubtful darkness. The outlook is anything but inviting to a stranger. The street lamps do little to relieve the gloom and the stores and houses, with wavering gas jets behind murky windows, do nothing. Only before the saloon is there any degree of light and here the eye makes out a group of lounging figures that go well with the general gloom and darkness of the scene.[39]

The press was as equally critical of the people of Little Sicily as they were of the physical condition of the area. The *Chicago Record-Herald* reported that half of the residents were European ex-convicts or fugitives from justice, and that 60 percent of those who were not criminals were paying a monthly tribute to the Black Hand. *Tribune* feature writer Henry Hyde described Little Sicily as a place where "knots of dark, mustached, fierce-looking men with bold, sullen faces are gathered on the street corners. Some of them, red handkerchiefs twisted about their necks and little gold rings in their ears, look like Mediterranean pirates." They were former sulfur rats (miners), shepherds, goatherds, and brigands who worked in Chicago as laborers, peddlers, and in a dozen other occupations. In Little Sicily, they set up a community of their own with "almost all the immemorial customs and the dark and bloody rules of conduct which have made Sicilians feared—and misunderstood—throughout the world." In another report, the *Record-Herald* concluded, "Little Sicily was a tiny district four blocks square, which apparently knew no law except that of the vendetta and the Black Hand."[40]

Little Sicily was located within the Near North Side community of Chicago. The Near North Side was part of the original incorporation of the city in 1837. In 1856, a bridge was constructed across the Chicago River at Erie Street, bringing settlers to the district. By 1860, large numbers of German and Irish immigrants had settled there. They were soon followed by Swedes and other Scandinavians. Although most of the Near North Side was destroyed by the Chicago Fire, the area quickly rebuilt. Immediately after the fire, destitute and homeless families moved back into the district and built small wooden cottages in spite of a new ordinance defining "fire limits" where only brick and stone buildings were allowed.[41]

The turn of the century brought additional settlers to the Near North Side. Large numbers of Italians and, in particular, Sicilians moved into the community. The "dark people," as they were called, soon dominated the area. By 1910, the Sicilian community extended as far north as Division Street. Over 13,000 Sicilians and other Italians lived in the district. By 1920, Little Sicily, or "Little Hell" as the Sicilian community was also known, stretched from Sedgwick Street west to the Chicago River and north from Chicago Avenue to North Avenue.[42]

The name Little Hell was derived from the gashouse at Crosby and Hobbie streets whose belching flames lit the sky at night. Residents recalled how the skies ignited like a satanic specter when flames from the furnaces producing "water gas" would soar upward into the sky.[43] The roaring thunder of the furnaces could be heard for blocks around as coal was poured into the ovens and moistened with water from the Chicago River to create gas that was used for heating, cooking, and lighting. Enormous tanks stored the gas during the day. These gigantic cylinders grew many stories high as they filled with gas. During the night, the cylinders would descend back into their wells as the gas was dispersed throughout the neighborhood. The Little Sicily plant was eventually dismantled when natural gas was made available in Chicago. Much to the dismay of neighborhood residents, the name Little Hell remained. Both the press and government officials continued to use that designation to refer to the area.

Little Sicily was an area of first settlement, an area where immigrants came directly from Europe bringing with them their Old World language, dress, and customs. Those who came to Little Sicily were *contadini* (peasants) from the *Mezzogiorno*, as Sicily and the south of Italy were called. Most had worked in the fields as fruit and table gardeners, cultivators of grains and cereals, and sheepherders. The *contadini* often immigrated as a group and, once in the United States, settled among others from their native Sicilian town. People from Alta Villa Milicia settled on Larrabee Street. Those on Cambridge came from Alimenia, Cuisa, and Caccamo. On Milton were immigrants from Sambuca. Those on Townsend migrated from Bagheria and Burgio; those on Hobbie and Elm from Corleone. The attachment to others from one's native village was termed *campanilismo*, the spirit of dwelling under one's own church tower.[44]

Although the Sicilians exhibited camaraderie with those from their native towns, the interests of the family took precedence over those of the village. Intense family pride was their outstanding characteristic, and the family unit not only included those related by blood but those related by ritual bonds such as godmother and godfather as well. One social observer noted, "The extent to which family loyalty goes is beyond belief; no matter how disgraced or how disgraceful a member may be, he is never cast off; the unsuccessful are assisted; the selfish are indulged; the erratic patiently borne with. Old age is respected, and babies are objects of adoration."[45]

First-generation Italian immigrants in Little Sicily and other Italian colonies were reluctant to integrate with their American neighbors. The socialist, Italian-language newspaper *La Parola dei Socialisti* argued that Italians, like the Chinese, were difficult to assimilate. Many lived in America for twenty years without learning the language, manners, and customs of their new country. Italians traded at Italian grocery stores, spent evenings and Sundays in Italian saloons, deposited savings with Italian bankers, and got a shave from an Italian barber—all adding to their isolation from the larger American community. Anthropologist George Dorsey traced the source of this clannishness to Italy itself. The majority of Italians who came to America were from the south of Italy where their horizons enclosed the home, the family, and the native village. Beyond that, everyone was a stranger. As a result, those who came to the America sought to live among relatives and friends and exhibited little interest in cultural assimilation.[46]

The community that the Sicilian immigrant arrived in was in a desperate state. Many of the houses in the district were two- and three-story frame cottages that sat below street level. The streets had been raised three to six feet to accommodate a new sewer system. This caused the ground-floor apartments to become basement or cellar dwellings. These apartments were often damp, especially during the winter and spring months. In addition, the buildings in the district covered a large percentage of the available land space, and often more than one building was erected on each city lot, resulting in a large number of rear cottages. These rear cottages were mostly older frame buildings that had been moved back from the street. With the dilapidation of the buildings came a general lack of cleanliness in the yards and alleys. These conditions were a direct cause of phthisis, a form of pulmonary tuberculosis or consumption, which by 1917 was epidemic in the area.[47]

Sicilians, like many other immigrant groups, came to Chicago to find work. The legend grew that if a man could not "make it" in Chicago, he could not make it anywhere. The establishment of Little Sicily and other immigrant colonies was not haphazard, but was determined by the socioeconomic ecology of the city. The Chicago River with its north and south branches provided the basis for the industrial topography of Chicago. The river's twenty-four miles of shoreline provided access to both water transportation and waste disposal for the city's emerging industries. As a result, an industrial belt hugged the course of the river. So many industries were located along the North Branch of the Chicago River that smoke from the factories and the railway built along the river to service them caused the area to be named Smoky Hollow. With these new factories came a demand for labor that was filled by the rising tide of immigration. While the economic advances of earlier immigrants, including northern Italians, allowed them to move to newer areas of the city, Sicilians and other immigrant groups settled in the working-class slums that had sprung up adjacent to the factories alongside the Chicago River. These inner-city communities were called the River Wards.[48]

This semicircular belt between the downtown business area and the more desirable neighborhoods of Chicago was a "zone in transition." It was here that the poor settled to gain a foothold in American society. In addition, it was here that social conditions were the worst in the city. Sociologists at the University of Chicago described these areas as socially disorganized. They were disorganized because local families suffered from poverty, sickness, poor housing, crime, and the difficulties of adjusting to urban life.

Although people came to Chicago to better their lot by finding work, periods of unemployment were common. A 1919 report by the City of Chicago indicated that nearly one-quarter of the Italian immigrant population worked seasonal jobs that left them unemployed for several months each year. This unemployment led to great financial need, especially if there was a slowdown in the building trades and railroad construction. During one such period in 1914, a volunteer charity named the Good Fellows gave aid to nearly 400 families a month in the area.[49] Commenting on the poverty, Lenora Midler, the commissioner of public welfare, asked, "How can anything different be expected from the poor people, crowded as they are into miserable habituation in districts where the smoke hangs a large part of the time like a pall over gray broken-down houses and unkempt streets; where constantly recurring unemployment makes it impossible for them to obtain the basest necessities of life; where ignorance is unenlightened and despair seizes on many a heart?"[50]

Despite the difficulties encountered, the residents of Little Sicily sought to build a better life. Although many lived in run-down housing, the interiors of their homes were clean and orderly. There were fewer cases of family desertion among Chicago's Italians than any other ethnic group. Few Italians were street beggars, and Italian immigrants were unusually sober. Work was often a family affair. Sicilian women took in sewing in order to earn money while watching their young children. Older children sold nuts after school and gathered coal at nearby factories and railroad yards. It was also common for boys and girls to leave school at age fourteen to find jobs in local shops and industries. Reacting to the plight of the people of Little Sicily, a local settlement house worker commented, "But after all I wonder if there is as much happiness on the Gold Coasts as over in these basement rooms. When the father comes home at night, six or seven children run to meet him, and a warm supper is always ready; and summer nights—the streets—you would go a long way to hear the concertinas."[51]

Until 1914, the Sicilian colony in Chicago was also a foreign community. The food sold was distinctively different. Women rarely left home and the family arranged marriages. People lived as much as possible in groups that corresponded to their home villages in Sicily. They participated in religious societies with other immigrants from their native town. The foreign nature of the community limited police protection. The police and public alike generally did not understand the foreign customs, language, and traditions of the Sicilian immigrant. The older people in the community were superstitious. For example, a number of Italian women living near Death Corner reported to the Chicago police that they heard strange noises coming from the passageway where the men who had killed Antonio Dugo and Phillip Maniscalsco, victims of the so-called Shotgun Man, hid and fired their shotguns. The women asserted that the "spirit voices" of the dead men were talking to one another.[52]

Cultural differences between the Italian immigrant community and other ethnic groups in Chicago undoubtedly contributed to the isolation of the Little Sicily community. This isolation was not entirely bad. Noted sociologist Robert Park argued that immigrant colonies served a useful function in the social organization of the city.[53] Neighborhoods such as Little Sicily eased transition and allowed newcomers to settle among fellow countrymen who understood their cultural habits and shared their views on life. Little Sicily provided a place where first-generation immigrants were able to maintain their cultural heritage in diverse surroundings until they gained a foothold in American society. Cultural differences, however, were not the only reason for the isolation of the community. It could also be argued that the isolation of Little Sicily was directly related to the Italian immigrant's distrust of government.

Italian Immigrant's Distrust of Formal Authority

After the fall of the Roman Empire, the south of Italy and Sicily had a succession of foreign rulers that included the Arabs, Normans, French, and Spanish. The history of the region is one of a thousand years of political, social, and economic repression. Not being able to look upon their government or its laws as just or protective, the people of the south of Italy developed their own code of conduct. *Omerta*, the quality of being a man with honor and dignity, allowed a man to resolve his own problems without recourse to the law. A man who appealed to the law against his fellow man was seen as not only a fool but a coward. Such a code is common in societies that have been the victims of government persecution. *Omerta* allowed the people of southern Italy to cooperate individually to frustrate the efforts of a government that sought only to exploit them.[54]

Foreign domination had additional consequences for the development of Sicilian society. Christianity came later to Sicily than to the other areas of Europe. The Arabs conquered Sicily in 826 and remained for two hundred years. The Norman invasion of Sicily at the end of the eleventh century forced the Arab population to seek asylum in the western portion of the island. This fugitive existence contributed to the development of norms and values that were in opposition to the ruling government structure. Arab customs also contributed to the development of the Sicilian acceptance of private violence as a means of redressing social wrongs.[55]

The vendetta, or use of violence to settle personal disputes, was common in Sicily. The original purpose of the vendetta was retaliation against the foreign officials sent to rule the land. Because it was impossible to have their rulers punished for oppression, the Sicilian people would dispose of them by assassination, which became an honorable act. Over time, the use of the vendetta became a cultural phenomenon. Unable to seek justice from their foreign rulers, families and individuals took private vengeance against their enemies. A rhymed Sicilian proverb summed up this principle: "If I live, I will kill thee. If I die, I forgive thee."[56]

The custom of resorting to violence to settle private disputes carried over to Chicago's Sicilian colonies, where there were many examples of the vendetta. When his daughter was poisoned in a robbery scheme, Frank Renda vowed publicly to wreak vengeance upon the perpetrator of the crime, stating, "I am Sicilian and will not rest until I have avenged the death of my little girl." When Anthony Puccio and Rosario Dispenza were murdered on a sidewalk in Little Sicily, friends and relatives of the slain men dipped their fingers in the pools of blood and swore to avenge their deaths.[57]

In another case, a murder was committed in Chicago and the police identified the killer. In spite of weeks of searching, however, they were not able to apprehend the offender.[58] Finally, a detective saw the wanted man leave the home of the brother of the murder victim. The home had been the criminal's refuge for weeks. When the police questioned the brother regarding this strange behavior, he declared that the killer of his brother had been wounded and that he and his family had nursed him back to health. He did so in order to personally kill the offender and avenge the death of his brother.

When a society fails to punish criminals, the populace is likely to take the law into its own hands, resulting in private acts of retribution. Such was the case in Sicily and the south of Italy in the late nineteenth century because of the absence of effective state government. In Chicago, an Italian killed the abductor of his wife after the courts failed to convict the kidnapper and dismissed the case. Believing that justice had not been served, he took the law into his own hands and murdered the kidnapper. Philosophers have argued that the problem with retributive justice is that it often lacks proportionality. It is generally agreed that punishment is necessary to restore the unfair advantage gained by the offender and to prevent future crime. The punishment, however, must not exceed the harm caused by the initial act, which often occurs in private acts of vengeance. Take the classic example of cultural deviance provided by Thorsten Sellin. In his study *Culture, Conflict, and Crime*, Sellin described a Sicilian father in New Jersey who killed the sixteen-year-old seducer of his daughter. The father expressed surprise at his arrest since he had merely defended his family honor in the traditional way. Not only did the father fail to realize that American law did not recognize the right of private vengeance, but the penalty he meted out was not proportional to the crime. Requiring retribution to be proportional to the crime serves a real purpose—it helps to prevent the escalating violence of blood feuds and further vendettas.[59]

Distrust of government was also related to the harsh conditions of life in the south of Italy and Sicily. In the *Mezzogiorno*, extreme poverty led to the development of a fatalistic, alienated view of life—"*La Miseria*"—in which a man conceived of himself as having little if any control over his life. Such a view prevented people from cooperating with their neighbors, because in so doing they jeopardized their positions in a competitive world where goods were scarce. Banfield described this inability to act together for the common good, or for any end transcending the material interest of the nuclear family, as "amoral familism." So exclusive was the demand of the family for the loyalty of its members that it precluded allegiance to other social institutions, including the government. This tradition of undivided loyalty to the family was deep-rooted in the culture of southern Italy, which emphasized individual freedom from discipline or restraint by any group other than the family.[60]

The Italian's distrust of government even extended to Chicago. The political nature of municipal government often exploited those in need of government services. An investigation by the City of Chicago reported that whenever Italians encountered the judicial machinery, politics interfered and made them feel that money was the key that unlocked all doors.[61] For example, the mother of a boy who was arrested for stealing lead pipe sought the help of a local political leader. The "Big Man," as he was described, told her that he would talk to the judge and prosecuting attorney, but it would cost her $75. The boy was a first-time offender and received probation, which he probably would have received anyway. The "Big Man" later came by and collected an additional $25 from the mother. In another instance, a young man deserted his wife and children, leaving them penniless. Instead of going to the welfare department and asking for aid, the woman went to a local political leader and paid him a small sum to ensure that she received her rightful public assistance. Actions such as these served to reinforce the Italian immigrant's suspicion of government.

Cairoli Gigliotti, an attorney and member of the Italian community, also noted the difficulty that Italians were having with Chicago's judicial system. Writing in 1916, Gigliotti charged that the political nature of the court system prevented Italians and other poor litigants from finding justice. Police officers were regularly charged with connivance when politically connected criminals were arrested, prosecutors were always willing to help politically sponsored criminals escape punishment, and judges were tied, body and soul, to political bosses. As a result, groups that were not politically organized, especially recent immigrant groups, were at the mercy of the political system. The corrupt political system in Chicago so disenchanted Gigliotti that he quit the practice of law to work exclusively on reforming Chicago's judiciary.[62]

An important implication of Italian immigrants' lack of trust in government authority was their reluctance to cooperate with the police. When asked about a crime that had occurred, residents of Little Sicily often replied with "No speaka da English" or an equally illuminating shake of the head, even though they may have known who was responsible for the offense. The police and the press attributed this unwillingness to the code of *omerta*, but in reality, people were probably just too frightened to cooperate with authorities. One reason for this fear was the failure of the American police to cope with the Black Hand gangs. This failure was remarked in the Italian community and caused many to fear for their lives. In one case, police reported that three men walked into a flat in Little Sicily and shot a man as he lay in bed. His wife, who witnessed the murder, refused to cooperate with the police in identifying the killers. She was afraid to "squeal" for fear that she would be marked for vengeance and the Chicago police would be unable to protect her.[63]

The Reverend Graham Taylor, founder of the Chicago Commons Settlement House, provides a different view of the southern Italian's willingness to cooperate with the law. It was his experience that Sicilians were willing to cooperate with the authorities when assured of protection by the courts and the police, and that they even risked death to testify against Mafia and Camorra extortionists and kidnapers.[64] Taylor found that most Sicilians strongly objected to the parasites of their race from whose lawlessness they themselves suffered most. Located in the Italian settlement along West Grand Avenue in Chicago's Near Northwest Side, Taylor and his Chicago Commons settlement workers had intimate knowledge of the Italian immigrant community and provide what should be considered an unbiased view of Sicilian immigrant life.

Saloons and Saloonkeepers with Powerful
Political Connections

The existence of bawdy saloons and politically connected saloonkeepers within Chicago's Little Sicily community also contributed to Black Hand crime. Italian saloons generally had a bad reputation. Whether deserved or not, the appellation "dago bar" was a common synonym for saloons in exposés about Chicago's criminal element. Six saloons were believed to be the locations where most Black Hand conspirators met to plan their crimes. Chicago police identified the saloonkeepers as Coniglio and Manina, 926 Milton Avenue; Charles Plumeri, 924 Milton Avenue; Philip and John, 860 Milton Avenue; I. G. Le Vatino, 872 Milton Avenue; Salvatore Pinachi, 501 W. Oak; and Rosario Dispenza, 1021 Milton Avenue. All of these saloons were located in the immediate vicinity of Death Corner. They were the places of retreat for the worst elements of the Italian colonies. Some of the saloons were also houses of prostitution and other immoral traffic.[65]

The keepers of these saloons were powerful political forces in their areas. They took an active role in political campaigns, contributed money to political candidates, and assisted ward leaders and the candidates that they represented. So many saloonkeepers were active in Chicago politics that Lincoln Stephens wrote in *The Shame of the Cities*, "The quickest way to clear the city council was to stand at the door and yell your saloon's on fire." As a result, it was common for the police department, because of entangling alliances with corrupt politicians, to adopt a "let alone" attitude towards those saloons and saloonkeepers who supported successful candidates. The profound indifference to the law exhibited by saloon proprietors created an atmosphere in which Black Hand criminals were able to operate with the expectation of some degree of immunity.[66]

Another factor that contributed to the ability of saloonkeepers to disregard the law was the fact that the saloonkeeper was often an agent of the liquor distributor, who was obviously interested in keeping the saloon open. Distributors often loaned money to saloons to pay for remodeling and new equipment. As such, they were willing to exert their own political influence with local authorities to keep bawdy saloons open in order to protect their investments. The extent of the political influence exerted by the saloonkeepers was demonstrated when Chicago police raided several Little Sicily saloons in connection with the murder of Benedetto Cinene. It was hoped that the raids would induce the proprietors to stop gambling and liquor law violations, but the proprietors "only laughed at the officers" when confronted about their vice activity.[67]

Saloons were viewed as "crime factories" because of the relationship between vice and crime. They also contributed to Black Hand crime in a very direct way, particularly Black Hand crime in the Little Sicily area. Criminals from other cities or neighborhoods in Chicago were drawn to these locations by their reputations. They were not only known for their wine, women, and gambling tables but as the place to meet new coconspirators to carry out Black Hand crimes.[68] These saloons were additionally useful for identifying potential Black Hand victims. They provided a place to talk about those in the area who had exhibited any sign of prosperity. There were numerous small businesses in the community, particularly ethnic shops supporting the Sicilian community. Each became a potential victim of Black Hand extortion, and each was readily visible to the clientele of these saloons.

The connection between saloons in Little Sicily and Black Hand crime was positively established by the shooting of Joseph Sutero in December 1911. Sutero had come to the attention of the police and agreed to aid them in their efforts against Black Hand crime, which led to his becoming a marked man. One night, Sutero was approached by Pietro Distenzo and Joseph Ilordi, proprietors of a saloon at Hobbie and Townsend streets, who warned him that unless he refrained from helping the police they would "get him." Sutero laughed at the men and their threats. As he passed their saloon the next night, the basement door suddenly opened, the end of a sawed-off rifle was thrust through the opening, and a volley of bullets fired into the street. Two pedestrians and a teamster were struck. Sutero escaped without a scratch. The police raided the saloon within minutes after the shooting, and both Distenzo and Ilordi were arrested. A few days later, police received an anonymous letter identifying Vito Barone and Vito Ingraffia as the shooters. They were arrested and charged, along with Distenzo and Ilordi, for threatening Sutero and wounding the three bystanders.[69]

The connection between saloons in Little Sicily and Black Hand activity contributed to the perception that the Black Hand and the Mafia were the sources of vice and crime in Chicago. The Italian community challenged this perception, arguing that the press was overlooking police corruption while focusing attention on the Mafia and Black Hand. For example, *L'Italia* reported that a local Italian saloonkeeper, Battista Pizzi, had paid Chicago police $300 to remedy a prostitution arrest that had occurred in his tavern. There were even allegations of police corruption in Black Hand investigations. In one instance, patrolman James McGrath was accused of stealing a package of ransom money from its hiding place. Assigned to investigate an extortion demand against Isaac

Wechaler of South Commercial Avenue, McGrath was caught taking the ransom money after the blackmailers failed to retrieve it. In a separate investigation, Charles De Woody of the Justice Department's Bureau of Investigation reported to the Chicago Civil Service Commission that Chicago police officers had blocked federal investigations of white slavery and Black Hand crimes.[70]

Corruption in Chicago was by no means restricted to Italian saloons. In his 1894 exposé of vice conditions in Chicago's Levee district, noted evangelist William Stead charged that every member of the police force neglected to perform his duty when it came to the saloon, the gaming house, and the house of ill fame. Describing Chicago as "Satan's Sanctum," L. O. Curon listed the amounts charged by the police in 1899 to protect vice activities in Chicago. Gambling houses paid fifty dollars a month. Panel and badger houses (bordellos) paid thirty-five. Houses of ill fame paid $100. Crap games and opium dens paid ten to twenty-five dollars, depending on their income.[71]

Corruption was not limited to vice activities. Everyone connected to the reigning political party benefited from the corrupt government system when it came to the administration of justice. According to Stead, "The mayor, the aldermen, the saloon keeper, the heeler, everybody in fact who is anybody or anything in Chicago has got a 'pull' when justice is to be administered excepting that abstract entity justice herself. Justice has no pull." A police officer had explained to Stead how the system worked: every judge was a political appointee and under the thumb of the alderman and politician. A tough who was always prominent at ward meetings and fought for the candidates of his party got the protection of his party. Hence, when he was arrested and taken to court, the judge reduced the charge, administered a fine, and later suspended it. The police officer who resisted temptation or fought the system found himself abused, hounded, and eventually out of a job.[72]

Chicago was notoriously corrupt: a 1909 editorial in the *Chicago Daily Tribune* charged that Democratic politics in Chicago was under the control of the vicious, criminal, and predatory elements of the city that included rum sellers, gamblers, and the men who supported and owned the saloons. A similar editorial in a 1911 edition of the *Chicago Record-Herald* charged that although Chicago's system of payoffs was not as extensive as New York's, it appeared to be organized and growing. Citizens openly wondered whether graft was systematically levied. Were detectives directly or indirectly paid for not seeing or knowing too much? Did police administrators issue orders without expecting them to be obeyed? Were certain groups too politically powerful to be subject to police interference? These questions were asked by thousands of perplexed and indignant Chicagoans. The public asked these questions because they believed that the police could have chosen to suppress professional crime and clear up centers of gambling and other vice activity.[73]

Vice was so rampant in Chicago that Judge William Gemmili of the municipal court charged that police consciously fixed "limits" to crime.[74] By limits, he meant that police allowed crimes to occur in certain districts of the city. They included the First, Eighteenth, Nineteenth, and Twenty-first Wards. These areas contained the Levee, Chicago's red-light district; the Near West Side, which included Chicago's largest Italian community; and the Near North Side, which included Little Sicily. Judge Gemmili charged that in these wards criminals could act with impunity. These areas were the reserves in which Black Hand criminals, gamblers, and persons of every other criminal stripe could operate. They were set aside, he argued, by the police department to allow lawbreakers to commit unspeakable and innumerable crimes.

An investigation conducted by the Chicago Civil Service Commission in 1911 concluded that Judge Gemmili's views were well founded. The commission reported that they had uncovered 2,018 violations of police rules governing the operation of "gambling houses, prohibited dives, all night saloons, shady hotels, and drug dens."[75] One-third of these violations occurred in three of Chicago's police districts: the Cottage Grove, East Chicago Avenue, and Twenty-second Street stations. The East Chicago Avenue district, which contained Little Sicily, was described as the "most political ridden of any in the city" and found to contain more "shady" hotels and saloons that sheltered "disorderly women" than any other police district in the city.

Police allowed crimes to occur in certain districts because that is what political leaders wanted, and police were often powerless to act. City oil inspector James Aloysius Quinn was the political power in the Near North Side. Better known as "Hot Stove Jimmy Quinn," because of his use of the aphorism "he'd steal a hot stove" when referring to fellow politicians, Quinn reportedly controlled police assignments in the East Chicago Avenue district, and it is believed that police efforts against the North Side underworld were subject to his veto.[76]

A 1913 incident in the Near West Side demonstrated the influence that powerful political leaders had over police operations. When officers in the Maxwell Street District did not follow the direction of Twentieth Ward alderman Emanuel "Manny" Abrahams, he "sent everybody who was not with him to the tall timbers." The "cleaning out" of Maxwell Street meant transferring four sergeants, sixteen patrolmen, one police switchboard operator and six senior detectives "who knew every crook in the district." All of those transferred had good records, and the only reason they were transferred was that they were not "in right" with Alderman Abrahams. In other words, they refused to do the bidding of the alderman and protect his interests. A 1911 newspaper exposé charged that Abrahams controlled vice activity among the Orthodox Jews in the Maxwell Street precinct, which was the home of Chicago's immigrant Jewish population.[77]

Corruption in New York may have also affected Black Hand crime in Chicago. New York Mayor George B. McClellan Jr., the son of the famous Civil War general, withheld the penal certificates of more than 700 Italian ex-convicts then in the United States. These certificates were legal proof that the men had served prison sentences in Italy, making them ineligible for immigration to the United States and subject to immediate deportation if they had managed to immigrate anyway. McClellan reportedly withheld the certificates because he was afraid that the arrests would alienate Italian voters and affect his political future. McClellan also was concerned that the arrests would alienate his Tammany Hall backers, who often benefited from the support of Black Hand criminals. Had the police been allowed to round up these potential Black Hand offenders, the Black Hand problem might have been solved by 1910.[78]

Problems with vice and corruption had a direct affect on Black Hand crime, but they were not the only problems confronting the criminal justice system in Chicago and other American cities. Some charged that the criminal justice system itself was ineffective in controlling Black Hand crime.

Ineffective Criminal Justice System

Detective Sergeant Julian Bernacchi reported that of the thirty-six murderers that the Chicago Police Black Hand Squad had taken to court from Little Sicily, only four were convicted. The other thirty-two defendants were acquitted, jumped bond, or released for some other reason. Even when an arrest was made and the offenders taken to court, police could not guarantee the safety of the witnesses against them. Threats against their lives were common. The difficulty that the police and courts experienced was made apparent by the murder trial of Joseph Bertucci and Bruno Nardi. Bertucci and Nardi were on trial for the murder of Vito Umbrello, who was found shot to death in an alley near Twenty-third and La Salle streets on January 19, 1909. Police arrested Bertucci and Nardi after hearing gunshots and seeing the defendants running out of the alley where Umbrello's body was found. Police also found Black Hand letters in Umbrello's clothing and copies of the same letters in a trunk belonging to Bertucci. At the trial, Nardi turned state's evidence against Bertucci. While Nardi was on the witness stand, a stranger entered the courtroom and stopped at the rail directly in front of him. The stranger covered his face with a handkerchief, eyed the witness, and then left the courtroom. The acts of the stranger terrified Nardi into silence.His subsequent answers to questions were "I can't say anything; I can't talk; or I'll get into trouble and I'm afraid." Such brazen attempts at intimidation were a new challenge for the American justice system.[79]

The Italian community placed part of the responsibility for Black Hand crime on the shoulders of the Chicago police. Black Hand crimes occurred, they argued, because there was no one to stop them. Italians could not understand why American detectives did not investigate idlers who never worked but always wore the best clothes, had diamond rings on their fingers, had pockets full of money, and were armed with revolvers, razors, and knives. Why couldn't the police investigate where the money came from? *L'Italia* went so far as to charge that the police were as much to blame as the criminals for Black Hand crime—their inability to control Black Hand extortion gave criminals the courage to strike again.[80]

Italians were particularly critical of the police dragnet as a method of controlling Black Hand crime.[81] Although the dragnet often brought in suspiciously armed Sicilians on minor weapons charges and made good newspaper copy, it failed to solve any crimes. Police, however, believed that holding suspects on vagrancy and minor weapons charges was an important law enforcement tool that allowed them to detain and question a variety of suspects. Italians were also critical of the police service in the United States. While European countries had called well-trained men to the police service and raised it to a profession, police in the United States were often political appointees controlled by corrupt political organizations.

Police cooperation with the press was also criticized. Robert Watchorn, writing in *The Outlook*, argued that newspapers aided lawlessness by prematurely publishing news relating to impending action in Black Hand cases. The newspapers were trying to best competing news organizations, but the headlines informed suspects of the progress of an investigation. Newspapers often reported each new suspect or each new step in an investigation in the morning edition in order to scoop their evening rivals. For example, on March 4, 1910, the early edition of the *Chicago Daily News* reported that police recovered an overcoat containing a handkerchief with the initials "PG" near the scene of the alleged Black Hand shooting of police officer John Wren. The afternoon edition of the *Chicago American* reported that a button made in Italy was also recovered near the crime scene. The next day, the *American* reported that the police had found the home of the owner of the button and discovered that his initials were "PG," the same as those found on the handkerchief. The *American* also announced that the police knew the identity of "PG" and were seeking his arrest. Although the public had an interest in crime news, the play-by-play description of this investigation could have certainly facilitated the escape of the suspect. The wanted man had only to read the daily newspapers to determine if he was sought for the crime.[82]

Italian immigrants were also struck by the difference between the American and Italian justice systems. In Chicago, the court released a man on a $100,000 bond after he had signed a written statement confessing to a murder. Such a thing could not have occurred in Italy, where the courts often denied criminals the benefit of bail. In another case, one of the few Death Corner murders to be solved by the Chicago police, the offender was granted a new trial despite the fact that a police officer witnessed the crime. Patrol Sergeant William Byrnes saw Joseph Cutello walk up behind Frank Ciccia and place a revolver to his head and fire. A jury found Cutello guilty of murder and sentenced him to fourteen years imprisonment. One month later, a new trial was granted. Former judge and county commissioner Charles Goodnow represented Cutello, which probably had something to do with the granting of the new trial.[83]

In another case, a Sicilian was charged with killing a fellow countryman in the Near North Side was tried in Chicago for the murder and acquitted.[84] The family of the victim followed the shooter back to Sicily and complained to the police there. The authorities in Italy arrested the offender, tried him for murder, and sentenced him to thirty years in prison. In still another case, a Sicilian who had murdered a man in Chicago escaped arrest in America and went back to Italy, where the Italian police arrested him. The prosecutor in Italy sent for the evidence. Chicago police prepared the necessary affidavits and forwarded them to the Italian authorities. The Italian courts then convicted the offender and sentenced him to prison.

Italian criminal justice varied greatly from that of the United States in a number of ways. First and foremost was that the United States operates under an adversarial system of justice, a battle between two opposing parties. Based on English common law, this system evolved out of the use of trial by combat.[85] Each side is expected to pursue its self-interest to the fullest. The burden of proof is on the prosecutor, who must prove the defendant guilty beyond a reasonable doubt, while the defense attorney is responsible for arguing the defendant's innocence. The judge serves as a neutral arbitrator who stands above the fight ensuring that each side plays by the established rules. Italian courts, and those of most European countries except Great Britain, operate under the inquisitorial or Roman system of justice. Under the inquisitorial system, the judge is the center of the fact-finding process. Both parties provide evidence to the court and the judge or judges, not the attorneys, call and examine witnesses. In essence, the court acts as the investigative body.

Another way that Italian criminal justice varied from that of the United States was that a man convicted of a crime in Italy was placed under *vigilato* or "special surveillance." Special surveillance was a form of parole that required ex-convicts to remain at home for a period of two to four years after their release from prison, to report to local police authorities two or three times a week, and to be in their home before 6 o'clock every evening. If they were picked up with weapons, were intoxicated, or were found in a suspicious place or in the company of suspicious people, they were sent back to prison. Criminals lived in continual dread of the police, who could appear at their bedside at any hour of the night to make sure that they were at home. Violation of special surveillance resulted in imprisonment. It is not surprising that an Italian criminal may have found America attractive. In Italy, in addition to convicted criminals, vagabonds (those with no visible means of support), persons arrested for less serious crimes, and those acquitted of serious crimes were placed under "admonition," a less severe form of surveillance. In the United States, the experienced Italian criminal learned that no law could limit an individual's liberty or force him to remain where he would be harmless. In the United States, there was no possibility of detaining bad men for extended periods.[86]

Parole in the United States differed greatly from the Italian *vigilato*. Italy was the home of the classical school of criminology, which held people entirely accountable for their crimes. The American criminal justice system was moving toward positive thought, which argued that conditions external to the individual caused crime. One of the characteristics of this new view of justice was indeterminate sentencing that allowed offenders to serve only a portion of their penalty behind bars. The idea was that the offender who showed evidence of rehabilitation would be released from prison sooner. Both the White Hand and Italian civic leaders charged that parole boards were subject to political influence and, if enough pressure and money were applied, dangerous offenders could be paroled after serving only a minimal amount of their sentence.[87]

There is substantial evidence to support allegations of corruption in the Illinois parole system. A 1928 report on parole abuses in Illinois, written by such notables as Andrew Bruce of Northwestern University, Dean Albert Harno of the University of Illinois, and Ernest W. Burgess of the University of Chicago, attributed abuses in the parole system to politics.[88] The report found that state representatives and senators often represented prisoners at their parole hearings. Although they were attorneys, inmates did not retain the members of the state legislature because of their legal acumen but because of their political influence. One state representative told the parole board that the robbery offender he represented lived in his legislative district and that the offender's parole was important for his reelection.

Sociologist John Landesco reported in his 1935 study of Eddie Jackson, "the immune pickpocket," that Jackson received an early release from parole because of his usefulness on election day.[89] Jackson, a known thief, had significant political power because of his control of "repeat" voters. Jackson's twenty-five followers could steal as many as 800 votes on election day. His ability to organize groups of repeaters, who he took from precinct to precinct to roll up the vote, made him a valuable party member.

A glaring example of parole corruption was the release of Joseph Novello and John Barone. In May 1915, police sergeants George De Mar and Joseph McGuire arrested Tony Titcola, a known Black Hand gunman, for carrying a concealed firearm. While waiting for a patrol wagon to transport Titcola to the police station, two men approached the detectives and began shooting. A bullet struck Sergeant McGuire in his right hip. Titcola then joined the shooters and the three men fled. Police identified the two gunmen as Joseph Novello and John Barone. Both Novello and Barone were also suspect Black Hand offenders. An anonymous letter received by the police not only identified Novello as McGuire's assailant but also implicated Novello in the murders of William Moore, Fanny Bracciavento, Pietro Castello, and Detective Frank Daly. Correctly anticipating a guilty verdict, Novello jumped bond on the last day of his trial. The court sentenced Novello and Barone to a maximum of fourteen years of imprisonment at the Joliet penitentiary but acquitted Tony Titcola of the charge. Regular court watchers were surprised at the verdict. No one could remember the last time that a jury had come in against two men from the Near North Side.

However, the conviction was not the end of the story. Two weeks later, a disgruntled bondsman tipped off the police that Novello was hiding at a farm in the South Side near Kensington. When detectives arrived at the farm, Novello opened fire on them with poisoned dumdum bullets. Police returned fire, striking Novello in the leg. Following a short hearing, the court sent Novello to the Joliet penitentiary to begin his prison sentence. While Novello and Barone were in prison, a sawed-off shotgun blast killed Titcola as he walked through the darkened streets of Little Sicily in September 1918. East Chicago Avenue police found Titcola sprawled on the pavement when they arrived. He died without making a statement.[90]

The parole board released Novello and Barone after serving only four years of their prison sentence. As soon as they were released from prison, Novello and Barone became involved in another extortion attempt. Brothers John and Michael Gagliardo, owners of a wholesale grocery business on West Randolph Street, were the targets.[91] On the afternoon of February 5, 1919, Peter Montalbano, a cousin of John Gagliardo's wife, came to the brothers and told them that Joe Novello had sent him to collect $1,000 and that they could have a little time to think it over. Two days later, John Gagliardo received a telephone call from Novello, who asked him if he had thought the matter over. Gagliardo replied that he did, and that he was not going to pay the money. As the brothers were closing their store at 6 o'clock that evening, a man fired a revolver at them from across the street, and two other men shot at them with sawed-off shotguns. Both brothers reached the shelter of their doorway unharmed. The assailants fled. At Peoria Street, the two shotgun men mistook a mailman for a police officer and shot him in the left cheek. They shot another man standing nearby in the leg.

John Gagliardo called the police when he arrived home later that night. When the police arrived at the Gagliardo residence, they found Gagliardo in conference with Augustino Morici, another West Side merchant. Gagliardo told the police the story of the attack and that he was willing to press charges. On the morning of February 18, Montalbano, the intermediary, told John Gagliardo that he had heard that Morici was going to die that day. Gagliardo called Morici and relayed what he had heard. Morici immediately left his office. At noontime, Novello entered Morici's business and asked for him. A clerk told Novello that Morici was not in the building. Morici then called the office and Novello requested that he return immediately. Morici did, but with the police. They found Novello hiding in the basement with a loaded revolver. A few days later, Montalbano came to the Gagliardo store, where he was detained at gunpoint for the police.

It later came out that Novello, who was paroled to work at the Rock

Island arsenal, came to Chicago and became involved with Augustino and his brother Antonio Morici, both wholesale grocers in the Near West Side. It is believed that the Moricis were behind the Gagliardo extortion attempt. Based on the testimony of John Gagliardo, Joseph Novello received five years in prison for violating his parole and an additional five years and eight months for the Gagliardo extortion. Stephen A. Malato, now in private practice, assisted the state in prosecuting the case. Six months later, John Gagliardo was murdered as he stood in a grocery store at 900 North Milton. Also killed was Charles Ramondy, a sales clerk in Gagliardo's employ. It is believed that the murders were carried out by the fugitives Montelbano and Barone. The nefarious activities of the Morici brothers proved to be their ultimate undoing. Both were the victims of a 1926 shotgun attack that killed Augustino and left Antonio severely wounded.[92]

Another factor favorable to Black Hand criminals was the lack of a unified criminal justice system in the United States. The White Hand argued that the many separate justice systems allowed Black Hand criminals to move from one American city to another with little chance of the various police agencies sharing information.[93] Policing was very different at the turn of the last century than it is today. There were no radios or computers. Police had difficulty sharing information within their own police departments, let alone with other agencies.

The Italian criminal also knew that there was no possibility of prosecuting a case with nothing more than circumstantial evidence. The experienced Italian criminal was aware that police in America could not keep him in prison while they interviewed his accomplices looking for contradictions in their testimony in order to place responsibility for the crime.[94] In the United States, police could detain a suspect for only a few days, during which time they must provide evidence of his guilt, and the whole burden of proof rested on the prosecution. The defendant was under no obligation at any time to prove his innocence. In the United States, unlike Italy, the defendant had the right to refuse to answer the questions of the magistrate. Even if he did choose to answer, the language barrier, the fact that the answers had to pass through an interpreter, made it difficult for American magistrates to comprehend the testimony of Black Hand defendants.

The White Hand Society also argued that the requirement of proof beyond a reasonable doubt often aided Black Hand offenders because the complexities of Black Hand crime often confused American juries.[95] Take the example of the so-called friend, who acted as a mediator between the victim and Black Hand offenders. This friend often invoked the defense that he was only trying to help the victim, while the whole time he was an integral part of the criminal conspiracy. Additionally, Illinois law required severe penalties for those convicted of Black Hand crimes, which the White Hand believed prevented many juries from entering a guilty finding for fear that the punishment was too harsh. Further, the jury system itself may have been an encouragement to Black Hand criminals. American law requires the unanimous vote of the jury to convict a defendant, and a trial without a guilty verdict resulted in the freedom of the defendant. Violent Black Hand criminals knew that all they had to do to win a case was to intimidate one juror into voting not guilty.

Another problem faced by the American justice system was the sophisticated manner in which some Black Hand gangs worked. Professional Black Hand gangs used a well-thought-out procedure to carry out their crimes. Their method of operation began with the blackmailing letter. The letter in its classic form was short and contained a request for money and an indication of the place where the victim was to deliver the money. The letter also contained a threat that was sometimes veiled by mysterious allusions and sometimes expressed with a brutal lack of reserve. Most of these letters did not leave the area in which they were written. A good number went to a house in the immediate neighborhood of the offender. Others went to the post office to be returned to another floor in the same building from which they were sent. There had even been cases of Black Hand letters delivered to a relative of the writer. Most, but not all, were from the same neighborhood or contiguous community in cities where Italians were numerous.

If a victim decided to conform to the blackmailing demand and deliver the requested money, he often did not find anyone at the designated place of the payoff, but received a second letter a few days later. The second letter typically repeated the request for money and aggravated the threat. After a brief interval, a third and sometimes even a fourth letter was received containing more violent threats expressed in words and symbols such as drawings of pierced hearts, pistols, daggers, skulls and crossbones, and bombs. All of the letters were prepared with some degree of skill, with an intentional system of progression, in order to intimidate the victim to the point that he could not refuse the blackmailers' demands.[96]

The following letters were sent by Gianni Alongi to Carmino Marsalo during the summer of 1910. They provide an excellent example of the method followed by experienced Black Hand gangs:

First Letter

Dear Friend

You are too thick but we swear that we send your head to the air and will do the same as we done to your townsman, Cinena. After five days, but

you will die before. You are mistaken about this—you think this over well and walk on the street. You were in the right way but be careful. Think of your head if you want to live a little more. Confide yourself with somebody that you know and Pig of Madonna we swear that in three or four days you will be in other world. Be careful—we will leave this to your will. The amount of $500, and this is the death you have coming.
        Black Hand
        This is your death that is coming to you.

Second Letter

Dear Friends
Look this is our last. Confide yourself as quick as you can with friends. Otherwise you'll go into the air. Pig of Madonna. If you do not bring the amount you must die of the same death of your townsmen and these are the tools of your death.
        Black Hand

Third Letter

Dear Friend
We want to have $500 and if you do not send it—will be trouble for you, pig of Madonna. If you do not come this week your head will go to the air. If you want to live confide yourself with some friend. God damn you must die the same as your townsman, and these are the tools, of your death.
        Black Hand

Fourth Letter

Friend
Pig of Madonna; you would not understand. This is a bell that rings. We will stop it when you bring the said amount, or in a short time you will pass a bad fate. Confide yourself with some friend and they will fix all.
        Black Hand
        This is the last.[97]

Professional Black Hand criminals almost never went to the appointed place to retrieve the requested money. They knew that the frightened victim probably notified the police or was delivering the ransom money under the watchful eyes of equally dangerous friends and relatives who hoped to catch the blackmailer in the act. Instead the blackmailer was either safe at home or watching the movements of the victim from a distance. The failed trap often gave the blackmailer an opportunity to write a new letter in which he ridiculed the victim for the failure and added that the eyes and ears of the Black Hand were everywhere. This new letter warned the victim to refrain from further contact with the police or anyone else, lest he suffer a worse fate. Sometimes the persistent pressure of the Black Hand letters was supplemented with acts of violence in order to remove any doubts about the efficacy of the threats—a window was broken, a gun fired, or a bomb exploded under a stairway or in the cellar of the building where the victim lived.[98]

Black Hand offenders often instructed their victims to seek a "friend" who could help them solve their extortion problem.[99] This friend appeared at the height of the intimidation when the victim felt that neither his relatives nor the police were powerful enough to disrupt the extortion plot. The friend provided a glimmer of hope that somebody might intervene between the victim and the murderous blackmailers. The friend knew many mysterious people and, being wise to the activities of the underworld, knew that the police and the authorities often closed their eyes to these crimes because Black Hand criminals had powerful political patrons. This new friend usually was acquainted with someone who could intercede on the part of the intended victim and possibly "adjust" the matter. The friend was always happy to act as an intermediary for the victim. In reality, the new friend was part of the blackmailing scheme.

Sometimes the friend offered to deliver the blackmailing money. In the case of Black Hand victim Giovanni Castello, Antonio Schiro wrote the following letter appealing to the blackmailers to accept a lesser amount than demanded.[100]

> My dear children, I answer your dear letter which stated that you wanted this flower. So my dear children I cannot. I can only give you this flower of two hundred because I am not a person like you, gentlemen, believe. You must excuse me if I cannot make you content because I am a laborer and have nothing else to say but salute you friendly and sign. Your friend Giovanni. You can get this letter in the place you know, because I cannot go there. Good bye, good bye and make a good life.

The professional Black Hand extortionist used the progression of threats and letters to soften his victim through psychological intimidation. This process was supplemented through the supposedly benevolent activities of the friend. There was, however, another aspect to the activities of the friend that only became apparent when the conspirators were arrested and brought to trial. In some cases, the friend appeared to become a victim himself as Black Hand criminals forced him deeper into the conspiracy through his actions as an intermediary. Once this occurred, the ability of the state to prosecute the case successfully was in jeopardy. Although it did not take the police long to realize that the so-called friend was part of the criminal conspiracy, it was often difficult to prove the blackmailing case against him. The friend did not always offer himself as a mediator, but was often appealed to by the victim. In fact, he often advised against yielding to Black Hand demands and was reluctant to intervene. He only did so after the victim begged, entreated, and implored, and only gave in seemingly out of consideration for the victim. These facts created doubt in the minds of the jurors who heard Black Hand cases. Who was the criminal when the victim asked the defendant to intervene? For example, Isadore Carlino, accused of extorting $300 from Joseph Macaluso, testified in his own defense that the victim was willing to pay the extortion money and had asked him to be his agent. Carlino initially refused, stating that he feared that Black Hand offenders might beat him, but when Mrs. Macaluso began to cry, he agreed to deliver the money. Chicago police arrested Carlino on his way to deliver the extortion demand.[101]

The psychological intimidation of Black Hand victims was intensified by the concentration of Black Hand offenders in specific neighborhood areas, particularly in Little Sicily. Victims refused to go to the police out of fear that Black Hand criminals would find out about their cooperation with the authorities. "The Black Hand knows everything" was a familiar refrain in the Italian community.[102] The ability of the Black Hand to "know everything" was based on their presence in the insular Italian community. Black Hand offenders were vigilant and always on the lookout for new victims. Once identified, victims were kept under close watch in order to monitor their activities and their efforts to contact authorities. The close proximity of Black Hand offenders to victims was unsettling. As reported in the *Chicago Daily Tribune*, so deep and wide were the incursions of Black Hand criminals that "the Italian shoveling snow in the streets knows not that the man at his elbow may be a Black Hand man" and "the merchant does not know but his clerk is the same."

Fear of the Black Hand was so strong in Little Sicily that all strangers were viewed with suspicion.[103] Sicilian parents were particularly suspicious of outsiders because they feared harm to their children. Parents viewed strangers with a look of inquiry, a look that told of suspicion and the stress of dwelling under the shadow of a terrible fear. Fear also affected the manner in which the people lived. Little Sicily was a poor neighborhood, but poverty was not the only reason for the lack of comfort that was evident everywhere. People refrained from exhibiting signs of wealth for fear that Black Hand criminals would regard them as a target once they displayed any evidence of prosperity. As a result, many Italians who would have been considered well off went about shabbily dressed or lived in small, poorly furnished rooms, ate poor food, and bemoaned their lack of wealth.

Fear of the Black Hand was so powerful that Pietro Rossano committed suicide after receiving an extortion note.[104] Rossano, a poor carpenter with six children, could not understand why he had received a demand for $500. His inability to pay and the dire threats in the letters began to affect his mental condition. On the advice of his brother, Rossano went to Mother Cabrini Hospital, where he became violent. The hospital attendants called the police, but they arrived too late. Rossano had shaken off the attendants and jumped from a second story window, killing himself.

An article appearing in *L'Eco deli Emigrazione*, an Italian emigration newsletter, repeated many of the views of the White Hand Society regarding the causes of Black Hand extortion.[105] The article denied the existence of a Black Hand organization and charged the United States with being too lenient in enforcing its immigration laws. Thus, criminals could enter the country. Although the Black Hand was not organized, the *L'Eco* article argued that Black Hand criminals thrived on the natural conditions that existed wherever Italians came together in large numbers. It argued that the immigrant knew nothing of American laws, nothing of the English language, and lived in the poorest sections of cities where police protection was the least efficient. Confronted by the whirl of American life, the Italian immigrant was unable to protect himself against the criminal element that preyed upon him, criminals that were confident that they were safe from the American police.

The views of the White Hand Society were also supported by a study conducted by Jeremiah Jenks of Cornell University in conjunction with an undisclosed expert on Italian immigration.[106] The Jenks report argued that those who constitute what was commonly called the Black Hand were habitual Italian criminals who had immigrated to America. The report divided Italian criminals who came to the United States into three classes:

1. Italians who came to the United States to avoid special surveillance after having served time in an Italian prison.
2. Italians who had committed crimes in Italy and fled to the United States before their trial began.
3. Italians who authorities in Italy universally regarded as criminals but were never charged with a crime. Such men took refuge in the United States either because they were forced to flee by public opinion or because they feared possible incrimination or revenge by their enemies.

Support for the argument that criminals in Italy were fleeing to the United States was provided in an article written for the *Chicago Daily*

Tribune by George Dorsey during his nearly three-year study of immigration. While visiting Calabria, Dorsey was told that many local criminals had moved to New York and Chicago. Just as America was considered a promised land for the Italian immigrant, so it was also considered a haven of refuge for the criminal. The White Hand argued that many Black Hand offenders were fugitives from Italian justice. These fugitives, having fled to the United States, were encouraged by the conditions that they found here—including a large immigrant population and an inefficient criminal justice system.[107]

The Jenks report, like the White Hand report, also stressed the difference between American and Italian justice systems. Just like the White Hand, Jenks stressed that Italian criminals often left Italy to avoid special surveillance.[108] Another reason offered by the Jenks report for the Italian criminal's attraction to America was the ease with which it was possible to evade punishment. In the United States, surveillance by the police was virtually nonexistent, it was easy to get hold of firearms and explosives, and there was no penalty for giving a false name. In addition, it was easy to hide because of the vast size of the country and density of the population in the larger cities. The variability of laws from state to state and the ease with which bail was granted often made police action long, drawn out, and fruitless. Another factor highlighted by the Jenks report that echoed the findings of the White Hand investigation was the fact that many hardened Italian criminals became associated with political cliques, such as New York's Tammany Hall, for whom they worked and from whom they received political protection in return.

Jenks's belief that the easy availability of bail and the vast size of the United States facilitated Black Hand crime was demonstrated in Chicago in April 1910 when Charles Moraizze, Rozien Romacciotti, William Lorenzoni, and John Morisi were arrested for attempting to extort $2,000 from a prosperous Sicilian merchant.[109] Moraizze was the first to be caught and was immediately recognized by one of the detectives as a member of a trio of extortionists who had escaped prosecution some years earlier. It seems that Moraizze and two of the other men had been arrested for extorting $15,000 from South Side Italians, but had fled when released on bond. Moraizze told the police that after traveling throughout Europe, they returned to the United States and again engaged in blackmailing in many American cities.

Another problem faced by the American justice system in its efforts to combat Black Hand crime was the ineffectiveness of immigration law itself. Frank Marshall White went so far as to charge that responsibility for the Black Hand rested at door of the U.S. Congress. Their failure to pass immigration legislation allowed the "jailbirds" of Italy, who were driven from their native land by rigorous police supervision, to immigrate to the United States. Although the United States precluded persons convicted of crimes of "moral turpitude" from entering the country, determined criminals were able to circumvent immigration regulations. Italian criminals reached the United States with passports obtained through political connections and bribery, with passports issued under false names, or by boarding ships clandestinely as stowaways. If discovered, those who had come to this country illegally could be deported. The problem was that they had to be discovered within three years of arriving in the United States. If they could avoid coming to the attention of the authorities in those three years, it made no difference how they came to the United States. They even could have spent the three years in an American prison. Even if identified, the burden of proof fell upon the government to prove that the offender had not been in the country for three years rather than the offender having to prove that he was.[110]

Additionally, the United States did not require that persons entering the country have a valid passport.[111] In fact, the United States itself did not even issue passports to its own citizens until 1915. An Italian entering the United States had only to answer three questions: Are you an anarchist? Are you an ex-convict? Are you a contract laborer? If the reply to these was no, you could enter the United States. This was unlike Italy where, as early as 1901, a royal decree had been issued forbidding prefects and other authorities from granting passports to persons likely to be rejected from the country of their destination. In addition, no Italian subject was legally allowed to leave from an Italian seaport without a passport.

Some blamed the Italian government for the large number of Italian criminals entering the United States. George Dorsey charged that Italy was not strictly enforcing its emigration laws. Dorsey argued that the Italian government was more than happy to let its criminal element leave the country and become someone else's problem. The Italian community did not share this position. Attorney and author Gino Speranza had challenged this belief one year prior to Dorsey's accusations, arguing that Italy could not have any interest in exporting its criminals because such an action would jeopardize the interests, safety, and influence of the millions of honest immigrants that had settled abroad.[112]

The ready availability of firearms was also thought to contribute to Black Hand crime in Chicago. So extensive was gun-related crime in the city that Ozora Davis, the president of the Chicago Theological Seminary, pointed out that young boys often played the game of "holdup" using toy pistols.[113] Davis believed that these games played an important part in shaping the lives of the children. The Reverend Smith Ford of the Englewood Baptist Church took the argument a step further by adding that an "unchaste attitude" toward human life existed in the city. Street crime, tavern brawls, and disturbances in gambling houses all contributed to the crime rate in Chicago. The police response to these concerns was typical of the times. Sparked by newspaper headlines and the demands of the clergy, police dragnets often spread out across the city to arrest suspects and unsavory characters. One such dragnet resulted in the searching of 2,000 suspects and the arrest of eight of them for carrying concealed weapons.

The absence of effective gun control laws was also viewed as a factor contributing to gun violence. Efforts to pass effective gun control legislation had been fought by local hardware dealers, who were not willing to forsake their profits. A local ordinance requiring all persons wishing to buy firearms to obtain a permit from the superintendent of police was struck down by the Illinois Supreme Court. Even Chicago's mayor was opposed to the legislation, arguing that controlling firearm sales in Chicago would only force purchasers to buy their guns in Evanston, in Indianapolis, or from a mail-order house.[114]

Problems with the American system of justice did not go unrecognized. Meeting at Northwestern University in June 1909, many of America's leading jurists, including Roscoe Pound and Supreme Court Justice Orin Carter, considered a list of legal reforms that included measures for the investigation of those suspected of Black Hand crimes. It is unclear what effect the conference had on Black Hand crime, but it is clear that legal scholars recognized that Black Hand extortion was a challenge to the American legal system. That same month, a bill was introduced in the House of Representatives calling for the life imprisonment of Black Hand offenders who used the U.S. mail to carry out their blackmailing crimes. The bill, introduced by Representative Kennedy of Ohio, also recommended that victims who failed to turn Black Hand letters over to federal authorities be subjected to a $100 fine.[115]

Chicago newspapers also supported strict enforcement against Black Hand crime.[116] An editorial appearing in the *Chicago Daily Tribune* reported that New Orleans had long been the scene of attempts at extortion, blackmail, kidnapping, bomb throwing, incendiarism, and murder, but authorities there had suppressed Black Hand villains through swift punishment. In one case involving the murder of a young boy, two of the assassins were promptly hanged and four others sent to the penitentiary for life. This was followed by the imprisonment of two or three more for thirty years and the hanging of another killer. These speedy executions, the newspaper argued, had not only ended Black Hand crime in New Orleans but caused the exodus of Black Hand criminals to other cities where they might ply their business more safely. The *Tribune* concluded that Chicago and other cities could control the Black Hand crime problem by adopting the same measures.

An editorial appearing in the *Chicago Record-Herald* presented a similar argument.[117] Recognizing the difficulties of combating Black Hand crime, the newspaper argued that strict enforcement would end the problem in Chicago. The newspaper also argued that the problems faced by the police when dealing with Black Hand crimes were multiplied tenfold when the criminals, living together in overcrowded immigrant colonies, enjoyed the protection of police and public ignorance of the ways, customs, language, and traditions of their victims. These problems, however, could be overcome by law enforcement through persistence, skill, courage, and experience. Immigrant criminals were no different from native-born criminals. A few spectacular and impressive police successes in uncovering Black Hand conspiracies could make a difference. Efficiency in dealing with these criminals would help to overcome the timidity of the Italian community and give the victims confidence and determination.

Frank Marshall White summarized the ineffectiveness of the justice system's response to Black Hand extortion in a 1909 article titled, "How the United States Fosters the Black Hand." White wrote, "It is time, however, that Americans should realize that the frequency of Italian names in our criminal news is not so much a proof of unfitness in the immigrants as of the failure of the machinery of American justice to give him the protection to which he is entitled."[118]

Until the time of the White Hand report, Black Hand crime was explained from one viewpoint only, that of the criminality of the Italian immigrant. The White Hand report, however, furnished a different view. The White Hand was convinced that the cause of Black Hand crime was directly related to social conditions in American society. It even argued that Black Hand crime did not exist in other countries hosting large Italian immigrant populations. Black Hand crime flourished only in the United States because social and political conditions were favorable to its existence and provided a fertile arena for experienced criminals to ply their trade.

Attributing Black Hand crime to the Mafia and the Camorra was consistent with the criminology of the time. The idea that crime was related to social structural conditions was a revolutionary idea. Although earlier studies had related environmental forces to the incidence of crime, it was not until the formation of the Chicago School of Sociology, at the dawn of the twentieth century, that researchers sought to understand the relationship between crime and the organization of the urban environment. Using the city as their laboratory, researchers at the University of Chicago studied a myriad of crime-related problems including youth gangs, vice, and organized crime. Although there is no evidence of contact between Chicago School researchers and the White Hand Society, the social structural influences identified by the White Hand as the causes of Black Hand extortion fit perfectly with Chicago School beliefs.

Attributing Black Hand crime to the Mafia and Camorra may have reflected the state of criminology at the time, but it was not consistent with the facts. The leaders of the Italian immigrant community could not have been the only ones to see the connection between Black Hand crime and social structural conditions, yet their views were never accepted. Society focused on culturally based explanations for the alleged criminal tendencies of the southern Italian. Why? The Italian community blamed the American press for the inaccurate definition of Black Hand crime.

6 The Social Construction of Deviance

How did the acts of so-called Black Hand groups, which were in reality small gangs of criminals and individual offenders, many of whom were not even Italian, become defined as the work of the Mafia and Camorra? How did the acts of a small number of Black Hand gangs and a limited number of copycat criminals become defined as the acts of an international criminal organization? Through what mechanisms did apocryphal stories and urban legends become the public understanding of the Black Hand? The Italian community believed that the American press was responsible for the improper definition of Black Hand crime. Gaetano D'Amato took this line of reasoning a step further, arguing that the press actually facilitated the commission of Black Hand crime by making it appear that all the evil done by Italian criminals was the work of a powerful criminal society that the victim was powerless to resist.[1]

Research has shown that the media is the basic source of information on crime, criminals, and the criminal justice system.[2] Research also suggests that the media provides a distorted view of the amount and type of crime in society, with its focus on violent crime. Sensational and rare crimes such as white slavery, satanic and serial murders, and organized crime are particularly popular with media outlets. The focus on sensational and unusual stories suggests that the media plays a vital role in the social construction of beliefs about crime. Additionally, false beliefs and myths about crime abound in the United States and are often tied to immigrant groups.[3] Historically, problems of opiate addiction were blamed on Chinese immigrants and marijuana consumption was linked to Mexican farm laborers. This suggests that "crime scares" can be traced to xenophobia and anti-immigrant prejudice in American society. In summary, crime myths have been found to focus on unpopular, minority, and deviant groups in society.

Crime myths are particularly important in the development of what has been described as the "social reality of crime."[4] This theory argues that crime is a definition of human conduct that is created by authorized agents in a politically organized society. Those who possess the ability to have their interests represented in public policy regulate the formation of criminal definitions. As a result, myths can be used by the powerful segments of society to support their positions. In the case of the Black Hand, the mythical association with the Mafia and the Camorra provided "evidence" that Black Hand offenders were alien conspirators and not products of an ineffective American justice system.

Crime myths also provide answers to questions that social science either cannot answer or has failed to address, particularly when science, empirical evidence, and education fail to provide answers to the public's concerns. Black Hand crimes occurred at a period in history before social organizational explanations of deviance were common. The only suitable explanation for Black Hand crime that existed at the time was the Lombrosian view that crime was the result of the characteristics of the offender.[5]

It has been argued that the news media creates crime myths by fitting isolated and rare incidents into "news themes" through selective interviewing and reporting.[6] News themes are unifying concepts. They present a specific event in terms of some broader idea. In the case of immigrant crime, offenses committed by Italians were often organized under the heading of Mafia activity. News themes allow us to make some sense out of an individual crime by placing it in a larger framework. Telling us that an Italian killed someone provides little information. Telling us that the murder was part of a Mafia or Black Hand conspiracy implies a myriad of other details about the crime that may or may not be true. Themes also place crime in a rational context. We don't have to wonder why a person was shot if we can attribute the crime to the Black Hand. News themes can also define crime waves. Repeatedly attributing crime to the Black Hand, whether true or not, led to the construction of the Black Hand as a social problem. Crime myths typify reality to make comprehensible what is inherently complicated and obscure.

Violent crime is particularly susceptible to inaccurate claims making.[7] The meaning that we attach to a violent act is often grounded in a social and cultural context, so that our understanding is a reflection of our own experience. Take the case of vendetta crime. Many alleged Black Hand crimes were in fact acts of vengeance that were common in Sicily and the south of Italy but uncommon in the United States. Unable to find a sufficient explanation for these crimes in American culture, claims makers—those with the power to form public opinion—attributed such acts of violence to the Mafia and Black Hand.

Crime myths also cause social problems other than the crimes themselves. In the case of the Black Hand, it could be argued that the labeling of Black Hand crime as solely the work of Italian criminals led to discrimination against Italian Americans. Additionally, labeling organized crime activity as the work of an alien Italian conspiracy led to our nation's inability to recognize that the genesis of organized crime lay within machine politics and corruption in municipal government. The labeling of organized criminality as the work of the Mafia and Black Hand diverted government attention away from the social and structural forces that allowed organized crime to flourish and placed the blame on culture and the individual pathologies of immigrant minorities.

The most powerful Black Hand gangs in Chicago were those in Little Sicily. These gangs apparently had some degree of political protection. In spite of the efforts of the White Hand Society, little was made of the fact that official corruption contributed to their success. Official protection of Black Hand criminals never became a theme in the American press. Newspaper attention was given to the relatively powerless Italian community as the source of Black Hand crime. The press rarely upset the status quo by attacking the police or local government. This lack of attention to official corruption may have been due to the fact that journalists and news media professionals interpret news and complex issues in a way that is consistent with the dominant culture and with the interests of powerful groups.[8] Thus, the media plays an important role in enforcing hegemony (dominant beliefs) in society.

There is ample evidence to support the position that the societal definition of Black Hand crime was the work of the Chicago press. In his book *Come into My Parlor*, Charles Washburn reported that Black Hand murders were invented by a Chicago reporter in order to advance his own career.[9] Washburn related that Charlie Johnson, a police reporter for the *Chicago Examiner* (later renamed the *Herald and Examiner* and still later the *Herald-American*), used the Black Hand label to give "page-one punch" to ordinary Sicilian and Italian killings such as an Italian father slaying his daughter's lover because he refused to marry the girl. Johnson reportedly had discovered that "wop" murders were too frequent and used the Black Hand angle to gain the attention of his rewrite men and editors. As a result, every routine Italian or Sicilian shooting soon turned into a Black Hand crime. Washburn obtained this information in a 1936 interview with Minna and Ada Everleigh, proprietors of the famous Everleigh brothel that operated in Chicago from 1900 to 1911. Charlie Johnson was a regular customer of the Everleigh sisters, who obtained the information about the Black Hand from Johnson firsthand.

Washburn's story is supported by Murray's history of the Hearst newspapers in Chicago. The *Chicago Examiner*, where Charlie Johnson worked, was owned by William Randolph Hearst and famous for sensationally reporting an editor's interpretation of the news rather than the objective facts. Murray reports that rewrite men and headline writers at the newspaper were instructed to seize on the most fantastic aspect of any story and compress it into a "capsule jolt" in order to obtain the utmost shock value and make the stories unique.[10]

There is even a report that the term *Black Hand* was entirely made up by a Chicago newspaper reporter in order to create an attention-grabbing story. Noted feature writer Jack Lait, who became famous for his book *Chicago Confidential*, wrote a copyrighted article in 1918 in which he claimed that a fellow reporter was responsible for the Black Hand name.[11] Lait explained that it was common for newspaper reporters to embellish articles in order to get their editor's attention and that it was a common practice to use Italian words for headline purposes. "You call a vendetta a grudge and it doesn't sound like much, but you call a grudge a vendetta and it gets on page 1 where crimes of violence among foreigners with unpronounceable names seldom carry. Have a peddler stabbed with a knife and it's worth a paragraph; call the weapon a stiletto and it takes on the dignity of a spicy episode. . . . A robbery in that section [Little Italy] was done by *banditti*, not plain holdup men; a street fight was between Sicilians, not Italians—a Sicilian lends himself somehow so much better to the narrative than does a Venetian, for instance. . . . When the term Little Italy grew stale, they called it Little Hell and one crossing where two men had died in five years we denominated Death Corner." Lait wrote that reporters did not regard this activity as unethical but simply as a mechanism for lengthening a one-inch story to three.

Regarding the Black Hand, Lait explained that a fellow reporter who was reluctant to embellish his stories as other reporters commonly did needed to produce something out of the ordinary in order to keep his job.[12] So he sent a letter to an Italian banker demanding money. He knew that the incident would not get more than casual attention unless he signed it with a terrifying and high-sounding name, so he thought up the Black

Hand. He then went on to write an article about the blackmailing incident, having never once talked to the alleged victim. When confronted by other newspaper men, the banker admitted receiving the letter, but he denied having talked to anyone about it. Questioned by his fellow reporters, the author of the article admitted to the scheme, adding that he had sent a second letter to the banker advising him that the whole incident was a hoax. When asked why he created such a hoax, the reporter explained that it had occurred to him that "one need not fake the news—one can make the news." The innovative reporter, who Lait referred to as the "Walrus" because of his long moustache, died soon after the incident. He was honored by his fellow reporters with a floral piece in the shape of a black hand. And that, according to Lait, is how the Black Hand was born, as succeeding generations of professional extortionists adopted the blackmailing letter as their method of operation.

Chicago Daily Tribune columnist Henry Hyde also supports the argument that the Black Hand was a media construction. In fact, he wrote a series of three articles in 1914 denouncing the Black Hand as a "bit of newspaper fiction."[13] Hyde argued that the seemingly endless series of deaths in Chicago's Sicilian colony were the result of vendettas, and that there had never truly been a Black Hand murder in Chicago. There were attempts to extort money, and bombs had been placed; but as far as police records showed, Black Hand criminals had never actually carried out their threats. He claimed many Black Hand letters were written by the supposed victim in order to obtain a police permit to carry a firearm. Hyde concluded that the Black Hand was a creation of "sensation mongers" and that the terror aroused by Black Hand stories was used by blackmailers of many races.

Hyde's position is supported by the data collected here. Of the 280 alleged Black Hand incidents identified in this analysis, only forty-nine involve murder. Of these, only three had concrete evidence that the murder victim was killed because of Black Hand extortion. Four additional cases provided some evidence; only seven incidents had any evidence that the victims were murdered for not complying with Black Hand extortion demands—less than one percent of the cases reviewed!

The Black Hand crime wave also began at the height of "yellow journalism" in the United States. The 1890s were marked by the rise of crusading newspapers, often called "yellow" because they emphasized crime, sex, and sports with a sensational appeal to the emotions. In his book *Yellow Journalism and the Gilded Age*, Sidney Kobre argues that enterprising publishers recognized that cities bred crime and that children growing up in slum districts often became involved in delinquency, which could escalate from petty thievery to robbery to murder. Gangs grew and crimes mushroomed. Publishers recognized that this type of news built circulation, and editors became known for their exploitation of crime.[14]

Writing in 1904, Italian commentator Gino Speranza argued that the American press was unfriendly towards the Italian immigrant. Why is it, Speranza asked a prominent journalist, that the press prints news about Italians that it would not print about other nationalities? The journalist is said to have replied that if we publish derogatory news about the Irish or Germans, we would be buried with letters of protest. The Italians do not seem to object, probably because they have learned the uselessness of objecting unless they can back up their objections by a solid Italian vote—something the Italians did not have. This fact was recognized by the Italian community as early as 1889, when *L'Italia* reported that of the 20,000 Italians in Chicago, only 700 had become citizens and earned the right to vote.[15]

As can be seen, social problems are not always a reflection of objective facts about a social condition and can be depicted in more than one way. For example, rape can be depicted as a sex crime or a crime of violence. Sociologists argue that the characteristics of a social problem emerge through a process of claims making and that claims typically originate with those who have a vested interest in bringing attention to the problem, such as a reform group. Claims about the characteristics of a social problem can also originate with the press, who can act as primary claims makers, discovering and constructing social problems on their own. For instance, police found the "fearfully mutilated" body of Joseph Salvo in a wine shop on South Clark Street. The body had been literally chopped to pieces. The skull and chest had been crushed and the flesh had been hacked away from the bones in many places. Headlines read, "Black Hand Is Suspected." The article read "Private Feud Hinted" and "While there is evidence that a blackmailing society may have played a part in this murder [none was presented], the police believe a private feud may have been responsible for the midnight attack."[16]

The manner in which many crimes were incorrectly attributed to the Black Hand was recognized in 1911 by C. R. Knight, who wrote to the *Chicago Record-Herald* protesting that crimes ranging from street brawls to kidnapping and murder were often incorrectly attributed to the Black Hand.[17] He complained that the indiscriminate use of the term *Black Hand* in connection with crime reporting had an unwholesome effect on the popular mind. To support his argument, Knight cited the case of Joseph Vacek, who murdered his own father and then attributed the case to the Black Hand in an effort to cover up his part in the crime. He added that to name a thing was to fix it concretely in the mind. As a result, attributing Black Hand crime to an organized group could give the Black Hand a greater importance in the public mind than would arise if the crimes were treated as sporadic and independent occurrences. In essence, Knight was arguing that the manner in which newspapers reported crime was contributing to the social construction of the Black Hand. Knight closed his letter by challenging the press to reform the manner in which Black Hand activity was reported.

The *Record-Herald* responded to Knight's letter with a complete lack of sympathy for his position, arguing, "The best newspapers do not invent or distort details of crime; they do not seek to stimulate it, but to record and explain it. . . . They hold the mirror up to Nature and record what they see, not what they might see if the world were more moral." The *Record-Herald* concluded, "Newspapers did not invent the 'Black Hand.'"[18]

Following the social constructionist tradition, I argue that a series of newspaper articles that began in the early 1890s played a significant role in defining Black Hand crime as the work of a sinister foreign group. These articles attributed Italian criminality to the Mafia and the Camorra and include the newspaper coverage of the murder of David Hennessy, the New Orleans chief of police; the murder of New York police lieutenant Joseph Petrosino; and a series of articles on immigration written by George Dorsey, Ph.D., for the *Chicago Daily Tribune*. Author Richard Gambino writes that two of these incidents, the murder of David Hennessey and the murder of Joseph Petrosino, were responsible for the term Mafia becoming associated with Italian American crime. Michael Woodiwiss takes this argument a step further, writing that the assassinations of Hennesy and Petrosino magnified the relatively insignificant criminal activity of the Italian immigrant out of all proportion and forever established the mythology of the Mafia in American society.[19]

The Murder of David Hennessey

One incident more than any other event contributed to the beliefs about the Mafia in the United States. The murder of the chief of police in New Orleans resulted in a yearlong series of articles that presented the idea and power of the Mafia to virtually every newspaper-reading member of the American public. In Chicago, no less than forty-eight articles appeared in local newspapers covering the events in New Orleans. On October 15, 1890, Chief David C. Hennessy was murdered as he was returning home, allegedly by Mafia criminals.[20] He was attacked by three men who fired four shots into his stomach. Hennessy died the next morning without having identified any of his assailants. Four men, all Italian, were immediately arrested for the crime. The citizens of New Orleans were so outraged by the death of Hennessy that they established a committee of fifty prominent citizens to investigate the crime. Within three days of the killing, a total of seventeen men were arrested. Eleven were charged with the murder and eight with being accessories before and after the fact.

The authorities believed that Hennessey was killed because he had obtained evidence that a witness in a recent murder case had perjured himself. The case involved two alleged Mafia groups, the Matrangas and the Provenzanos. The Matrangas had accused the Provenzanos of killing several members of their gang. An interview with the Provenzanos, however, alleged that the Matrangas killed Chief Hennessy because he had received information from Italy that would expose their Mafia connections. The informant told the police that there were about twenty leaders of the Mafia in New Orleans and about 300 "greenhorns" who had to do the leaders' bidding. The greenhorns were allegedly paid from $10 to $100 for each murder directed by the committee. If he refused, the greenhorn was himself murdered in order to prevent him from informing the police. Some questioned the claims of New Orleans officials that the killing of Chief Hennessy was the work of the Mafia. In Chicago, for example, the Italian press condemned the wholesale arrest of Italians during the Hennessey investigation and the accusation that the murder was the work of a sinister foreign group.[21]

On October 25, the *Tribune* reported that a dead Italian was found in a sack floating in a river near Konnerville, Louisiana.[22] Police speculated that the dead man was either the victim of a vendetta or a witness in the murder of Chief Hennessey. The same article noted that a great effort toward secrecy was being maintained in the Hennessy investigation and that the Committee of Fifty, which had been appointed to investigate the crime, often acted without public approval. The article also indicated that suspicion against Italians was growing because of the Hennessy murder. The steamship Elysia with 1,038 Italian immigrants had arrived at the New Orleans quarantine station, and a revenue cutter, with federal, state, and local authorities aboard, went down to meet the vessel to ensure that not one of the Italian immigrants was entering the country improperly.

Three days later, Chicago newspapers reprinted a statement made by the Committee of Fifty at an open-air meeting held in New Orleans.[23] Although they never specifically used the word *Mafia*, committee members stated that they were charged with investigating "the existence of murder societies" in the city and that they had been promised the full cooperation of the "Italian government and the leading Italian citizens and societies." The committee asked for $30,000 to fund the investigation of the "murder societies and discover whether they exist or not"; if found to exist, the report continued, "we must destroy them at any hazard."

The New Orleans district attorney eventually brought the eleven Hennessey defendants to trial. The roll of witnesses for the state numbered ninety-one. The roll of witnesses for the defense was 228. The state's case rested solely on circumstantial evidence. Although authorities had admittedly failed to uncover evidence of the existence of the Mafia, one of the alleged conspirators, a Sicilian named Polizzi, who was "acting like a madman for fear of the Mafia," admitted to the existence of the organization. The trial began on February 16, 1891, and lasted twenty-five days. It took the jury less than two days to reach a verdict of not guilty for six of the defendants. The fate of three others was left undecided, and the remaining two were severed from the trial. A cry went up immediately that jury tampering had occurred. A private detective named Dominick O'Malley, whose "special forte" was subornation and perjury, had allegedly bribed one or more of the jurors. Additionally, he and Hennessy were deadly enemies, and it was generally believed that he was an agent of the "Sicilians" whenever they appeared in court.[24]

As a result of the alleged jury tampering, a group of 100 leading New Orleans citizens led by Colonel W. S. Parkerson, editor of the *New Delta* newspaper, called for a mass meeting on March 14 to take steps "to remedy the failure of justice in the Hennessy case."[25] The announcement appeared in every New Orleans newspaper with the notice, "Come prepared for action." The fact that violence was expected was made evident by the title of an article appearing in the *Chicago Daily Tribune* the day before the meeting that read, "May Lynch the Mafia Thugs." The *New Delta* also foreshadowed what was to occur. In a written editorial, Parkerson wrote that the citizens of New Orleans must decide whether they would be governed by their own laws or the laws of the Sicilian Mafia: "A perjured jury brought the law to naught, and today the officers who conducted the prosecution, the citizens who supported it, and the witnesses who testified at it are living at the mercy of the men who took the life of your officer. . . . Will you hold your life at the mercy of these law-proof murders, or will you protect it by the only means this foresworn jury have left you?"

The next morning, Parkerson addressed the large crowd gathered at

Clay Square, stating, "When courts fail, the people must act." He asked what protection was left for the people when their chief of police was murdered by the Mafia. He then challenged the crowd to follow him to see that the murder of Chief Hennessy was vindicated. Parkerson's speech was followed by those of other prominent men including attorneys Walter Denegre and John Wickliff, who both advocated that the crowd take justice into their own hands and avenge Hennessy's death. After warning that Dominick O'Malley should leave town or be killed, the crowd, now numbering 3,000, began to march on the parish jail where the suspects were being held. The Italians had not yet been released in spite of the not guilty verdict because the prosecutor's office was considering additional charges against them. In what newspapers described as the "New Orleans Horror," all eleven men were brutally murdered. Nine were shot to death in the prison and two were dragged out of their cells and hanged. Five were gunned down together in one cell. The vigilantes shot most of the men "through the brain" which "made a horrible sight as they lay weltering in blood and brains." In one of the most astonishing descriptions to appear in any newspaper article, the press reported, "The work of blood was accomplished without unnecessary disorder, without rioting, without pillaging, and without the infliction of suffering upon any innocent man, save one, and he was only slightly hurt. It was not an unruly midnight mob. It was simply a sullen, determined body of citizens who took into their own hands what justice had ominously failed to do." The article named the eleven victims of the "public indignation."[26]

The brutal actions of the mob were widely supported in New Orleans. The powerful Cotton Exchange adopted a resolution supporting the murders, stating, "That while we deplore at all times the resort to violence we consider the action taken by the citizens this morning to be proper and justifiable." The Stock Exchange, the Board of Trade, the Lumbermen's Exchange, and the Sugar Exchange also passed resolutions endorsing the mob action. The *New Orleans Times* wrote that the "thrilling events" of March 14 allowed the citizens of New Orleans "in complete and admirable self-control" to do for the "law and for the administration of justice what law and the administration of justice had confessedly been unable to do for themselves." The *Picayune* wrote that popular vengeance came only after every resource of government had been exhausted and that there was no other means but for the people to take the matter into their own hands. Brushing aside local officials, the public "took into their own hands the sword of justice," and did not lay it aside until they had executed vengeance upon the criminals whom corruption had set free. The *New Orleans Delta* reported, "The Mafia had triumphed over the laws of the State. The people rose in their might and put down the Mafia. What has been done meets the approval of all law-abiding citizens. The verdict of the country cannot be otherwise." The *New Orleans States* carried an editorial supporting the killings, writing, "Yesterday the cancer, which for years had been gnawing at our social system until good men's hearts had near despaired—the hideous Mafia—was rooted-out by the people's strong arm and with the people's instruments." Apparently, the *Italo Americano*, the official organ of the New Orleans Italian colony, was the only newspaper to condemn the event, calling for the resignation of the government officials who had permitted the massacre.[27]

Even the *London Times* supported the actions of the New Orleans mob.[28] In an editorial, the *Times* wrote that the people of New Orleans had no choice but to resort to violence. What good was trial by jury, the newspaper argued, if every juryman knew he was in danger if he convicted a Mafia member? All laws rest ultimately upon force. Where the courts are dominated by criminals, nothing remains but to revert to force to affect justice. In regard to the guilt or innocence of the slain Sicilians, the *Times* added that it did not matter whether or not they were the actual murderers of Chief Hennessey. The fact that they were all members of the Mafia made them complicit in the Hennessy killing.

A study of newspaper editorials addressing the incident that appeared in the *Louisiana Historical Quarterly* identified four themes that had emerged justifying the murder of the eleven men.[29] First, the revulsion against lynching that had developed in the South because of its use against Negroes was silent in view of the alleged Mafia connections of the victims. Second, those that had been put to death were considered guilty of the crime for which they had been tried. The failure of the jury to convict them was caused by a dread of the vengeance of the Mafia. Third, the outbreak was a warning to all evildoers. It contained a lesson for the unscrupulous court, attorney, jury-briber, and corrupt juryman. Finally, life and property were safer in New Orleans after the outbreak than they previously had been or would have been if the acquitted criminals had been released.

The jurors in the Hennessy case were also the subject of public indignation. Walter Livandais, a clerk with the Southern Pacific Railroad, was discharged from his job because his fellow clerks refused to work with him. Jacob Seligman, the foreman of the jury, was a partner with his brother in a jewelry business. The brother dissolved the business and Seligman left town. Dominick O'Malley, who had supposedly "fixed" the jury, also fled New Orleans. One week later he was found in Memphis, where he told reporters that he had nothing to do with the bribing of the jurors and that he intended to return to New Orleans and tell all he knew about the Mafia.[30]

One of the chief causes of the indignation in connection with the Mafia trial was the belief that someone had bribed the jury to secure the release of the accused murderers. It was alleged that $75,000 to $100,000 had been contributed by Italians all over the country to be used as a corruption fund, including thousands of dollars from Chicago Italians. Italian laborers in New Orleans were reportedly taxed $2.00 each as a contribution to the fund. In fact, the New Orleans *Italo Americano* had appealed to Italians throughout the country to aid in the defense of the nineteen prisoners. The New York Italian newspaper *Il Progresso Italo Americano* also joined in the appeal. In spite of these efforts, it is not clear that any money was ever collected. Italians in Boston and St. Louis were reticent and apparently efforts to collect money in Pittsburg and Philadelphia were unsuccessful.[31]

In Chicago, the editor of Chicago's *L'Italia* newspaper, Oscar Durante, refused to support the effort for fear that the American press would label it a corruption fund and imperil the prisoner's chances of acquittal. Durante also strongly denounced the American belief in the Mafia, stating, "The statement that there is a secret society, the Mafia, organized to commit murder, among my countrymen is a lie. I believe I represent the feeling of the majority of my countrymen in Chicago and the nation when I denounce the published statements about the Mafia as false throughout." Although Chicago's Italian community refused to contribute to the New Orleans defense fund, a storm of indignation rose among the leading members of the colony.[32] A banquet to honor the forty-seventh birthday of the Italian king was turned, instead, into a strategy session in which it was decided that a letter would be sent to the Italian minister of foreign affairs condemning the New Orleans massacre. Camillo Volini, who would later lead the White Hand Society, delivered a forceful speech demanding a full investigation of the affair. A mass protest was also called for the following Sunday, which all Italians in Chicago were invited to attend.

Durante was not alone in his condemnation of the American press. Italian American leaders throughout the country denounced the New Orleans murders and the so-called corruption fund. In Chicago, a group of prominent Italians labeled the press coverage of the New Orleans events "unprovoked abuse" against a hardworking and unoffending class of citizens. One New York Italian journal, however, did not help the Italian cause. *Le d'Italia* issued an extra edition on March 14, 1891, telling the story of the assassinations in New Orleans followed by an editorial calling for all brave Italians to raise a vendetta against those responsible for the New Orleans massacre.

An insightful editorial in the *Chicago Daily Tribune* presented the New Orleans massacre in a different light. The *Tribune* reported that the murder of Chief Hennessy, the rumors of Mafia intrigue, and the allegations of jury tampering went a long way to fuel the fires of indignation among the people of New Orleans. But there was more to the story, argued the *Tribune*. In back of it all was a "race hatred and class prejudice even more bitter than that which the people feel towards the Negroes." Considering the general spirit of lawlessness that prevails in the South, the *Tribune* concluded, "it is not remarkable that this horrible tragedy was perpetrated." This theme was repeated in several other newspapers. The *Philadelphia Press* stated, "Murders have been common in New Orleans for years past and punishment only too infrequent. So long as the victims were innocent colored men and women the community looked on unconcerned, but these violences were sure to breed a reckless spirit and a disregard for the sanctity of human life which was one day certain to result in just such a tragedy as that which occurred yesterday."

The *Baltimore American* editorialized that the New Orleans tragedy was the result of "lawlessness in a city where the law is not strictly or honestly administered. A place that licenses lotteries and gambling hells and other criminal institutions is not in good health. The public sentiment is depraved and the mob spirit comes forth as a reaction from the reign of disorder."[33]

In spite of these challenges to southern culture, the overwhelming press coverage contributed more to the view that the words Italian and Mafia were synonymous. The American people believed that a police official had been killed, that a jury had been corrupted, and that the Mafia had entrenched itself in American society.[34] The link between the New Orleans massacre and the American understanding of the Mafia and Italian crime cannot be underestimated. The biased reporting of the events in New Orleans forever established a link between Italians and the Mafia in American society. For example, the *New York Times* described Sicilians as "the descendants of bandits and assassins, who have transported to this country the lawless passions, the cut-throat practices, and the oath-bound societies of their native country." In Toledo, the *Blade* wrote that the New Orleans events should be "the cause of a movement to stop the immigration of undesirable classes of foreigners" and that "such men as the Sicilian brigands in New Orleans can never make good American citizens. They should never have been allowed to come." The

Minneapolis Tribune reported that "the Camorra, the Mafia, and bands of like character . . . fled to America and brought their infamous system of blackmail and assassination with them." The *Nashville American* wrote, "The Mafia had instituted a reign of terror in New Orleans . . . and had defeated the punishment of the courts of justice through bribery and corruption . . . giving to organized crime an assurance of impunity." The *Kansas City Times* wrote, "It is the Sicilian vendettas, conspiracies, and disregard of law which are disliked." The *Kansas City Star* reported that the rapid improvement of social conditions in Italy has been due as much to the emigration of her "mendicants and criminals" to the United States as to any other cause.[35]

The events in New Orleans continued to dominate the news for months. In Chicago, a *Tribune* editorial commenting on "The Italian Question" stated that instant measures should be taken to protect the peaceful Italians of New Orleans, but it must be remembered that only 15 percent of the Italian population is from the north of Italy.[36] The rest come from the south and the two Sicilies (Naples and Sicily) where a "more passionate people" reside. Those from the north were described as peaceful tradesmen and shopkeepers, while those from the south were described as members of the peasant class. It was from this peasant class that the people of New Orleans came. Quoting an Italian periodical, the *Tribune* attributed part of the reason for the New Orleans trouble to the fact that America's coastal cities were "infested with the ex-galley slaves of Europe," referring to southern Italian and Sicilian immigrants.

In a "special cable to the *Tribune*" from London, John Brenon, who had made a study of secret societies in Italy, wrote to the newspaper that he supported the New Orleans lynchings.[37] In lynching the Mafia, Brenon argued, the New Orleans people took the only course open to them if they wished to rid the city of the murderous gang. He then went on to describe how Italy treated them, "shooting them down in the streets of Sicily like mad-dogs—dozens of them at a time." Brenon related that the Mafia had flourished under Bourbon rule but was forced from Italy when Garibaldi liberated Palermo in 1860. The gangs then were exiled from Italy and took refuge in the United States. Brenon explained that the Mafia differed from the Camorra in that the Mafia was always in league with brigands. They existed to defy the law and to despise the judiciary. The Mafia controlled elections and robbed indiscriminately for purposes of plunder and revenge, and it had a code of honor called *Omerta* by which all who were members of the Mafia bound themselves and swore never to give evidence in a court of law or seek legal redress for any injury.

The fact that four of the New Orleans murder victims were Italian citizens made the killings an international scandal. There was even talk that Italy would boycott the upcoming Columbian Exposition in Chicago if the Italian government did not receive reparations for the murder of its citizens. Some argued that the federal government was powerless to intervene in the affairs of the individual states and that the national government was in no way responsible for the actions of the city of New Orleans or the state of Louisiana. The Italian government found this position to be absurd, declaring that the United States was treaty bound to afford protection to Italian subjects residing on American soil. The problem for the American government was that it had never passed legislation granting the authority to enforce the treaty provisions and prosecute their infraction. Further, there was little support for the Italian claims in the United States. One Chicago newspaper wrote that rather than pay reparations, we should hold up the victims of the New Orleans massacre as a warning to others and as an object lesson testifying to the dangers of adopting murder as a profession in this country. With a condescending tone, that paper concluded, "There has been a little too much of this organ-grinder and monkey business for American patience" and if the American people had their way, "they would send back all organ-grinders of this kind to their native land, where they can kill to their hearts' content."[38]

Although much of the country condoned the New Orleans massacre, enough pressure was brought upon officials in New Orleans that a grand jury investigation was begun of the affair. From its inception, the grand jury was more concerned with placing blame for the alleged jury tampering than with the murders of the purported Mafia conspirators. News accounts reported that it would be difficult to obtain indictment. The prison keepers and the police stated that they did not recognize anyone in the crowd of rioters, and the citizens who called the meeting were not present at the time of the murders. As a result of its deliberations, the grand jury indicted Dominick O'Malley for his alleged attempt to bribe the jurors. O'Malley, who had returned to New Orleans, responded that he was innocent and so were the men murdered at the jail. The only one lying, according to O'Malley, was Manuel Politz (aka Polizzi)—the one accused assassin who had confessed any knowledge of the Hennessey murder. Politz had told authorities that he did not take part in the murder, but he had heard about it from one of the conspirators. Politz related that he was a member of a "society" organized by Charles Matranga and that Matranga had planned the murder of Chief Hennessey. Ten men were reportedly chosen by lot to carry out the crime. Each was paid $200. The actual murderers, according to Politz, were Antonio Scaffedi, Antonio Marchesi, Antonio Bagnetto, and Pietro Monastero.[39]

Despite the fact that the prosecutor reported that there were so many contradictions in Politz's testimony that it was of limited value, as well as the fact that there was some question about his sanity, the court accepted his revelations as proof that there was a Mafia conspiracy to kill David Hennessey. The "proof" of the existence of the Mafia in New Orleans, Politz's testimony, contributed to the belief that the Mafia had become a menacing force in the United States. The belief was reflected in a *Chicago Daily Tribune* editorial stating that repression of the Mafia in Italy had led a considerable number of these scoundrels to make their way to the United States. As a result, the U.S. government estimated that by the close of 1885, 54,974 Italian convicts and felons had come to this country. America's recourse, the *Tribune* added, was to "collect the Mafias and Mala Vitas and the whole unsavory crowd of Italian criminals, banditti, and cutthroats, place them on board steam vessels, and send them to Naples and Palermo."[40]

In spite of strong public support for the New Orleans vigilantes, Italian communities throughout the country continued to call for reparations and an investigation. In Chicago, *L'Italia* called for the formation of a national committee of representatives, from all Italian groups across the nation, to present their concerns to the federal government. Seven prominent members of the Italian community in Chicago made up the committee, including Stephan Malato and Camillo Volini. However, actions in communities throughout the country showed the extent to which Mafia stereotyping and prejudice against Italians had spread. In Troy, New York, when 150 Italians gathered to protest the lynchings in New Orleans, a spontaneous crowd gathered and, hearing the object of the meeting, began to stone the Italians, describing the assembly as a Mafia meeting. A meeting of Methodist ministers called to pass a resolution condemning the lynching resulted in a debate over the appropriateness of the murders. Even the clergymen could not agree on the morality of the murders of the eleven Sicilians.[41]

A harbinger of future Mafia stereotyping appeared in an April 1891 *Chicago Daily Tribune* article describing the corrupt practices of the Cregier administration in Chicago.[42] Mayor Cregier's followers had set up a campaign fund, and every city employee was required to contribute a portion of their salaries, including the members of the police force. Nobody could deal faro or stud poker or twirl a roulette wheel without submitting to an assessment from city hall. As a result, the gamblers facetiously call the Cregier administration the "City-Hall Mafia."

There was so much interest in the New Orleans murders that the *Tribune* sent a correspondent to Italy to obtain the Italian government's position on the incident.[43] Reporting from Sicily, the *Tribune* showed some insight: although the Mafia is generally not what it is supposed to be, it did exist, and it was easy to detect the spirit of such secret societies, "common to the people of all mountainous countries," in Sicily. This spirit, according to the *Tribune*, took many forms. Sometimes a gang of rowdies was employed by a bidder at an auction to keep other bidders away. Sometimes it was a voluntary refusal on the part of an entire village to give information to the police. Sometimes it was an improvised arrangement between cabdriver, hotel porter, and storekeeper to fleece the tourist. Sometimes it was political influence used to control public contracts. The old form of the Mafia, however, with its brigandage and slaughter had been rooted out, and no doubt most of its leaders had fled to America. Even so, concluded the *Tribune*, there was no proof that any of the men lynched in New Orleans were *mafiosi* in Sicily, and it was only natural for Sicilians to band together in small groups in the United States.

Suspicion of Italians was also fueled by the so-called *Mala Vita* (evil life) trials that were taking place in Italy at the time. The *Mala Vita* was described as an association of criminals similar to the Camorra of Naples and the Mafia of Sicily. In an article titled "The Mala Vita Dagos at Home," the *Chicago Daily Tribune* reported that the Italian courts had sentenced 165 people to terms of imprisonment varying from eight to fifteen years for being members of the society. The article then stated that Americans did not understand why the government with the largest batch of convictions against such people would demand reparations from the country that had "removed" similar criminals from the world. Instead of complaining, the *Tribune* argued, the Italian government should give a vote of confidence to the citizens of New Orleans. Two weeks later, newspapers reported that 179 members of another *Mala Vita* group had been brought to trial in the province of Bari. Centered in the town of Apulia, the group's objectives were theft, robbery, and other crimes. In yet another case, more than 200 persons were on trial in Trani for being members of the *Mala Vita* of Anaren. According to the testimony, the members met in the catacombs of Santa Margherita, where mysterious rites were performed. In that investigation, the constitution of the society, consisting of twenty articles with oaths and penalties governing the conduct of the members, was discovered and laid before the courts.[44]

The report of the New Orleans grand jury investigation into the events surrounding the Hennessey murder trial was made public on May 6, 1891.[45] Although the jurors found that "no visible act was committed," they indicted six men for attempting to bribe members of the Hennessey jury. Dominick O'Malley, the private detective thought to have masterminded the bribery scheme, was not among them. The state's case rested on the fact that O'Malley had received the names of the potential jurors and that men in his employ let it be known that money could be made by being a jury member in the Hennessey case. It seems that O'Malley and others had routinely been involved in influencing juries and jury pools. Regarding the murders of the eleven Sicilian prisoners, the New Orleans grand jury failed to identify anyone responsible for the killings, stating, "The magnitude of the affair makes it a difficult task to fix the guilt upon any number of the participants—in fact, the act seemed to involve the entire people of the Parish and City of New Orleans, so profuse was their sympathy and extended connection with the affair."

The grand jury report was a disappointment. The conservative *New Orleans Picayune* reported that it ignored the corruption of juries, declared the evil of immigration laws that enabled nations to deport their criminal and pauper classes to the United States, and asserted the existence of the Sicilian Mafia. But the practical results were disappointingly meager. In spite of having uncovered collusion between the offices of the jury commissioners, the sheriff, and the defense bar, only a few indictments were issued and no effort was made to reform the criminal court, let alone to condemn the violent acts of March 14. The lack of concern for the deaths of the eleven alleged murderers may have been due to the fact that members of the grand jury had been in the mob and they were trying to cover up their actions. Pascal Corte, the Italian consul in New Orleans, charged that nothing was done because the mayor and other public officials contributed directly to the actions of the mob.[46]

The reality was that public corruption was responsible for the deaths of the eleven Sicilians, not their alleged Mafia connections. Jury tampering appears to have been a routine occurrence in New Orleans. The evidence before the grand jury revealed that O'Malley and a leading criminal attorney, Lionel Adams, had a panel of thirty jurors in the jury pool who were in their employ and expected to vote in support of their clients.[47] It was not the Mafia that corrupted justice in New Orleans but the corrupt legal profession. There is little doubt that local Italians had been involved in the death of Hennessey, but there is no proof that the murders were the work of the Mafia. Soon every crime committed by an Italian was attributed to this mysterious organization.

In Chicago, a man waiting for a streetcar told three men that the Italians who were shot and hanged in New Orleans deserved their fate.[48] To his surprise, the three men, who were Italian, assaulted him. He attributed the beating to the Mafia. The New Orleans affair undoubtedly gave birth to the American stereotype of Italians, particularly southern Italians and Sicilians, as violent, hot-tempered criminals with extensive underworld connections. Not only were all Italian crimes now regularly believed to be the work of the Mafia, but Italians themselves became suspected members of the mythical secret organization.

An in-depth study of the New Orleans incident that appeared in a 1939 issue of the *Louisiana Historical Quarterly* concluded that three of the murdered men, Manuel Polizzi, Antonio Marchese, and Antonio Scaffidi, "probably deserved their fate."[49] They had been placed at the scene of the murder by two eyewitnesses. There was also evidence that Pietro Monastero had been involved in the plot. As for the rest, "the slaughter was unjustified."

Articles about the Mafia continued to appear in Chicago newspapers after the Hennessey affair. In May 1891, the *Tribune* reprinted a story appearing in the *St. Louis Republic* titled "The Origin of the Mafia." This story recounted the "legend" of the Night of the Sicilian Vespers described in chapter 4. The article ran again two months later in July 1891 under the title "Reputed Origin of the Mafia." The ceaseless publicity given to the Mafia affected Italians in a number of ways. Not only was suspicion of the Italian immigrant heightened, discrimination grew in the work place. In New Orleans, the Stevedores' and Longshoremen's Association began a campaign to take over the business of unloading fruits and vegetables from ships docked at the port. The business had traditionally been controlled by nonunion Italian labor.[50]

In October 1892, the New Orleans jury-tampering trial was back in the news. Two members of the jury, Bernard Glandi and Thomas Mc Chrystol, were convicted and sentenced to the penitentiary for their parts in the alleged conspiracy.[51] The district attorney in New Orleans, however, dropped the indictment against Detective O'Malley because of the refusal of the convicted defendants to testify against him. Little was heard about the New Orleans affair after that.

The Killing of Joseph Petrosino

Another incident that contributed to the societal definition of the Black Hand as an alien criminal group was the death of Joseph Petrosino. In March 1909, the *Chicago Daily Tribune's* New York bureau reported,

"Lieutenant Joseph Petrosino of the New York detective force, who has sent more men to the electric chair than any other member of the force, was slain in Palermo, Sicily. He was shot down by members of the Black Hand." The policeman was allegedly marked for death by the "Black Hand, the Mafia, and the Camorra, and the hundred and one offshoots of these organizations of Italian bandits formed to prey on their country-men." Petrosino had gone to Italy to establish a system by which American authorities would be notified whenever a known criminal left Italy for the United States. He was also gathering information on fugitives from Italian justice with an eye towards having them deported back to Italy upon his return. Nobody in Italy supposedly knew of Petrosino's mission except for the chief of the Palermo police, although word was leaked to the press in New York.[52]

A number of theories developed to explain Petrosino's murder. The Italian government initially reported that Petrosino was in Sicily to prevent a possible plot against the life of President Theodore Roosevelt, who was planning to visit to view recent earthquake damage. Petrosino and Roosevelt had become friends when Roosevelt served as New York City's commissioner of police. Petrosino's connection to the upcoming visit of the American president, however, was vehemently denied by the police in New York, who had begun a roundup of known Black Hand criminals in an effort to obtain information on the murder of their officer. The plot against Petrosino was even traced to Chicago. Assistant Chief Schuettler found information that Petrosino was killed at the instigation of Joseph Scriuba of Marion, Illinois. It was believed that Scriuba was in Palermo at the time of Petrosino's death, which heightened police suspicion.[53]

Information in Chicago alternatively suggested that Petrosino was murdered by the followers of an anarchist group that had used extortion to fund their activities. Arguing that there was "no regular Black Hand organization," an unnamed foreign police official visiting Chicago who had made a twelve-year study of Black Hand crime traced the evolution of Black Hand extortion to two men who had emigrated from France. These two men reportedly formed a number of anarchist societies in the United States, and it was from their teachings that the Black Hand was born. They reportedly used the Black Hand scheme to extort money from their countrymen for the purpose of printing anarchist literature and otherwise carrying on their work.[54]

The lack of information coming from Italy regarding the murder so frustrated New York police that plans were made to send local officers to Italy to assist in the investigation. Italian police objected to criticism of the way they were handling the murder investigation. In fact, the police in Italy had begun to seek information in cities throughout the Mediterranean where criminal bands were known to operate, as well as throughout Italy itself. In addition, the general inspector of police had been sent to Palermo to supervise the investigation personally and the chief of police in Palermo had been removed from office for failing to protect Petrosino. The Italian investigation led to a witness to the shooting. The witness claimed that two men came upon Petrosino and shot at him when they were only a few feet away. The assassins then fled. The witness was unable to identify the murderers, except that they were both short in stature.[55]

On March 20, 1909, police in Palermo, after arresting more than 100 suspects, announced that neither the Mafia nor the Black Hand had anything to do with the murder of Petrosino. The police discovered that on the day of the murder, Petrosino had gone to Caltanisetta to search the judicial archives. While there, Petrosino received a telegram urging him to return to Palermo. Two men, recently returned from America and suspected of looting at Messina after the earthquake, were seen talking to the originator of the telegram. Police believed they were Petrosino's killers. A few days later, police in Palermo arrested Carlo Constantino for "complicity" in the Petrosino murder. Constantino had recently returned from New York, where he had lived for two years and had been the subject of an investigation by Petrosino's men.[56]

In Columbus, Ohio, postal authorities theorized that Black Hand criminals Antonio Marrfesi and Collogero Vicario were involved in the Petrosino murder. Both were alleged to be members of the "Society of the Banana," an Ohio Black Hand gang, and both men were in Sicily at the time of the Petrosino murder. The men were also linked to receiving nineteen money orders, eighteen for $1,000 and one for $80, that were traced to a fund in Italy allegedly collected to protect the slayers of the New York police lieutenant. Further investigation, however, discounted any involvement in the Petrosino slaying and concluded that the money orders simply represented the division of the spoils made through Black Hand activities that were sent to innocent relatives abroad for safekeeping.[57]

The last report to come from Italy regarding the Petrosino affair described a meeting of the Camorra in Naples that had been called to discuss measures to guard against the investigation into the Petrosino murder.[58] The meeting was prompted by the presence of New York police lieutenant Antonio Vachris, Petrosino's trusted assistant, who had gone to Italy to assist in the investigation. It was alleged that members of the Camorra followed Vachris while he was in Italy in order to learn of his activities.

The Camorra had decided to do everything in its power to check the actions of the New York police, whether in Italy or in America, resulting from the death of Lieutenant Petrosino.

Although Petrosino's murder has never been officially solved, the Italian police had a number of theories about motive, including personal vengeance (criminals that Petrosino had deported to Sicily had become aware of his mission and sought retribution), the survival of the "black bridge" between Palermo and New York over which criminals had fled Italian justice, and the rescue of Black Hand criminals in the United States who would be threatened with deportation by Petrosino's discoveries. His biographer, however, provided another explanation. In his book *Joe Petrosino*, Arrigo Petacco argues that Petrosino was killed by Vito Cascio Ferro. Ferro had been identified by Petrosino six years earlier in New York City as one of the suspects in what became known as "the man in the barrel" murder case, so named because the victim was found stuffed in a wooden barrel. Arrigo reports that Ferro, while serving out his last years in prison, admitted killing Petrosino. Although Ferro, who had risen to a position of authority in the Palermo Mafia, intimated that he had killed Petrosino for daring to come to Sicily to investigate Italian criminals, he probably arranged for the murder to prevent his own extradition to the United States for his part in the barrel murder.

Whatever the cause of the tragic death of Joseph Petrosino, the blame was placed squarely at the feet of the Black Hand and the Mafia in spite of the fact that the most likely explanation was that Petrosino was killed to protect Vito Cascio Ferro from extradition. Because it was believed that the murder was the result of a plot that had its inception in the United States, police in New York declared a "war to the finish" with Black Hand criminals and sent telegrams to the police chiefs of all the major American cities asking for the arrest of known Black Hand offenders. There was also a renewed outcry for immigration reform that would make it more difficult for foreign criminals to enter the United States. There was even a rumor in Italy that the United States intended to expel a large number of Italian immigrants in revenge for the death of Petrosino.[59]

In Chicago, the *Record-Herald* reported that Petrosino had established that the Black Hand, the Mafia, and the Camorra were international organizations, headquartered in southern Italy and directed by a "wonderfully organized, secret, vengeful, and relentless central committee which directed the carrying out of crimes, including arson, bomb throwing, blackmail and murder, and which was actuated by thirst for revenge as often as by mercenary reasons."[60] These statements were made in spite of the fact that it was widely known that Petrosino believed that Black Hand crimes were perpetrated by isolated groups of blackmailers and petty spoilers. Petrosino's position on the Black Hand can be summed up in a statement attributed to him by Arrigo Petacco. When questioned by reporters about Black Hand crime, Petrosino is said to have responded, "I've told you many times before that the 'Black Hand' doesn't exist as a functioning organization. It's the newspapers that have built up the myth of an octopus that's supposed to have the whole city of New York in its tentacles. What does actually exist is gangs, mostly very small, and not concerned with one another, that have appropriated this name that the anarchists invented to frighten their victims."[61]

The body of Lieutenant Joseph Petrosino was returned to New York on April 9, 1909. The headline appearing in the *Chicago Daily Tribune* read, "Bring Victim of the Black Hand Home." His funeral, three days later, was remarkable. A crowd of approximately 200,000 people attended the funeral in New York City. No one other than the leading men of the country has ever received the honors that were bestowed on the Italian policeman that day. Between 7,000 and 8,000 men walked before and behind the hearse that bore his body. They included 1,200 police officers, four mounted troops of police cavalry riding four abreast, 350 firemen, two military bands, and more than sixty Italian religious and fraternal societies. The procession was nearly five miles in length. A massive candle, expected to burn for five years, was created in his honor. The candle stood nine feet tall and had a circumference of three feet, six inches, and weighed 178 pounds. When it was learned that he had died a poor man, the people of New York reportedly collected $10,000 for his widow, Adelina, and the city awarded her a pension of $1,000 a month. Years later, Ernest Borgnine portrayed Petrosino in a Hollywood film titled *Pay or Die.*[62]

Two months after Joseph Petrosino's death, Mayor des Planches, the Italian ambassador, informed the U.S. government that his country planned to organize an international conference on immigration aimed at stopping the victimization of Italian immigrants by Black Hand and other such criminal groups. The proposed conference would consider the idea, first conceived by Petrosino, of establishing bureaus of information in Italy whereby police authorities in the United States would immediately be notified of the emigration of every person suspected of having any connection with criminal activity.[63]

George Dorsey

Although not as widely known as the murders of David Hennessey and Joseph Petrosino, the writings of George Dorsey had an equally important impact on American views of the southern Italian and Sicilian immigrant. In 646 articles written over a three-year period (1909–1912), George Amos Dorsey, a member of the editorial staff and a foreign correspondent of the *Chicago Daily Tribune*, traveled throughout the world studying the customs and "sources" of the people who were immigrating to the United States.[64] Next to the "Negro problem," Dorsey considered immigration to be the most important social problem facing the United States at the beginning of the twentieth century.[65] He was concerned about the growth of immigration and the nature of the people who were coming to the United States because of their effect on the future "physique" and culture of the American people.

Dorsey was an intellectual heavyweight. Educated at Harvard, he had taught at the University of Chicago and Northwestern University as well as Harvard itself.[66] He was the author of five books and had led a number of field expeditions in California and South America for the World's Columbian Exposition and the Field Museum. A pioneer in forensic anthropology, Dorsey is believed to have been the first anthropologist ever to testify in a criminal trial. In 1897, Louise Luetgert, the wife of a Chicago meatpacker, disappeared. Although no body was ever found, police believed that her husband Adolph, the owner of a sausage factory, had murdered her. It was believed that Adolph had destroyed his wife's body in one of his factory's meat grinders. At Adolph Luetgert's trial, Dorsey testified that small bone fragments found at the Luetgert sausage factory were in fact those of a woman.

In no less than 141 newspaper articles, Dorsey maligned the suitability of the Italian immigrant. From March through August 1910, the readers of the *Chicago Daily Tribune* were presented with a series of articles describing the often unsavory characteristics of the southern Italian and Sicilian people. It just so happened that these articles appeared at the height of Black Hand activity in Chicago. Over one-third of the alleged Black Hand crimes identified in my analysis were committed between 1910 and 1911. Nearly one out of four had no evidence of extortion, yet they were described as Black Hand crimes in the media. It is my contention that Dorsey's articles contributed to the public's belief in the Mafia, and to a lesser extent the Camorra, as the origin of Black Hand crime in Chicago. Consider the following exerpts from Dorsey's articles:

APRIL 13, 1910 CULTURE OF SICILIANS THAT OF ANCIENT GREECE

Our interest in Sicily is real, even serious; if we can get the key to Sicily we have the key to one large section of a solution of the problem of immigration. If the Sicilian is a desirable immigrant, if we can assimilate him, we need not worry much about the remaining Italians. . . . But the Sicilian is in a class by himself. He and his first cousin just across the straits [North Africa], and the Jews, in my estimation, represent the extreme poles of present day immigrants. With clear ideas of the best course to pursue toward these two groups, we cannot go far astray in coming to a decision as to the rest of European immigrants.[67]

APRIL 14, 1910 PROCESSION OF RULERS IN HISTORY OF SICILY

More than half the men in Sicily are in blood of the Greek type. The prevailing culture of the Sicilian is fundamentally Greek. . . . The number of men showing Greek influence is nearly equaled by those showing traces of African and Arabian blood. These descendants of Saracen influence are of short stature, lithe and slender, with black hair, black fiery eyes, and screwed twisted faces. They have the agility of a cat and an alertness of mind truly oriental. . . . The third element of Sicilian blood and culture is the Norman. The descendants of the fresh importation of blood at this period are seen in the tall men, with brood chests, grey eyes, light hair, broad heads, and finely molded faces, in stature they are not unlike Northern Italians.[68]

APRIL 15, 1910 SICILIAN CODE OF HONOR SERVES TO HIDE CRIME

The Sicilian has been characterized as bold, fearless, vindictive, a lover of his children, a hater of spies, arrogant, insolent, vivid in imagination, affable, friendly, benevolent, cruel, a gambler, picturesque, poverty stricken, and sometimes a murderer and robber. We may explain the peculiar and to us abnormal traits of Sicilian character by reference to his history. . . . However, much we may withhold adverse judgment, we are still compelled to ask ourselves whether men of the character and disposition of the Sicilian form desirable additions to American blood and culture. . . . Can we assimilate the Sicilian? There is that in the Sicilian culture which stands for, encourages, or tolerates without protest, conditions of mentality and of cultures in general which not only hinder progress, but perpetuate vices which are neither primitive nor savage. . . . It is what they call omerta or manliness. . . . Crimes go unpunished, the police are helpless, even the brave carabinieri, or national police, are powerless to put down crime because evidence is not to be gotten. . . . They have their own way of settling their wrongs and grievances. These ways are not our ways. The vendetta flourishes, the Mafia thrives.[69]

APRIL 16, 1910 CENTURIES OF FIGHTING LEAVES MARK ON SICILY

Go where you will about town, you encounter lofty old gray walls, topped with sharp iron spikes or bits of glass bottles. . . . They [the Sicilians] have been protecting and fortifying themselves against the enemy, either a stranger or one from their midst, through endless generations. It has come to be part of their life. . . . They throw the same wall of evasion, of subterfuge, about their social and business life. It lacks directness, simplicity, straight-forwardness, openhandedness. It is strife of wit against wit, of force against force. . . . In a society with that peculiar point of view of honor, which is part of the Sicilian's code, it becomes necessary to have protection. This protection takes many forms, personal, legal, and organized. The offensive method of protection from crime is to become a criminal, a brigand, or thief. The defensive protection with us is supposed to be public sentiment and law; in Sicily it is insurance, the vendetta, and the Mafia.[70]

APRIL 17, 1910 MAFIA MYSTERIES TERRORIZE SICILY

It [the Mafia] is a vague, shadowy, ephemeral, irresponsible gang, which has usurped some of the functions of the government and often descends to the role of sneak thief and murderer. . . . Its existence is possible owing to the contempt which the average Sicilian has for the law and the sort of honor which not only enables a man to take the law into his own hands but to repay vengeance, however slight the original provocation may have been, by committing depredations on the property of the man he seeks to injure. . . . This hideous conception of Sicilian honor, which makes the conviction of criminals well nigh impossible, keeps these blackmailing gangs out of jail or the executioner's hands. . . . Many gangs exist in many towns in Sicily, perhaps in all the towns in the western half of the island. . . . Often a single city contains two mafias. Its membership does not consist of petty pickpockets or sneak thieves, and as a rule, it is not from the extremely poor classes. Among them will be found petty tradesmen, small landowners, native steamship agents, and politicians. It is an aristocracy of criminals, led generally by a skilled criminal, often an outlaw. . . . The functions of the Mafia are many; the chief among them is the levying of blackmail. . . . Failure to comply with the threatening extortion may lead to murder. I am informed that there is no town in Sicily where one may not have an enemy put out of the way by paying $200 and supplying the assassin with a ticket to some neighboring state or to America. I do not know how many Sicilian or Italian murderers are today in the United States, but, if I can believe only part of the evidence which comes from every side, there must be hundreds, if not thousands. . . . There are cities in Sicily, especially in the province of Caltanisetta, where murder is so common as to go unnoticed. . . . The Mafia thrives because it fits in with the Sicilian's conception of a square deal. . . . It is an attitude of mind which, while explainable on historic grounds, must be considered, from our point of view, as opposed and destructive of Anglo-Saxon culture.[71]

APRIL 18, 1910 SOME WAYS OF SICILIAN DUE TO LONG OPPRESSION

The Sicilian is neither childlike nor bland, but he is as lacking in naiveté as an Asiatic. I attribute the eccentricities of his culture not to his blood, but to his social environment. He is the inheritor of the evil traits of a dozen masters. He has been exploited for 2,000 years by tax gatherers. Wrongs could not be addressed by law. Each man became his own judge and executioner. . . . A favorite method of carrying out vengeance is for a young man to select for the time of a murder the wedding day of a friend, at which function he appears, perhaps as the best man. Another method, well recognized in Sicily, is for the man who proposes to commit murder to sell his house and immigrate to America. Over there, he arranges with certain friends for an absence of three or four weeks. They are ready to prove that during his absence he has been with them. In the meantime, he quietly returns to Sicily, perhaps through France, commits the murder, hides the body and, before the community is aware of it, is on his way back to the states. . . . It is said that all the young men [in Sicily] go armed. . . . With the average man, a revolver is as much a part of his costume as his shirt. . . . It [the Mafia] is a spirit, a state of mind, a feature of Sicilian society.[72]

APRIL 19, 1910 LAW FAILS TO KEEP OUT MEN CONVICTED OF CRIME

A ship sailed from Palermo today with a cargo of lemons and Sicilians. I have no knowledge of the value of the lemons, but the odds are in favor of the presence of one or more criminals and one or more individuals afflicted with trachoma amongst the Sicilians. . . . The storm of indignation which followed the assassination [of Joseph Petrosino] brought the Italian government to its feet. As I understand the situation the thing they least desire is the return of Italian criminals now in New York or elsewhere in the United States. Likewise he [the American consul in Italy] has expressed his surprise at the apparent indifference of our authorities to the offenses of the Italian government in aiding and abetting the departures of criminals to the United States. . . . We are dealing with authorities who are not only weak kneed, because they are only too often serving their own interests in tolerating or abetting the escape of criminals, but with authorities who belong to a culture one of the ideals of which is omerta. . . . The most interesting chart which could be made of Sicilian criminology would be one which would record the ascending wave of crime whenever the tide of returning Sicilians sets in strongly this way. According to a German banker, the number of criminals sometimes increases with the return of a few from the United States, but it never diminishes because they are bred [in Italy] as fast as they go.[73]

APRIL 20, 1910 HOW EMIGRANTS EVADE LAWS THAT BAR THEM

You may think I am prejudiced against Italians. I am not. . . . I like Italy. I respect conditions which make for the Camorra in Naples and the Mafia

in Palermo. But however one may sympathize with certain conditions
. . . it does not imply that one is not entitled to form a judgment as to the
desirability of the people of this culture [Sicilian] as playmates or work-
mates. . . . The fact that conditions, intolerable to our way of thinking,
and incompatible with our ideals exist in Sicily does not even imply that
I think Sicilians better or worse than we are. . . . The real question is to
what extent we care to work or play with those who are accustomed to
act in accordance with a different set of rules. . . . You may even think
that I am striving for the sensational in this preliminary observation of
the Sicilians. I am not. I admit that the statements I have made which
imply judgment are to a certain extent the result not of personal observation gained through sense impression, but have been based in part
on conversation with those in whose judgment I have confidence. . . .
Sicilian women rarely commit crime. But as instigators of murder it is
said they surpass the men.[74]

APRIL 22, 1910 SICILIANS ARE INSPIRED BY GRIM DETERMINATION

Perhaps the most striking characteristic of the Sicilian's mental makeup
is the quality of spirit which prompts him to action . . . having once made
up his mind, it takes a great deal to stop him. . . . The Sicilian robs or
commits murder according to a similar mental process. A Sicilian murderer or brigand is a man of character. His act differs fundamentally from
the murder committed, for example, by a Hungarian peasant when under
the influence of alcohol. The Sicilian is more deliberate. . . . With the
growing consciousness of his courage and his physical strength he casts
about for some objective method of putting this courage and strength to
use . . . to avenge a death or to slay someone whose existence is a menace. No one questions the Sicilian's intelligence. He comes from good
stock, but an infusion of blood from Africa and Spain has not helped
him to expend wisely his intelligence. . . . The culture which exists is
the result not so much of a commingling of the excellent traits of the
Phoenicians, Greeks, Romans, Saracens, Normans, Spanish, and French
as it is a combined product of the attitude which these rulers took toward
the common people. Few of them came as true colonists, but rather as
exploiters of the island. As a result, the Sicilian has had to look out for
himself. His peculiar conception of honor, his taking the law into his own
hands, have been the result. All of this has not only tended to develop
conceptions of life radically different from those of northern Europe, but
the acquisition of oriental blood has helped strengthen this attitude and
mark the foundations of his social structure. The capacity for good or
evil of the Sicilian is great. But the training which is to convert him to
American ideals must be long and will necessarily be difficult. We cannot afford to tolerate him. We cannot afford to let him go on and follow
his own inclinations. To do so is to encourage ever growing areas in our
cities of an element fundamentally at variance with American ideals.

Our attitude toward him must not be one of toleration. A halfway attitude like this is not helpful to him; it is dangerous to us.[75]

MAY 8, 1910 SICILY'S ONE HOPE IN ITS EMIGRANTS

As I have watched the long lines of emigrants offering themselves to our medical examiner I kept asking myself, what have they of value for us? We have a right to ask this question. We did it in the case of the Chinese, we did it with the Japanese, I believe either the Chinese or Japanese to be far superior to the Sicilians I have seen entering ships destined for New York. Physically they [the Orientals] are vastly superior, and I believe them to be superior mentally and morally. . . . To admit freely Sicilians to the right to compete in the economic life of the United States, to grant them citizenship after they have been subjected to a meaningless and perfunctory test is, in my estimation, to offer them that to which they are not, by their own acts and own worth, entitled . . . the culture from which they spring is perhaps not as far removed from ours as that is of the Brahmans or Mohammedans of India, but it is certainly not better than half way. . . . They fight and cut at each other's throats for the sake of honor. They rob and pillage for the sake of gain. They destroy crops, vineyards, and other property for spite. They threaten and kidnap for blackmail.[76]

JUNE 2, 1910 SICILIAN EMIGRANT BRINGS IDEAS STRANGE
TO AMERICA

Physically, the Sicilian is inferior to all other European emigrants of whom I have personal knowledge. On the average, his stature is not only less, but he lacks the ruggedness of physique which is especially characteristic of the southern Slavs. . . . My observations are not sufficient to enable me to state definitely what percentage of those who emigrate show traces of African blood. . . . I believe that a conservative estimate would be one in twenty. This African blood was probably introduced during the time of the Saracens. It is not unreasonable that some of it may be a survival of the Negroid element which once, perhaps, covered all of southern Europe. . . . The later infusion of African blood is seen in the character of the hair and a weak development of the nose. . . . Their short stature I believe to be due to selection, and possibly to an aboriginal population of short stature. . . . Whatever may be the cause of the low physical development of the Sicilian, his physical condition is such as to make him an easy prey to disease. . . . The Sicilian's conception of bodily cleanliness is peculiar. He likes to wear a moustache, but otherwise has a clean shaven face. . . . The average Sicilian never bathes. . . . Often he shares his one room [house] with his donkey or mule, his pig, and a few chickens. . . . In blood, the Sicilian brings us no strength, except that which his dogged persistence enables him to exist in pushing a cart or wielding a shovel.[77]

JUNE 3, 1910 SICILIAN EMIGRANT HAS STRONG AND WEAK POINTS

Physically, Sicilian immigrants are below the standard. With their cousins of lower Italy, they are except for the Jews, perhaps the physically poorest people entering the United States today. Grant that their children may improve in stature and strength; they cannot contribute to the physique of American manhood. The material and mental culture from which Sicilian emigrants come suffers in comparison with American ideals even more than does their blood. . . . We owe it to ourselves to ask whether the standard of material and mental life, which the Sicilian brings with him, is such as to make him a desirable addition to American society.[78]

JUNE 7, 1910 IDEAS OF EAST AND WEST RUB SHOULDERS IN NAPLES

The east meets the west in Naples and Naples is not unique. It is characteristic of the south of Europe. . . . Here begins the Orient. . . . There is a great difference between Naples and Milan. . . . The real difference between the east and the west is the attitude toward or the conception of life held by the two groups. . . . It is commonly believed that the north Italian immigrants are superior.[79]

JUNE 10, 1910 BIG OUTPUT OF COLONISTS DOESN'T
DEPOPULATE ITALY

We consider the south Italian peasant almost a barbarian. . . . The south Italian peasant occupies the same position in Italian society that the "poor whites" of the south held toward the aristocratic planter. You are hard pushed to recall the names of men of genius who have sprung from south Italian soil in the last 1,500 years. . . . Society in south Italy is organized on different lines. It has its own conceptions of revenge, love, marriage, religion, chastity, honor, and manliness.[80]

JUNE 11, 1910 CALABRIA THE HABITAT OF EXTREMEST POVERTY

A map of Europe showing the distribution of crime in proportion to population places Italy as the blackest spot. An enlarged map of Italy, showing the same features, makes the south equally black. . . . With the fact before us that measured by nearly every standard of civilization, southern Italy is much lower than northern Italy, and that in southern Italy Calabria occupies front rank in many ways in its lack of civilization.[81]

JULY 18, 1910 CAMORRA, ONCE PROTECTIVE, NOW
LEVYING BLACKMAIL

They say that the modern Camorra had its germ in a little organization of Neapolitan artists who long had suffered from the tyranny of Spanish artists. They did not band together for protection, but collectively took an oath that each day one member should kill at least one Spaniard. . . . The original crowd grew in size and unity and purpose. It assumed the right to regulate society. . . . One of its chief sources of revenue was the share the Camorra demanded of gambling. . . . Having paid tribute, gambler, cabman, fisherman, and the hundred and one groups of petty life could go on their way. . . . Since 1860, the Camorra has gradually declined in power and influence. . . . The Camorra exists today. Its chief function is blackmail. It levies tribute on women of the town, on usurers, gamblers, thieves—in short, on every form of vice and crime. . . . The Camorra recruits itself from the Mala Vita. Naples like southern Italy is tainted with this "bad life."[82]

AUGUST 19, 1910 IMMIGRATION OF ITALIANS MAY BRING
BIG RESULTS

Italians are among the poorest of our immigrants. They are poor in health, stature, strength, initiative, education, and money. They are of questionable value from a mental, moral, or physical standpoint. . . . They are like invaders from a poverty stricken, disease ridden country. . . . They add to our burden. They underbid the labor market. They help to strain our charity and to break down the freedom and independence of the individual. They increase the cost of government and add seriously to the problems of our slums . . . judged by every standard by which we can measure physical strength and quality of mind, the Italian is low as compared with the average immigrant from Europe . . . If we set up as the ideal American a well formed man of tall stature, the admixture of hundreds of thousands of short Italians will not improve this standard but be certain, in the long run, to lower it. . . . Of more concern and much greater importance is the quality of blood the Italian brings. No amount of compassion, induced by a knowledge of history which is responsible for his condition, will reduce the danger confronting us with a continued influx of Italians who are not physically sound. . . . But for centuries upon centuries the Italian has been inbred in the midst of unfavorable and unsanitary conditions. He remains a primitive man. . . . Selection has not worked to improve his race.[83]

AUGUST 22, 1910 AMERICA A FERTILE FIELD FOR CRIMINALS
OF ITALY

I am not trying to prove that every Italian is a criminal or even has criminal instincts. . . . But I do believe that the Italians peculiar way of looking at the truth, his peculiar conception of business are such as to make him, on the whole, an undesirable citizen, or one who must be looked after. . . . In short, we can make the Italian a good citizen if we surround him with the legal restraints to which he is accustomed. . . . There are honest Italians, but they have not yet learned to regard an assassin as a diseased member of society rather than as a hero. . . . The criminal is only unfortunate. It is not wrong to lie, steal, or fight. One is only unlucky if caught. . . . In minor offenses, at any rate, the number of Italians in penal institutions is proportionality much less than that of other nationalities. The real crimes of Italians in the United States are homicides and a general category of criminality which travels under the name of the Black Hand.[84]

Although Dorsey held a doctorate in anthropology and may have had some sociological insight into the development of norms within southern Italian society, his articles were severely critical of Sicilians and southern Italians and they no doubt had a significant impact on the reading public. How could anyone reading this series of reports not come away with the idea that the average Sicilian held cultural values that differed strongly from those of American society? How could the average American, who at this time in history had little, if any, understanding of anthropology or sociology, come away with anything but the idea that Sicilian and southern Italian immigrants were a threat to American ideals? Even if the reader had a university education, his thoughts were dominated by early positive school theories that placed the blame for criminality on the individual and his culture, not on the social structural conditions that contributed to criminality in complex urban environments.

Additionally, southern Italians and Sicilians were the only people that Dorsey attacked continually in his series of 646 articles. Traveling to over fourteen countries and a countless number of smaller ethnic regions within each, Dorsey condemned few people other than the Italian and Sicilian. He found Hungarians to be "Good Material for Citizens," "Slavs the Greatest People of Europe," and "Emigrants from Bulgaria the Best of People." Dorsey did not like "Roumanians" because they led primitive lives, held ideas unlike those held by Americans, and had a material culture that was "low." Nor did he favor Egyptians because Orientals had "devious minds." He disliked the people of India because they were "mentally and physically inferior to the Indians of Mexico and Peru" and thought that the people of the Philippines had a "lazy streak." Dorsey's criticisms of these groups, however, were limited to no more than two articles apiece at best, in comparison to thirty-nine severely critical articles about Italians.[85]

Dorsey's observations were undoubtedly influenced by the work of Lombrosian criminologists, who had linked racial inferiority to southern Italian culture. As an anthropologist, he was certainly aware of the work of Sergi, Niceforo, and other members of the Italian school—and its resulting scientific racism. In fact, Dorsey's investigation came at the height of the Italian school's influence upon American public policy. Both the Dillingham Commission and the Immigration Restriction League were at the height of their efforts to limit southern Italian immigration when

Dorsey published his reports. As a result, it could be argued that Dorsey's work for the *Chicago Daily Tribune* directly contributed to the negative view of the Italian immigrant held by the American reading public.

Dorsey's writings did not go unchallenged. In a letter to the *Tribune*, Sam Barbaro, a Chicago Italian, questioned the accuracy of Dorsey's reports.[86] Criticizing Dorsey's writings as gross misstatements of fact, Barbaro challenged the reporter to provide data comparing southern Italian criminality with that of other countries in the world. Barbaro argued that Dorsey's ability to travel unmolested in Italy was clear proof that his claims about the Black Hand, Mafia, and *Mala Vita* were untrue.

Although Dorsey's writings showed some insight into southern Italian culture, they painted an alien, often racist, picture of the southern Italian and Sicilian immigrant, one that characterized the Italian as a small dark man of mysterious origins, destined for menial employment and quick to pull a knife. There is no question that most Black Hand crimes were committed by Italians and that Chicago's Near North Side contained a concentration of Black Hand offenders, but newspaper fixation with the Mafia and Camorra and the idea of Italian "secret societies" dominated the news. No one outside of the White Hand Society identified Black Hand outrages as a method of crime rather than a group. Part of the confusion on the part of the press may be related to the fact that a small number of "professional" Black Hand groups were centered in the Little Sicily area. These groups, however, were more akin to robbery gangs than they were to organized crime in spite of some limited political protection.

In spite of the fact that there is little proof that the Mafia was involved in the killing of David Hennessey or that the Black Hand killed Joseph Petrosino, their alleged involvement crystallized into an explanation that has been recycled from one popular book to the next. Just as the deaths of Hennessey and Petrosino heightened concerns about the existence of the Mafia and the Black Hand, so did the writings of George Dorsey. Coupled with the growing canon of scientific racism, Dorsey's reports raised serious concerns about the criminal tendencies of the southern Italian and Sicilian immigrant, concerns that became part of the institutional legacy of Black Hand crime.

Conclusion

By 1930, the Black Hand as a method of extortion had virtually vanished. There are a number of reasons for the disappearance of Black Hand crime in Chicago. The most important was the prosecution of the Nicolosi gang and the exposure of their association with Chicago alderman John Powers. Another important reason was the intervention of the federal government, which began prosecuting Black Hand offenders in 1911. Local politicians did not have the power to interfere in federal prosecutions.

Although Black Hand crime had ended, the societal response to Black Hand extortion impacted American society in two important ways. The first involved Italian immigrants themselves. Italian families who had received a blackmail letter lived in constant dread of the unknown danger that hung over their heads. No one knew whom the crime would fall upon first: the father, one of the children, a relative, or the whole family via the bombing of their house or shop. Entire families wept in despair, fearing the loss of the money that they had gathered through so many hardships only to be taken away by the barbarous activities of Black Hand criminals. Others armed themselves and, with the assistance of family and friends, stood guard through the night. Armed to the teeth, their minds steeped in vengeance, some were driven to criminality themselves in order to defend against Black Hand terror. Take the example of Joseph Cristiano, who received an extortion letter demanding $2,000 from the "Iron Hand." Joseph and his brother Dominick owned a grocery in the Near South Side. The writer said that he would call on the brothers at their store to receive the money. Giovanni Mataleano and Giuseppe Leto entered the grocery a few days later and asked for a $2,000 pound of liver. Joseph Cristiano, never a loss for words, replied, "Here is the liver you will get." He then killed them both using a revolver that he had kept under the grocery counter.[1]

Others sold their belongings and fled to Italy to find safety from Black Hand retribution.[2] Among those who could not afford to flee, the effect was devastating. Not only were they forced to live in fear among feelings of hatred and vengeance, but the transgressions of Black Hand criminals reminded them of the tyranny that they had left in the south of Italy. As a result, the American government was discredited in their eyes. Rumors of political protection of Black Hand criminals and the failure of the American government to control Black Hand crime alienated Italian immigrants and prevented them from participating fully in American society. It may even have encouraged some to join the ranks of Black Hand criminals. Even the business and professional people who were strong enough to stand up to the demands of Black Hand gangs lived in fear, which had a detrimental effect on their daily lives.

The second major effect of Black Hand crime involved the response of American society to Black Hand extortion. Public opinion and the press showed little sympathy for the Italian immigrant. Every deed of the Italian criminal was seen as a manifestation of the Black Hand, which fueled prejudice and animosity against Italians throughout the nation. The feeling that they were not welcome compounded the problem, leading many Italians to turn inward, further isolating them from American society. It has even been argued that this isolation may have contributed to Italian crime as the hotheaded among them, cut off from American life and distrustful of American justice, took the law into their own hands.[3]

Distrust of southern Italians was so great that between 1886 and 1910, Southern lynch mobs murdered twenty-nine Sicilians. The motive for several of these killings was the suspicion that the murdered men were members of the Sicilian Mafia. In 1891, eleven men charged in the killing of New Orleans police chief David Hennessey were murdered. Three Sicilians were lynched by a mob in Hahnville, Louisiana. On August 8, 1896, a lynch mob stormed the jail and seized a Sicilian accused of murdering a local man. When the mob discovered two other Sicilians awaiting trial in the jail, they suspected a Mafia plot and hanged all three of the prisoners. Five more Sicilians were lynched by a mob in Tallulah, Louisiana in 1899. The murders were the result of a quarrel over a goat. Rather than condemning the murders, the *New Orleans Picayune* reported that the people of Louisiana acted out of outrage that the Mafia had again begun operation in the state, and that they were determined to crush it whenever it showed its dreadful head.[4]

Echoing the Hennessey affair, two Tampa, Florida, Italians were the victims of a lynch mob in September 1910.[5] Castenge Ficarrotta and Angelo Albano were hanged by a mob of sixty after being taken from two deputy sheriffs who were transferring them from the city lockup to the county jail. Reinforced by city police, the sheriff's deputies later found the bodies of the two Italians swinging from the limb of a tree in a forest at the edge of a swamp. Ficarrotta and Albano had been charged with the attempted murder of Frank Easterling, a bookkeeper for a local cigar manufacturer. The attempt on Easterling's life was attributed to an ongoing strike at the cigar plant. Ficarrotta had been a suspect in the alleged Black Hand murder of another man, but there was insufficient evidence to convict him at the trial.

In 1908, 150 Italians were told to leave Reeds Station, Indiana, or suffer death. Signs had been posted on doors throughout the colony warning, "All Italians must vacate and not be found here after Feb. 20. Those that stay will suffer the penalty." It was signed the "Committee." In 1920, twenty Italians were beaten by a mob in West Frankfort, Illinois, after the discovery of the murders of two young boys. A barbershop, a poolroom, and a saloon in the Italian district of the town were also damaged. The local sheriff supported the actions of the mob, arguing that these places were nothing but "dens of vice and places where anarchists and black-mailers met to hatch their extortion and robbery plots." Local hospitals refused to treat the wounded Italians. Many hid in a nearby forest until the U.S. Army arrived from Danville, Illinois, and restored order.[6]

To their credit, Chicago newspapers printed an occasional defense of the Italian immigrant, usually after a letter written to the editor from a local Italian. For example, in March 1910 attorney John De Grazia wrote the *Chicago Record-Herald* protesting the unfair notoriety given to offenses committed by Chicago's Italians.[7] De Grazia charged that every time a mysterious crime was committed near an Italian settlement, the newspapers unjustly attributed the crime to the Italians, or to the so-called Black Hand, as though Italians were the only ones capable of committing these offenses. Such an attitude, argued De Grazia, brought all Italians into ill repute, caused hatred, and affected race relations in many areas of the city. Regarding the Black Hand, De Grazia reiterated the position of the Italian community, arguing that the Black Hand as a secret criminal organization did not exist. De Grazia also reminded the newspaper that few Italians were involved in traditional forms of crime such as robbery, burglary, and theft. He concluded that the attitude of the press was hurting the Italian people who had contributed much to Western civilization and the building of industrial America.

The inappropriate response to Black Hand crime not only led to violence and discrimination against America's Italian population but also contributed to the creation of the alien conspiracy theory and the establishment of the Mafia as the folk devil of American crime. Italian immigrants in Chicago and elsewhere were routinely stereotyped as members of the Mafia and Black Hand. To be an Italian was to be a member of a foreign criminal group. Chicago attorney Bernard Barasa reported that he had difficulty defending Italians in criminal court because of the prejudice caused by Black Hand activities.[8]

Southern Italians and Sicilians were not the first immigrant groups to engage in crime. Every immigrant group brought their own share of criminals, but most were excused on the grounds that their lawlessness was bred by poverty and their inability to gain an economic foothold in American society. Only the Italians were cursed as a race by a society that ignored the reality of crime and organized crime in particular. It is a common misconception that American organized crime began with the importation of the Sicilian Mafia. But organized crime was an outgrowth of machine politics. Many criminal rackets flowed from the daily workings of the machine, not the Mafia, and these became the basis for organized crime in the United States. Municipal corruption, graft, and the proceeds of illegal gambling and prostitution were the basis of a vast underworld of saloonkeepers, bootleggers, compliant politicians, corrupt police officials, and gangsters.[9]

The incorrect definition of Black Hand crime added new words to the American vocabulary. The words Black Hand were not only a method of extortion but came to represent all manner of evil conspiracies. In October 1907, a headline in the *Chicago Daily Tribune* read, "Hist! Black Hand for Primary Law: Political Mafia Starts to Springfield with Murder in Its Heart." The headline referred to a bill pending in the Illinois state legislature that would allow the direct election of primary candidates without party sponsorship. Opponents of the bill, who were party regulars, were described as hatching "Black Hand" and all sorts of other plots against the measure. From Chicago to Springfield, "Mafia" bands of conspirators were reported to be considering ways to pass a bill that would appease the public but save their own political hides. Two years later, another bill in the Illinois legislature calling for the centralization of purchasing at the Joliet, Pontiac, and Chester penitentiaries was amended to protect the purchasing power of local prison officials. The bill was reportedly "mauled" by members of the "B. Gardner Black Hand Association," who sought to prevent competitive bidding. Once again, the term *Black Hand* was used to describe a group of persons working towards a questionable goal.[10]

In Gary, Indiana, just over the border from Chicago, the editor of the *Gary Times* received an anonymous "Black Hand" letter in July 1909 threatening that "his body would be riddled with bullets" if his paper did not desist from exposing a local vice ring.[11] Gary had recently been incorporated as a city, and it was in the midst of a campaign to close local gambling and prostitution dens. The use of the term "Black Hand" to describe the letter was not connected to any form of extortion, nor was any group of Italian criminals identified in the plot. The *Tribune* simply applied the term to the story because of the threatening letter and the fact that organized groups of criminals were involved.

The Black Hand also became a useful theme around which newspapers organized Italian crime consistent with early positivist theories of deviance. No one argued that Black Hand activity was the result of conditions in American society. Theoretical explanations for this position were only just being formulated under the rubric of the Chicago School. Although Italians argued that there was no such thing as the Mafia or the Black Hand, they did not have the ability to make their views known. What news they did control was published in Italian and thus inaccessible to the American reading public.

Some have argued that the United States' failure to provide its growing Italian population with effective police protection led to an increase in crime in Italian communities as the success of Black Hand criminals emboldened further Black Hand crime.[12] Americans, however, chose to interpret Italian crime differently. They believed that the growing frequency of crimes committed by individual lawbreakers and small groups were manifestations of the moral and educational deficiencies of the southern Italian community, a community that tolerated the activities of a vast criminal conspiracy in America as it had done in the Old World.

No one attacked the political system that allowed Black Hand crime to flourish. Society's attention remained focused on the relatively powerless Italian community while ignoring the social conditions that fostered Black Hand crime. The social constructionist perspective argues that those who have the power to turn their views into law determine what is deviant. The experience of the White Hand in Chicago highlights the fact that the ability to define and construct a social problem is also governed by those who hold power in a society. In spite of their efforts, the White Hand was unable to properly define Black Hand activity as the work of independent criminal gangs, let alone prevent the parole of politically connected Black Hand criminals.

The societal definition of Black Hand crime was the work of the Chicago press. The importance of the manner in which the press responded to crime cannot be understated. Every time a local newspaper reported a crime as being the work of the Black Hand, the publicity increased the power of Black Hand criminals. Whether the name originated in Italy or was made up by some ambitious newspaper reporter in the United States, the dark appellation conjured up thoughts of a mysterious foreign power beyond the control of local authorities.

Society's failure to control Black Hand crime is also worthy of note. Whether it was a lack of concern or simply racial prejudice, the city of Chicago tended to ignore the plight of the Italian community and the seriousness of the Black Hand menace. There is ample proof that this inaction was deliberate. When reform mayor William Dever took office in 1923, he directed the Chicago Police Department to hire a greater number of Italian police officers. Police commissioner Michael Hughes responded, in writing, that he had discussed the mayor's suggestion with his police captains and that they were, without exception, opposed to the idea.[13] It was the consensus of his command staff that the police department had been very fortunate in being able to recruit "Irishmen from overseas and narrow backs" (Irish Americans) and should stick with their success. Commissioner Hughes concluded, "Nothing I can presently think of would do more to ruin the Chicago Police Department than to start hiring Dagos in large numbers."

Grace Abbott, Chicago reformer and director of the Immigrants Protective League, blamed the Black Hand problem on the ineffectiveness of the Chicago police, arguing that the police method of preventing Black Hand crime was as unintelligent as it was unjust.[14] The result was that the Italian suffered at every turn. He was not protected against criminals inside or outside of his own ranks and the general public became increasingly indignant, not at the police but at all Italians. Had it not been for Chief Schuettler and his Black Hand Squad of Italian detectives and the work of Inspector John Revere, also an Italian, little would have been done to control Black Hand crime in Chicago.

Chicago's handling of Black Hand crime stood in stark contrast to that of other American cities. For example, an investigation by the Massachusetts Commission on Immigration found that despite the fact that a large proportion of the Italian population in that state had come from southern Italy and Sicily, Black Hand outrages were practically unknown in the city of Boston. The absence of Black Hand crime in Massachusetts supported the contention of the Italian community that local American conditions were responsible for Black Hand crime. It was police corruption, in the form of the protection of criminals, that enabled Italians and criminals of other nationalities to develop the Black Hand system of blackmail that was pervasive in America's Italian communities.[15]

The real cause of Black Hand crime was not the criminal tendencies of the southern Italian immigrant but conditions in American society. It was not the southern Italian's inclination to crime but his vulnerability to crime that explained the phenomenon known as the Black Hand. The effect that this inappropriate response has had on society is profound. Not only has it affected government policy because of the belief that the Black Hand was a transitional stage in the evolution of organized crime, it has also led to the creation of urban legends. Urban legends are stories that people tell as true and are widely believed, but lack factual verification.

An urban legend created by the societal response to Black Hand extortion appears to be that of the "Shotgun Man." Various authors have linked the story of the Shotgun Man to twelve to thirty-eight murders that occurred between January 1910 and March 1911.[16] There is no evidence, however, supporting the argument that the same person committed all of these crimes. In fact, police believed that two men had participated in the Shotgun Man murders. They based their theory on the fact that two sawed-off shotguns were recovered near the scene of the murders.[17]

There is even less evidence that a shotgun was used in all of the murders attributed to the so-called Black Hand Shotgun Man. The *Chicago Daily Tribune* reported on March 17, 1911, two days after the original shotgun incident, that the sawed-off shotgun was a "new" weapon in Black Hand extortion. The *Chicago Record-Herald* reported that the shotgun had replaced the bomb, stiletto, and revolver as the weapon of choice in Black Hand crime. A closer reading of the various newspaper accounts reveals that the press used the term Shotgun Man in a generic sense, that is, a man using a shotgun. Successive authors, however, interpreted the term to mean one person.

The earliest mention of the Shotgun Man theory appears in Asbury's 1940 book titled *The Gem of the Prairie*. This book was published again in 2002 under the title *The Gangs of Chicago*. The source of the information on the Shotgun Man murders is the March 17, 1911, edition of the *Chicago Daily Tribune*, which, by the way, never uses the term "Shotgun Man." Reporting on a fourth murder in seventy-two hours near Death Corner, the *Tribune* listed the murder as the thirty-fourth Black Hand killing in fifteen months and provided a list of the victims. A review of newspaper accounts of twenty-seven of the killings found that only six had been attributed to the Black Hand, and in only three cases was there evidence of extortion. The remaining murders were the result of a robbery, quarrel, or vendetta.[18]

The above information supports the argument that much of what was reported as Black Hand crime was the work of the press, but also demonstrates how the social reality of crime is constructed. For example, the *Encyclopedia of American Crime* reports that thirty-eight Black Hand murders occurred at Death Corner between January 1910 and March 1911.[19] The *Mafia Encyclopedia* reports that the Shotgun Man was responsible for fifteen of these murders. Both reports are based on an inaccurate interpretation of the initial press reports of the Shotgun Man incident and both have become part of hegemonic history of Black Hand crime, a history that has been further disseminated through the technological advance of the Internet. The following definition of the Shotgun Man appears in Wikipedia, the online Internet encyclopedia: "The Shotgun Man was a freelance Black Hand assassin and mass murderer to which 38 unsolved murder victims of Black Hand extortionists were attributed most notably gunning down 15 Sicilian and Italian immigrants between January 1–March 26, 1911 between Oak and Milton Street in Chicago's Little Italy (known as Death Corner). In March 1911, he reportedly murdered four people within a 72-hour period, also at the intersection of Oak and Milton Streets."[20]

The whole Shotgun Man legend is a fable! Yet the social construction of the Shotgun Man story and the attention given to Death Corner had real consequences for the residents of Little Sicily. The name Death Corner, like the name Little Hell, captured the imagination of newspaper reporters who repeatedly used the terms when referring to crime in the area. So effective was the use of these terms that they may have contributed to the destruction of the community. The City of Chicago eventually demolished Little Sicily and replaced it with public housing. There is evidence that the action was related to the community's sordid reputation.

Little Sicily was an old community and had been the location of an inordinate number of Black Hand crimes, to be sure, but much had been done to improve the area. The community had two critically important social institutions that played a major role in the advancement of the area, St. Philip Benizi Church and the North Side Civic Committee. St. Philip Benizi was the heart of Little Sicily. During its fifty years of operation, over 35,000 people were baptized, 6,273 couples were married, and 10, 854 funerals were performed. The pastor of St. Philip Benizi was a Servite priest named Father Luigi Giambastiani, an outspoken critic of crime and an energetic civic leader.[21]

Begun during the Great Depression, the North Side Civic Committee was an outgrowth of the Owl Indians Social-Athletic Club.[22] The Owl Indians began as a boy gang at Seward Park in the heart of Little Sicily during the early 1920s. The president of the Owl Indians was a dentist named Angelo Lendino. In September 1935, the Owl Indians were invited by the Illinois Institute for Juvenile Research to join the Chicago Area Project, a program begun by sociologists Clifford Shaw and Henry McKay to fight juvenile delinquency in Chicago. The program focused on using community members to fight delinquency through improved educational and recreational programs for youth and the improvement of the physical and social conditions of the community. Dr. Lendino invited seventy-five men to the boy's gymnasium in Seward Park. They were lawyers, policemen, machinists, physicians, truck drivers, carpenters, storekeepers, barbers, public officials, ditch-diggers, and tailors. The Chicago Area Project offered them a chance to make things better in their neighborhood, and they accepted the challenge. As a result, the North Side Civic Committee was formed with Lendino as its president.

Little Sicily was chosen as the first community in the Near North Side to participate in the Chicago Area Project on the assumption that the social life of the community and groups like the Owl Indians could support such a program. This social life is best described in the words of Dr. Lendino himself: "Perhaps nowhere else in the city is there to be found a neighborhood where as many people know each other as they do in our district. We have to a very great extent the same kind of warmth, friendliness and intimacy in our community life that was to be found in the small towns of Sicily from whence our parents came."[23]

The North Side Civic Committee wasted no time in setting up programs throughout the community. Seventeen subcommittees were formed to improve conditions in the area, including committees on delinquency, health and sanitation, civic responsibility, recreation, and camping.[24] A study by the Chicago Recreation Commission in 1938 reported that 3,100 boys, girls, and young men were participating in the programs sponsored by the North Side Civic Committee. Committee members worked with many other city organizations to improve services: with Chicago Park District officials to remodel Seward Park, with the Chicago Police Department to open a game room and craft shop on the third floor of the Hudson Avenue police station, with the Chicago Board of Education to improve conditions at Jenner School, and with Immaculate

Conception Church to build a playground at 1500 North Park Avenue. In addition, the committee created a summer camp program for local children in cooperation with the Salvation Army and the Italian Welfare Council. Boy Scout and Cub Scout troops were established, softball and basketball leagues formed, and educational trips were taken to Chicago museums and zoos. The committee also sponsored an eleven-day carnival at St. Philip Benizi to raise money to redecorate the church.

So successful was the work of the committee that it had a major impact on the field of sociology. Harvey Zorbaugh's 1929 study of Little Sicily supported social disorganization theory and the emerging Chicago school of sociology that viewed crime as the result of the failure of social control in community areas. This lack of control was brought about because community institutions such as the church, school, family, and local government ceased to function effectively. William Foote Whyte, a noted sociologist from the University of Oklahoma, challenged this position after observing the work of Lendino and the North Side Civic Committee. Whyte concluded that no one who read of the activities of this group could help but conclude that Zorbaugh neglected to see some of the most significant features of life in the area. This statement had a profound effect on the field of sociology and led to the recognition that even distressed neighborhoods can have an effective social organization of their own.[25]

In 1940, the City of Chicago approved plans to demolish a portion of Little Sicily and replace the homes there with low-rise public housing. Only St. Philip Benizi Church was to be spared. The initial plan was received with enthusiasm by residents of the area.[26] Only a small section of the community was to be razed, and jobs and new housing would be created for local residents. Due to Father Giambastiani's efforts, the new housing development would even be named for the Italian-born nun, Mother Frances X. Cabrini, who had worked tirelessly to serve Chicago's Italian community. In addition, many of the families who would eventually move into the public housing units would be Italian.

In the early 1950s, the Chicago Housing Authority decided to expand public housing in Little Sicily. The construction was to be in two phases. Phase one, the Cabrini Extension, consisted of fifteen seven-, ten-, and nineteen-story buildings. Phase two, the William Green Homes (named for the president of the American Federation of Labor), would add an additional eight buildings to the housing complex now known as Cabrini-Green. The people of Little Sicily felt deceived. Much had been done to rehabilitate the area. Lendino, as spokesman for the Near North Civic Committee, stated that 75 percent of the residents of the community were home owners who had done much to improve their property. Although well intended, the new public housing complex permanently altered the character of the neighborhood.[27]

The destruction of Little Sicily was viewed as a betrayal of the Sicilian community under the guise of progress. Many believe that the area's reputation for lawlessness led to the demise of the community. But as Lendino stated to federal housing officials, "We did have a reputation for crime and delinquency and at one time had the name of Little Hell, but our north side civic committee has been cleaning things up. We now have seven Boy Scout Troops." The development of Cabrini-Green, the construction of the Chicago expressway system, and the building of the Chicago campus of the University of Illinois have led many to conclude that no Chicago ethnic group other than African Americans was damaged as greatly by government policies as were the Italians. Perhaps as a result of the dispersion of the Sicilian and Italian populations, there has never been an Italian American candidate for mayor of Chicago or any other major city office.[28] It appears that all the good works could not overcome the stigma of the Black Hand.

The Black Hand was nothing more than a method of crime like armed robbery or safecracking. All that was needed to commit Black Hand extortion was a pen and paper. One did not even need to speak Italian. Ready victims were everywhere: the corner barber, the grocery storekeeper, or tenement owner were all potential Black Hand targets. There was no international association. There was no central organization. There was no connection to the Camorra or Mafia. There was, however, the press, which turned Black Hand crime into an international criminal conspiracy.

NOTES

The following abbreviations are used for frequently cited sources:

CA   *Chicago American*
CDN   *Chicago Daily News*
CFLPS   Chicago Foreign Language Press Survey
CR-H   *Chicago Record-Herald*
CDT   *Chicago Daily Tribune*
WHSC   White Hand Society of Chicago

Preface

1. Phillip Abrams, *Historical Sociology* (Somerset: Open Books, 1982).
2. C. Wright Mills, *The Sociological Imagination* (New York: Oxford University Press, 1959).

Introduction

1. "One Third of Chicago's Italians Paying Tribute to the Black Hand," *CDT*, 23 February 1908.
2. Britannica Encyclopedia (n.d.), s.v. "The Black Hand" (retrieved 1 August 2006 from http://www.answers.com/topic/black-hand); Columbia Encyclopedia (n.d.), s.v. "The Black Hand" (retrieved 1 August 2006 from http://www.answers.com/topic/black-hand).
3. "Scrubbing Italy's Black Hand," *Literary Digest* 50, no. 42 (April 1911): 1095; Tommaso Sassone, "Italy's Criminals in the United States," *Current History* 15 (October 1921): 23–31; quoting Marie Leavitt, *Report on the Sicilian Colony in Chicago*, n.d., quoted in Robert Park and Herbert Miller, *Old World Traits Transplanted* (New York: Arno Press, [1921] 1969), 241; Gaia Servadio, *Mafioso: A History of the Mafia from Its Origins to the Present Day* (New York: Stein and Day, 1967), 55–67.
4. Gaetano D'Amato, "The Black Hand Myth," *North American Review* 187 (April 1908): 543–49; U.S. Immigration Commission, *Immigration Conditions in Europe* (Washington, D.C.: U.S. Government Printing Office, 1911), 210; Diego Gambetta, *The Sicilian Mafia* (Cambridge: Harvard University Press, 1993), 140.
5. Gino Speranza, "Petrosino and the Black Hand," *Survey* 22 (1909): 11–14;

Arthur Woods, "The Problem of the Black Hand," *McClure's* 33 (May–October 1909): 40–47; Anonymous, "The Black Hand Scourge," *Cosmopolitan* (June 1909): 31–41.

6. Arthur Train, "The Story of the Camorra in America," *McClure's* (May 1912): 90–94.

7. Estes Kefauver, *Crime in America* (Garden City, N.Y.: Doubleday, 1951), 1.

8. FBI, "La Cosa Nostra; Italian Organized Crime" (retrieved 14 July 2006 from http://www.fbi.gov/hq/cid/orgcrime/lcn/lcn.htm).

9. Thomas Pitkin and Francesco Cordasco, *The Black Hand* (Totowa, N.J.: Littlefield, Adams, 1977); Robert Lombardo, "The Black Hand," *Journal of Contemporary Criminal Justice* 18, no. 4 (2002): 393–408; Joseph Albini, *The American Mafia* (New York: Appleton Century Crofts, 1971); Daniel Bell, *The End of Ideology* (New York: Free Press, 1960); Robert Merton, *Social Theory and Social Structure* (Glencoe, Ill.: Free Press, 1957); James O'Kane, *The Crooked Ladder* (New Brunswick: Transaction Publishers, 1992).

10. Victor Kappeler and Garry Potter, *The Mythology of Crime and Criminal Justice* (Prospect Heights, Ill.: Waveland Press, 1966), 111; Michael Woodiwiss, *Gangster Capitalism: The U.S. and the Global Rise of Organized Crime* (New York: Carroll and Graf, 2005), 75.

11. Park and Miller, *Old World Traits*, 241; "Cuneo Latest Target of Black Hand," *CR-H*, 12 April 1911; "Black Handers Flee as Cops Lie in Ambush," *CDT*, 20 December 1923; "Jury Terrorized by 'Black Hand'; Dragnet Closing," *CR-H*, 28 March 1911.

12. "Servant Is Black Hand," *CDT*, 17 November 1906; "Deserts Mafia; Slain in Street," *CDT*, 19 June 1911; "In Italians' Defense," *CR-H*, 16 November 1911; "The Black Hand," *CDT*, 18 November 1911.

13. White Hand Society of Chicago, *Studies, Actions, and Results* (Chicago: White Hand Society, 1908), 1; Jeffrey Adler, *First in Violence, Deepest in Dirt: Homicide in Chicago 1875–1920* (Cambridge: Harvard University Press, 2006), 174; Chicago City Council, *Report of the Committee on Crime*, 25 March 1915, 56.

14. John Higham, *Strangers in the Land: Patterns of American Nativism* (New York: Athenaeum, 1967), 138; Gino Speranza, "How It Feels to Be a Problem," *Charities* 12 (1904): 457–63.

15. Alexander De Conde, *Half Bitter, Half Sweet: An Excursion into Italian American History* (New York: Charles Scribner's Sons, 1971), 342.

Chapter 1. Italians in Chicago

1. U.S. Senate, *Reports of the Immigration Commission*, vol. 4, *Emigration Conditions in Europe* (Washington, D.C.: U.S. Government Printing Office, 1911), 137; "Races and Immigration," editorial, *Chicago Record-Herald*, 28 July 1909.

2. Rudolph Vecoli, "Chicago's Italians Prior to World War I" (unpublished manuscript; (Ann Arbor, University Microfilms, 1963), 81.

3. Robert Forester, *The Italian Emigration of Our Times* (New York: Arno Press 1968), 51, 371; Jerre Mangione and Ben Morreale, *La Storia: Five Centuries of the Italian American Experience* (New York: Harper Collins, 1992), 76.

4. Booker T. Washington, *The Man Farthest Down* (New York: Doubleday, 1912), 144.

5. *Emigration Conditions in Europe*, 228; Forester, *Italian Emigration*, 62, 91.

6. Rudolph Vecoli, "The Formation of Chicago's 'Little Italies,'" *Journal of American History* 2, no. 2 (1983): 7–20; "From Rome to Chicago," *CDT*, 23 February 1890.

7. Humbert Nelli, *The Italians in Chicago* (New York: Oxford, 1970), 24; "Testimonial Benefit to 'Lame Jimmy,'" *CDT*, 7 September 1926; "The Italians," *Illinois Staats Zeitung*, Chicago Foreign Language Press Survey, Chicago Historical Society.

8. Vecoli, "Formation," 7–20; "Italians in Chicago," *L'Italia*, 10 September 1898, CFLPS; "Testimonial Benefit to 'Lame Jimmy.'"

9. Frank Beck, *The Italian in Chicago* (Chicago: Department of Public Welfare II-3, 1919), 5.

10. Ibid., 5–7; City of Chicago, *Historic City* (Chicago: Department of Development and Planning, 1976), 69.

11. Roger Daniels, *Coming to America* (London: Harper Perennial, 1990); Joseph Gusfield, *Symbolic Crusade* (Champaign: University of Illinois Press, 1963); Joseph Feagin, "Old Wine in New Bottles," in Juan Perea, ed., *Immigrants Out* (New York: New York University Press, 1997); John Higham, *Strangers in the Land: Patterns of American Nativism, 1860–1925* (New York: Atheneum, 1967), 9.

12. Antonio Gramsci, *The Southern Question*, translated by Pasquale Verdicchio (West Lafayette, Ind.: Bordighera, 1995); Peter D'Agostino, "Craniums, Criminals, and the 'Cursed Race': Italian Anthropology in American Racial Thought, 1861–1924," *Society for Comparative Study of Society and History* 44 (April 2002): 326, quoting Guiseppe Sergi, *Attorno all'Italia preistorica* (Turin: Bocca, 1898).

13. Exerpt reprinted in David Richards, *Italian American: The Racializing of an Ethnic Identity* (New York: New York University Press, 1999), 107; D'Agostino, "Craniums," 326, quoting Alfredo Niceforo, *L'Italia barbara contemporanea* (Milano-Palermo: Remo Sandron, 1898).

14. D'Agostino, "Craniums," 44.

15. *Reports of the Immigration Commission*, vol. 5, *Dictionary of Races or Peoples* (Washington, D.C.: Government Printing Office, 1911), 81–85, 127.

16. Edward Ross, *The Old World in the New: The Significance of Past and Present Immigration to the American People* (New York: Century, 1914), 97.

17. *Webster's Encyclopedic Unabridged Dictionary*, 1994, s.v. "Dago"; Appelton Morgan, "What Shall We Do With the 'Dago'?" *Popular Science Monthly* 38 (1890): 172–79.

18. *Emigration Conditions in Europe*, 205–9.

19. *Emigration Conditions in Europe*, 18.

20. "Ample Proof," *L'Italia*, 6 February 1892; "Statistics Report," *L'Italia*, 4 June 1892, CFLPS; "No Italians in the House of Corrections," *L'Italia*, 24 February 1894, CFLPS; Edmund Dunne, *Memoirs of Ze Pré* (St. Louis: Herder, 1914).

21. "An Italian Vendetta," *CDT*, 29 July 1888.

22. "Italian Slave Dealers," *Illinois Staats-Zeitung*, 16 January 1877, CFLPS.

23. "Work on Sympathy," *CDT*, 20 August 1893.

24. "80,000 Italian Slaves," *CDT*, 27 February 1886; "The Padrone System," *CDT*, 28 February 1886.

25. "From Rome to Chicago," *CDT*, 23 February 1890.

26. "Italian Workers Defrauded," *L'Italia*, 16 September 1894; "Italian Workers Swindled," *L'Italia*, 4 May 1901; "Employment Agencies: The Guilty and Their Victims," *La Parola dei Socialisti*, CFLPS.

27. Carol Wright, *The Italians in Chicago: Ninth Special Report of the Commissioner of Labor* (Washington, D.C.: U.S. Government Printing Office, 1897), 49, 27; "Padrone Evil as It Exists in the Italian Colony in Chicago," *CDT*, 14 November 1897.

28. "Thee Camorra of Naples," *CDT*, 17 September 1877.

29. "Has Chicago a Mafia?" *CDT*, 24 October 1888; "Avengers of the Mafia," *CDT*, 22 October 1888.

30. "Has Chicago a Mafia?"; "In Defense of the Italians," *CDT*, 26 October 1888.

31. "Italian Assassins in Boston," *CDT*, 2 August 1890; "Another Victim of the Mafia," *CDT*, 5 September 1890.

32. "Mafia Murders Slain," *CDT*, 15 March 1891; Richard Gambino, *Vendetta* (New York: Doubleday, 1977), 138.

33. "Sentenced to Death," *CDT*, 12 November 1890; "Fearful of the Mafia," *CDT*, 17 February 1891.

34. "Hyde Park in a Panic," *CDT*, 19 February 1891.

35. "Murder on Tilden Avenue," *L'Italia*, 8 October 1892, CFLPS; "Does the Mafia Society Exist?" *CDT*, 6 October 1892.

36. "Mafia Active Again," *CDT*, 18 November 1892; "No Mafia Society in Chicago," *CDT*, 5 December 1892.

37. "De Bartolo Has Been Held Guilty," *L'Italia*, 23–24 March 1895, CFLPS; "Italians Sick of It," *CDT*, 19 October 1894; "Letters to Lure Him to Death," *CDT*, 6 February 1895.

38. "Most Dangerous Neighborhood in Chicago," *CDT*, 3 March 1901.

39. "Dreads Threat of Mafia," *CDT*, 14 May 1901.

40. "Italian Workmen Shot to Death," *CDT*, 20 September 1904; "Two Slain, Two Hurt in Feud," *CRH*, 20 September 1904; "Truce Assassinio di un Italiano," *L'Italia*, 19 November 1904, CFLPS.

41. "Truce Assassinio di un Italiano"; Pitkin and Cordasco, *The Black Hand*, 16.

42. "Receives 'Black Hand' Letter," *CDT*, 9 February 1905; "Crown of Chicago," *L'Italia*, 11 February 1905, CFLPS; "Second Letter Follows a Warning by 'Black Hand,'" *CDT*, 18 February 1905; "Italian Warned of Death," *CRH*, 18 February 1905.

43. "Justice Sees 'Black Hand,'" *CDT*, 19 May 1905; "Letter Threatens a Woman," *CDT*, 16 September 1905.

44. "Five Die in Fire Charged to Black Hand," *CRH*, 17 November 1905.

45. "Death Is Threatened Unless $10,000 Is Paid," *CRH*, 22 August 1904.

46. "Letters from 'Black Hand' Demand $300 of Italian," *CDT*, 10 July 1906.

47. "Brothers Are Threatened in Letter Demanding $300," *CDT*, 14 September 1906.

48. "Police Watch in Vain for Supposed Black Hand Man," *CDT*, 28 January 1907; "Taken as Black Hand Gang," *CDT*, 8 February 1907; "Black Hand Bomb a Joke, Is Theory of Police," *CDT*, 8 April 1907.

49. "Sleuths Seek Bomb Throwers," *CDN*, 11 April 1907; "Italian Refuses $2,000 Blackmail; Is Mailed Bomb," *CRH*, 20 April 1907.

50. "The Black Hand," *CDT*, 16 May; 1907; "East Appeals to Shippy," *CDT*, 30 July 1907.

51. Bernaldo De Quiros, "The Agrarian Sparticism of Andalusia," *Anales do Sociologia* (1968–1969), 4–5, 315–38; Pitkin and Cordasco, *The Black Hand*, 45; Gaetano D'Amato, "The Black Hand Myth," *North American Review* 187 (April 1908): 543–49; Gerald Brenan, *The Spanish Labyrinth* (London: Cambridge University Press, [1943] 1950), 160; "Black Hand Is a Hoax," *CRH*, 2 April 1908.

52. Dwight C. Smith, *The Mafia Mystique* (New York: Basic Books, 1975), 47.

53. D'Amato, "The Black Hand Myth."

54. Humbert Nelli, "Italians and Crime in Chicago: The Formative Years, 1890–1920," *American Journal of Sociology* 174 (1969): 373–91; D'Amato, "The Black Hand Myth."

Chapter 2. The White Hand Society

1. "Black Hand Foes Form White Hand," *CDT*, 18 November 1907.

2. "For a 'White Hand' Society," *La Tribuna Italiana*, 16 November 1907, CFLPS; "Black Hand Foes Form White Hand"; "Black Hand Is to Be Ousted," *Oakland Tribune*, 18 November 1907.

3. *WHSC*.

4. Ibid., 22; "Black Hand Foes Form White Hand."

5. "The White Hand Society," *La Tribuna Italiana*, 23 November 1907, CFLPS.

6. *WHSC*, 4.

7. "The White Hand Society," *La Tribuna Italiana*, 22 February 1908, CFLPS; "Black Hand Foes Form White Hand."

8. "Death by Dagger; Black Hand Acts," *CDT*, 19 November 1907.

9. "Police Chosen by White Hand," *CDT*, 20 November 1907.

10. Ibid.

11. "The White Hand Society," *La Tribuna Italiana*, 23 November 1907, CFLPS.

12. "'Black Hand' Letters Multiply," *CR-H*, 6 December 1907.

13. "White Hand Hot on Bravos Trail," *CDT*, 1 January 1908.

14. Ibid.

15. "The White Hand," *L'Italia*, 1 February 1908.

16. "Bingham Plan to End Black Hand," *CDT*, 7 February 1908; "Italy Endorses White Hand," *CDT*, 5 April 1908; *WHSC*, 22; "Police Chosen by White Hand," *CDT*, 20 November 1907.

17. "Black Hand Dooms Volini," *CDT*, 28 February 1908.

18. "Italians of Chicago," *CDT*, 3 May 1891; "A Family Gives Six Generations to Medical Art," *CDT*, 4 April 1948; "Move to Uplift Italian Youth," *CDT*, 11 November 1901.

19. "Police Seeking the 'Black Hand,'" *CDT*, 4 February 1908; "Called Leader of Black Hand," *CR-H*, 8 February 1908; Chicago Police Department, Personnel Division, Form P. D-4 15M 3-17 CA 87037, n.d.; Gabriel Longobardi; "Slash and Beat Black Hand's Foe," *CDT*, 2 May 1909; "Girl of Eight Dies as Mafia Bullets Fly," *CDT*, 3 May 1915.

20. "Rubber Stamps Murder Clew," *CR-H*, 4 February 1908; "Black Hand Gives White Hand Task," *CDT*, 3 February 1908.

21. "Black Hand Gives White Hand Task"; WHSC, 17; "See Black Hand End," *CR-H*, 15 May 1908.

22. "See Black Hand End."

23. "Gets 'Black Hand' Letters," *CDT*, 14 February 1908; "Mike McDonald at Death's Door," *CDT*, 8 August 1907; Humbert Nelli, *The Italians in Chicago* (London: Oxford University Press, 1970), 148.

24. "Black Hand Work Finds Imitators," *CDT*, 3 April 1908; "Italy Endorses White Hand," *CDT*, 5 April 1908.

25. "Boy in Black Hand Peril," *CDT*, 2 April 1908; "'Black Hand' Threats Reported," *CR-H*, 2 April 1908; "Rich Men as Victims of the 'Black Hand,'" *CR-H*, 3 April 1908; "Black Hand Work Finds Imitators."

26. "Black Hand Suspect Taken; May Solve Police Mystery," *CDT*, 13 April 1908; "Girl Sees 'Black Hand' Act," *CDT*, 9 April 1908.

27. "The Black Hand Blackmailers," Editorial, *CR-H*, 4 April 1908.

28. "Fear Black Hand; Pupils in Panic," *CDT*, 25 April 1908.

29. "Ghetto in Terror Over Bomb Tales," *CDT*, 26 May 1908.

30. "Bomb Scare Closes School," *CDT*, 27 May 1908; "Pupils in 'Black Hand' Panic," *CDT*, 29 May 1908; "Bomb Story Frightens Pupils," *CR-H*, 29 May 1908.

31. "Bold Lochinvars in Arms of Police," *CDT*, 1 May 1908.

32. "Pay Us $1,000 or Dynamite, Threat in Note to Woman," *CDT*, 24 May 1908.

33. "Two Men Are Arrested for Alleged Black Hand Plot," *CDT*, 7 July 1908.

34. "Arrest Made in Black Hand Plot," *CDT*, 18 August 1908; "The Police and Alien Ways," *CR-H*, 20 March 1911; John Landesco, *Organized Crime in Chicago* (Chicago: University of Chicago Press, 1968), 944; "Two More Dead; Mafia Tentacles Spread over City," *CR-H*, 27 March 1911.

35. "Arrest Made in Black Hand Plot"; "Says Black Hand Has Organ," *CDT*, 11 April 1908.

36. Ibid.

37. "Ambush Black Hand," *CR-H*, 18 August 1908.

38. "Drastic Measures for Black Hand," *CR-H*, 24 August 1908; "Italians in All Parts of World Celebrate Capitulation of Rome Thirty-Eight Years Ago," *CDT*, 20 September 1908.

39. "Boy Disappears as Sequel of 'Black Hand' Threats," *CDT*, 20 September 1908; "Call to Fight Black Hand," *CDT*, 22 September 1908; "More Italian Police Asked," *CR-H*, 24 September 1908.

40. "Black Hand Releases Boy," *CDT*, 14 October 1908.

41. "Need a 'Black Hand Squad,'" *CDT*, 24 September 1908; "More Italian Police Asked."

42. Editorial, "The Black Hand," *CDT*, 25 September 1908.

43. Jack Kuykendall, "The Municipal Police Detective: An Historical Analysis," *Criminology* 24, no. 1 (1986): 175; Eugene Rider, "The Denver Police Department 1858–1905," Ph.D. diss. (University of Denver, 1971).

44. "Need a 'Black Hand Squad.'"

45. "Police Scorn Threat," *CR-H*, 22 July 1909; "Second Black Hand Warning Follows Explosion of Bomb," *CDT*, 9 August 1909.

46. "Drastic Measures for Black Hand," *CR-H*, 24 August 1908; "America's Purse Opens to Italy," *CDT*, 30 December 1908; Nelli, *Italians in Chicago*, 113.

47. "Need a 'Black Hand Squad'"; "Avows Murder Just in Time," *CDT*, 21 November 1907.

48. *WHSC*.

49. "Wants Justice for Italians," *CR-H*, 19 December 1908.

50. "Threaten Bomb at Church," *CDT*, 6 December 1908; "Blackmailers Send Dead Men's Fingers," *CR-H*, 6 December 1908.

51. "White Death Letter as a Test of a Theory," *CR-H*, 12 December 1908.

52. Ibid.

53. Ibid.

54. *People of the State of Illinois v. Vincenzo Geraci*, Indictment, Term No. 3709 No. 90959A, 28 April 1909, Cook County Circuit Court Clerk; "Prisoner Called Black Hand Head," *CDT*, 3 April 1909; "Held on Blackmail Charge," *CR-H*, 3 April 1909.

55. *People of the State of Illinois v. Isadore Carlino*, Indictment, Term No. 3736 No. 90987A, 30 April 1909, Cook County Circuit Court Clerk.

56. "'Black Hand' Plot Leads to Arrest," *CDT*, 7 April 1909; "Alleged Blackmailer Caught," *CR-H*, 7 April 1909.

57. "Banker Declines to Act; Two Accused Men Released," *CDT*, 11 April 1909; "White Hand Society Presents New Evidence of Conspiracy," 19 March 1908.

58. "'Black Hand' War Brings Two Arrests," *CDT*, 14 April 1909; "Black Hand Is a Hoax," *CR-H*, 14 April 1909.

59. "'Black Hand' War Brings Two Arrests"; "The Black Hand," editorial, *CDT*, 14 April 1909.

60. "Near Black Hand Fate," *CR-H*, 2 May 1909; "Boy Slayer Bares Black Hand Death, Betrays Vendetta," 20 July 1909; "Slash and Beat Black Hand's Foe," *CDT*, 2 May 1909.

61. "Schuettler Takes Charge of Hunt for 'Black Hand,'" *CDT*, 3 May 1909; "Black Hand Eludes Pursuers," *CDT*, 3 May 1909.

62. "Detective Longobardi Is Informed He Is Under Society Death Sentence," *CDT*, 10 June 1909; "Black Hand Plot Likened to Mafia," *CDT*, 10 June 1909.

63. *People of the State of Illinois v. Antonio Baffa et al.*, Indictment, Term No. 3772 No. 91023A, May 1, 1909, Cook County Circuit Court Clerk; "Grocer Is Slain by Blackmailer," *CDT*, 13 April 1909.

64. "Boy Slayer Bares Black Hand Death, Betrays Vendetta," *CR-H*, 20 July 1909.

65. "Man Threatened with Death Accuses Black Hand Suspect," *CDT*, 2 October 1908.

66. "Light on Old Crimes," *CR-H*, 21 July 1909.

67. Ibid.

68. "Boy Slayer Bares Black Hand Death."
69. "Black Hand Plot Likened to Mafia."
70. "Dens of Black Hand Found in Many Cities," *CR-H*, 10 June 1909.
71. "Find Black Hand Lair; Arrest Supposed Chief," *CR-H*, 9 June 1909; "Scrubbing the 'Black Hand,'" *Literary Digest* 38, no. 25 (June 1909): 956–57.
72. "Boy Blackmailer Killed in the Act," *CDT*, 24 June 1909; "Boy Is Fatally Shot in Blackmail Ambush," *CR-H*, 24 June 1909.
73. "More Blackmail Boys Are Sought," *CDT*, 25 June 1909; "'Black Hand' Checked," *CR-H*, 25 June 1909.
74. Ibid.
75. "Boy Criminals," *CDT*, 25 June 1909.
76. "Dread 'Black Hand' Is Boy," *CDT*, 10 July 1909; "Two Boys Are Suspected of Black Hand Conspiracy," *CDT*, 15 August 1909; "'Black Hand' Boys Punished," *CDT*, 27 August 1909.
77. "Hundreds Pay in Fear," *CR-H*, 13 November 1909.
78. Ibid.
79. "Slain by Black Hand; Little Italy Raided," *CR-H*, 7 January 1910; "Hunt Black Hand Slayer; 154 in Jail," *CDT*, 7 January 1910; "Hide Facts in Murder," *CR-H*, 8 January 1910.
80. "Slain by Black Hand"; "Hunt Black Hand Slayer."
81. "Assassins Will Be Caught, Say White Hand Leaders," *CDT*, 9 January 1910.
82. "Hunt Black Hand Slayer"; "Hide Facts in Murder"; "Black Hand Clew Foiled by Fear," *CDT*, 8 January 1910.
83. "Slain Italian's Neighbor Gets Black Hand Message," *CDT*, 10 January 1910; "Black Hand on Trail of Slain Man's Friend," *CR-H*, 11 January 1910; "Try Again to Kill Longobardi," *CDT*, 23 January 1910.
84. "Arrested as 'Black Hand' Slayer," *CA*, 7 February 1910; "Murder Stirs the Italians," *CDT*, 8 February 1910; "Romance in Black Hand Killing," *CA*, 7 February 1910; "Slain by 'Black Hand'; Two Held," *CDN*, 7 February 1910.
85. "Murder Case Raid Traps Suspects," *CDT*, 13 February 1910.
86. "Legislator Gets Black Hand Demand but He's Too Busy," *CDT*, 15 February 1910.
87. "Two Detectives Shot," *CDN*, 4 March 1910; "Black Handers Shoot Two Police," *CA*, 4 March 1910; "Wren Dead, Black Hand Net Spread," *CA*, 5 March 1910.
88. "Black Handers Shoot Two Police"; "Two Detectives Shot."
89. "Detective Dying: Hunt Black Hand," *CA*, 4 March 1910; "Black Handers Shoot Two Police."
90. "Detective Dying"; "Detective Shot Is Dying," *CA*, 5 March 1910.
91. "Wounded Sleuth Blames Prisoner," *CDT*, 30 March 1910.
92. "Black Hand Shot Kills Detective," *CDT*, 5 March 1910; "Wounded Sleuth Blames Prisoner"; "Three Men Held as Robbers Now Suspected for a Murder," *CDT*, 12 March 1910.
93. "Two Detectives Shot," *CDN*, 4 March 1910; "Foreign Arm to Aid Police," *CDT*, 9 March 1910; "Detective Dying after Pistol Fight," *CA*, 4 March 1910; City of Chicago, Journal of the Proceedings of the City Council of Chicago, Regular

Meeting, 14 March 1910, 2340; "Bill Aims at Black Hand," *CDT*, 12 March 1910; "Theater Unsafe: City to Close It," *CDT*, 15 May 1910.

94. "100 Black Hand Brigands Terrorize 100,000 Italians and Sneer at the Chicago Police," *CDT*, 6 March 1910.

95. "Italian Club to Aid Police in Solving Crime Mysteries," *CDT*, 15 June 1910.

96. "New Bomb Wrecks Store," *CDT*, 21 September 1910; "Lack Bomb Theories; Also Short on Clews," *CR-H*, 22 September 1910.

97. "To Revive 'White Hand' against Blackmailers," *CDT*, 9 December 1910.

98. "35 Cents Turns George Bad; He Falls into Police Trap," *CDT*, 21 December 1910; *United States of America v. George Pavlick*, Indictment, December Term A.D. 1910, U.S. District Court, Northern District of Illinois, Eastern Division 22 December 1910; "Federal Grand Jury Completes Its Work," *CR-H*, 24 December 1910.

99. "Black Hand Men in Deadly Feud?" *CDT*, 28 January 1911.

100. "A Family Gives Six Generations to Medical Art," *CDT*, 4 April 1948.

101. "Olson Re-Elected as Chief Justice," *CDT*, 7 November 1912; "Accuses Malato in Italian Case," *CDT*, 26 June 1914.

102. "Auto Slayers Weep on Stand," *CDT*, 24 July 1913; "Uses High Case to Show Expert Testimony Folly," *CDT*, 30 September 1914; "Malato Assails Dunne Pardon," *CDT*, 29 October 1914.

103. *WHSC*, 2, 11, 20.

Chapter 3. The Black Hand Squad

1. Chicago Police Department, Personnel Division, Form P. D-4 15M 3-17 CA 87037, Paul Riccio, George De Mar, Michael De Vito, n.d.; "Fail to Catch Black Hand Band," *CDN*, 3 March 1909; John Landesco, *Organized Crime in Chicago* (Chicago: University of Chicago Press, 1968).

2. "Bomb Breaks Window Panes," *CDT*, 9 January 1911.

3. "Bomb Hurts Nine; Colony in Terror," *CR-H*, 19 January 1911; *United States of America v. Gianni Alongi*, Indictment, December Term A.D. 1910. U.S. District Court, Northern District of Illinois, Eastern Division 23 January 1911; "Shattered by a Bomb," *CR-H*, 24 January 1911; "Fake Bomb Is Found by Landis' Chambers," *CR-H*, 31 March 1911.

4. "Shattered by a Bomb."

5. Ibid.

6. "Black Hand Men in Deadly Feud?" *CDT*, 28 January 1911.

7. "Bombs Wreck a Store," *CR-H*, 29 January 1911; "Black Hand Still Active," *CDT*, 29 January 1911.

8. "Woman Terrified by Black Hand," *CDT*, 2 February 1911.

9. Ibid.; "Try for Secret Squad," *CR-H*, 3 February 1911.

10. "Try for Secret Squad"; "Shadows after 'Black Hand,'" *CDT*, 3 February 1911.

11. "Jury Tampering by Black Hand," *CR-H*, 28 March 1911.

12. "Two Men Are Slain in Camorra Plots," *CR-H*, 15 March 1911; "Black Hand

Gang Shoot Down Two; Police Get Clew," *CDT*, 15 March 1911; "Fourth Man Victim in Camorra War within 72 Hours," *CR-H*, 17 March 1911.

13. "Death a Ghastly Joke," *CR-H*, 16 March 1911; "Find Blackmail Plot in Double Death Mystery," *CA*, 15 March 1911; "Slain in Own 'Black Hand' Plot, Report," *CA*, 16 March 1911; "Italian Bound in Revenge Pact?" *CDT*, 16 March 1911; "Join Black Hand to End Murders," *CDT*, 19 March 1911; "Federal Spies Solve Black Hand Mystery," *CR-H*, 6 April 1911.

14. "Uses Deadly Slug to Shoot Italian," *CDT*, 17 March 1911; "Solves Black Hand Case," *CDT*, 18 March 1911.

15. "Black Hand Gang Shoot Down Two"; "Two Men Are Slain in Camorra Plots," *CR-H*, 15 March 1911; "Uses Deadly Slug to Shoot Italian."

16. "Black Hand Gang Shoot Down Two"; "Death a Ghastly Joke."

17. "Black Hand Gang Shoot Down Two"; "Bomb Exploded in South Side Italian Quarter," *L'Italia*, 4 February 1911, CFLPS.

18. "Slain in Own 'Black Hand' Plot, Report."

19. "Black Hand Bomb Reply to Scoffs," *CDT*, 22 March 1911; "Jar of Latest Bomb to Cost Boy's Life," *CR-H*, 23 March 1911; "Shot and Robbed on Open Prairie," *CDT*, 25 March 1911; "Bomb Again Weapon of Mafia Warriors," *CR-H*, 22 March 1911; "Federal Spies Solve Black Hand Mystery."

20. "Fears a Bomb, Will Flee; Persecuted by Black Hand," *CDT*, 25 February 1911; "Doctor Fears 'Black Hand,'" *CR-H*, 25 February 1911; "Gets Black Hand Letter; Her Husband's Clerk Held," *CDT*, 21 March 1911.

21. "Landis Warned by Black Hand," *CDT*, 26 March 1911; "Threat of Death Sent to Landis by 'Black Hand,'" *CR-H*, 26 March 1911; "Black Hand Stirs Officials; Invades Federal Building," *CDT*, 31 March 1911; "Fake Bomb Is Found by Landis' Chambers."

22. "Fake Bomb Is Found by Landis' Chambers"; "Black Hand Stirs Officials; Invades Federal Building"; "Full Confession by Blackmailer; Threat of Death," *CR-H*, 1 April 1911.

23. "Threat of Death Sent to Landis by 'Black Hand,'" *CR-H*, 26 March 1911; "Jury Tampering by Black Hand," *CR-H*, 28 March 1911; "Black Hand Case Fails," *CR-H*, 25 March 1911; "Mafia Chiefs Known," *CR-H*, 2 April 1911; "Think Murdered Man Was Enemy of Mafia," *CR-H*, 3 April 1911; "Alongi Found Guilty in 'Black Hand' Case," *CR-H*, 8 April 1911; "Black Hand Convict Is Taken to Prison," *CR-H*, 22 April 1911; "Secret Service Men on Hand to Block Attempt to Rescue the Prisoner," *CR-H*, 22 April 1911.

24. "Landis Warned by Black Hand," *CDT*, 26 March 1911; "Black Hand Kills Child and Toiler," *CDT*, 27 March 1911; "Push Work of Extermination," *CDT*, 28 March 1911; "Jury Tampering by Black Hand"; "Cuneo Long Target of the Black Hand," *CR-H*, 12 April 1911.

25. "Two More Are Dead; Mafia Tentacles Spread over City," *CR-H*, 27 March 1911.

26. Ibid.; "The Black Hand and the Federal Judge," *CR-H*, 26 February 1911.

27. "Window Thieves Steal $5,000 Gems," *CDT*, 28 March 1911; "Jury Tampering by Black Hand"; "Police Arrest Four in 'Black Hand' Move," *CR-H*, 27 May 1911.

28. "Police Arrest Four in 'Black Hand' Move."

29. "Camorra Agent Seeks $250,000 Aid," *CDT*, 29 March 1911.

30. "Camorra's Crimes Menace to Italy," *CDT*, 28 July 1907; "Camorra Trial Opens Soon," *CDT*, 26 February 1911.

31. "Fake Bomb Is Found by Landis' Chambers."

32. "Full Confession by Black Hander; Threat of Death," *CR-H*, 1 April 1911; "Landis Will Punish Men Who Told 'Silly Lies,'" *CDT*, 8 December 1911.

33. "The Individual 'Black Hand,'" *CR-H*, Editorial, 1 April 1911.

34. "Crimes of the Italian Colony," *L'Italia*, 1 April 1911, CFLPS; "Italians Strive to End Murders," *CDT*, 1 April 1911.

35. "Defends Police in Crime Data," *CDT*, 28 September 1910; "Blame on Police, Reply of Wayman," *CDT*, 29 September 1910; "Says Murderers Escape Capture," *CDT*, 1 October 1910.

36. "Another Italian Found Murdered at 'Death Corner,'" *CDT*, 2 April 1911; "Think Murdered Man Was Enemy of Mafia," *CR-H*, 3 April 1911.

37. "See Italian Die; Secrete Slayer," *CDT*, 3 April 1911.

38. "Deserts Mafia; Slain in Street," *CDT*, 19 June 1911; "'Black Hand' Death Starts War Anew," *CR-H*, 19 June 1911.

39. "Police Hope Now to Solve Puzzle of 'Black Hand,'" *CDT*, 21 April 1911; "Bomb Blast Victims are Held for Arson," *CR-H*, 21 April 1911.

40. Ibid.

41. "Police Hope Now to Solve Puzzle of 'Black Hand.'"

42. "Sons Slays Father, Confesses Crime; Says, 'I Hated Him,'" *CDT*, 5 August 1911.

43. *People of the State of Illinois v. Frank Mundo et al.*, Indictment, Term No. 1153 G. J. Nos. 80-81-82 PGD No. 97226:186, 187 September 14, 1911, Cook County Circuit Court Clerk; "Woman Outwits Black Hand Men," *CDT*, 26 July 1911; "Held on 'Black Hand' Charge," *CR-H*, 26 July 1911.

44. *People of the State of Illinois v. Mundo et al.*; "Woman Outwits Black Hand Men."

45. "Man Woman Shot Confesses," *CDT*, 28 July 1911.

46. "Futile Search for Kidnapper," *CR-H*, 7 August 1911; "Defies Police Guard," *CR-H*, 8 August 1911.

47. "Kidnapers Steal Child; Ask $5,000," *CDT*, 6 August 1911.

48. "Hunt for Boy Fails," *CR-H*, 7 August 1911; "Police Find Kidnapped Boy on North Side," *CDT*, 11 August 1911.

49. "Mareno Boy Returns Today?" *CDT*, 10 August 1911; "Police Find Kidnapped Boy on North Side."

50. "Mareno Exposes Bold Kidnapers," *CDT*, 12 August 1911.

51. "Ransomed Angelo Is Smiling Now; 'Pardon' Letter Father Received," *CDT*, 12 August 1911; "File Charges against Four Alleged Kidnappers," *CR-H*, 12 August 1911.

52. "Mareno Exposes Bold Kidnapers"; "Help to Free Man Held as Kidnapper," *CDT*, 13 August 1911.

53. "Mareno Exposes Bold Kidnapers"; "File Charges against Four Alleged Kidnappers."

54. "Help to Free Man Held as Kidnapper"; "After Ringleader of the Kidnappers," *CR-H*, 13 August 1911; "Kidnappers Now Menace Parent," *CDT*, 14 August 1911.

55. *People of the State of Illinois v. Giuseppe Nicolosi et al.*, Indictment, Term

No. 1062 G. J. No. 61 PGD No. 97137:176, 14 September 1911, Cook County Circuit Court Clerk; "Indict Five in Marino Case?" *CDT*, 12 September 1911; "Kidnapped Boy Tells His Story," *CDT*, 9 May 1914.

56. "Find Black Hand 'Clearing House,'" *CDT*, 11 October 1911.

57. "Sends Three Kidnapers to Prison," *CDT*, 13 October 1911; "Kidnappers Free: Victims Suffer," *CDT*, 4 May 1914; "Seek Jurors for Kidnapping Trial," *CDT*, 6 May 1914; Ray Baker, "Hull House and the Ward Boss," in Allen Davis and Mary Lyn McCree, eds., *Eighty Years at Hull House* (Chicago: Quadrangle Books, 1969), 62–65.

58. "Kidnappers Free: Victims Suffer."

59. Ibid.

60. "Kidnappers' Trial Reopens Today," *CDT*, 5 May 1914; "Kidnapped Boy's Father Exposes Reign of Terror," *CDT*, 7 May 1914.

61. "Kidnapped Boy's Father Exposes Reign of Terror"; "Free Italians in Kidnapping Case," *CDT*, 10 May 1914.

62. "Free Italians in Kidnapping Case."

63. "Hotel Man Pays $450,000 for Glengyle Flats," *CDT*, 26 June 1927.

64. "Officers Tell of North Side Dives," *CDT*, 15 November 1911; "War on 'Black Hand' Is Revere's Defense," *CR-H*, 19 December 1911; "Baer Says Chief Balked Cleanup," *CDT*, 20 December 1911.

65. Richard Lindberg, *To Serve and Collect: Chicago Politics and Police Corruption from the Lager Beer Riot to the Summerdale Scandal* (New York: Praeger, 1991).

66. "Praise for Revere at Trial," *CDT*, 19 December 1911; "War on 'Black Hand' Is Revere's Defense."

67. "Nab 'Black Hander,'" *CR-H*, 3 September 1911; "In Italians Defense," *CR-H*, 16 November 1911.

68. "'Blackmail' Pair Caught in Trap," *CDT*, 7 July 1912.

69. "Slain by Black Hand," *CR-H*, 1 January 1912; "Black Hand Gets New Year Victim," *CDT*, 1 January 1912.

70. "Think Private Feud Caused 'Death Corner' Assassination," *CDT*, 5 August 1912.

71. "Bomb Wrecks Grocery Store," *CR-H*, 15 May 1912; "Policies Cancelled," *CR-H*, 28 May 1912; "Lays Blast to Labor War," *CR-H*, 16 May 1912; "The Three Brothers Accused of Arson," *L'Italia*, 23 March 1913, CFLPS.

72. "Hoyne Traps Aid Charging He Sold Secrets of Office," *CDT*, 18 September 1913.

73. "Policies Cancelled; 'Black Hand' Cause," *CR-H*, 28 May 1912.

74. "Another Murder at Death Corner," *CDT*, 7 April 1912; "Another Man Found Slain Near Notorious Death Corner," *CDT*, 22 February 1913; "Killed Near 'Death Corner' by Rapid Fire of Bullets," *CDT*, 17 April 1913. "Silence Balks Police Seeking Mafia Gunmen," *CR-H*, 23 January 1914; "Three Murders Within One Hour," *CDT*, 23 January 1914.

75. "Double Shooting in Little Italy," *CDT*, 3 February 1914.

76. *United States of America v. Paul Mennite and Pietro Mecca*, Indictment, U.S. District Court, Northern District of Illinois, Eastern Division, 1915; "Held in 'Black Hand' Case; Big Step by U.S.," *CDN*, 7 June 1915; "Uncle Sam Starts Black Hand War," *CR-H*, 2 June 1915.

77. "Uncle Sam Starts Black Hand War."

78. Landesco, *Organized Crime*, 941.

79. "Uncle Sam to Fight the Black Hand," *Literary Digest* 50, no. 25 (1915): 1313.

80. "Assassin Kills 'Silver King' of Black Handers," *CDT*, 12 June 1915.

81. "Women Killed by Avengers of 'Silver King,'" *CDT*, 13 June 1915.

82. Ibid.

83. "Gunman at Bay; Taken as Mob Circles House," *CDT*, 14 June 1915.

84. "How to Stop Black Hand and White Slave Trade," *CDT*, 24 June 1908; "City for Aliens?" *CR-H*, 5 January 1905.

85. "Italian Feudist Murders Son of 'Silver King,'" *CDT*, 20 November 1916.

86. "Trailer of Men in Slaying Case Shot in the Back," *CDT*, 24 June 1914; "Accuses Malato in Italian Case," *CDT*, 26 June 1914.

87. "Police Open War on Mafia Gunmen," *CDT*, 25 June 1914.

88. Ibid.

89. "Trap Laid for Blackmailers of Bride-to-Be," *CDT*, 18 June 1915.

90. Ibid.

91. "Murder Starts Black Handers, Police Predict," *CDT*, 16 February 1916.

92. Ibid.; "New Black Hand Murder, Eight since December," *CDT*, 26 March 1916; "Woman Shot Dead in 'Black Hand' Murder Region," *CDT*, 8 April 1916; "Italian Murder Roster Grows," *CDT*, 12 April 1916.

93. "Mafia Murder No. 11 in 1916," *CDT*, 5 May 1916.

94. "Two Murders by Mafia at Death Corner," *CDT*, 23 November 1916.

95. "Vendetta Murders Baffle," *CDT*, 24 November 1916.

96. "Another Italian Murder; Police May Have Slayers," *CDT*, 25 November 1916; "Italian Slain; No One Tells Who or Why," *CDT*, 26 November 1916.

97. "Three Murdered as Police Start Gunmen Roundup," *CDT*, 27 November 1916.

98. "Schuettler Picked for Police Chief," *CDT*, 19 December 1916; "Herman Schuettler," editorial, *CDT*, 20 December 1916; "Chief of Police H. F. Schuettler Taken by Death," *CDT*, 23 August 1918; "Brand Saloons Akin Crime Factories," *CDT*, 8 February 1918.

99. "Self Sacrifice of Captain Schuettler," *CDT*, 10 February 1902; "Our Chief of Police," editorial, *CDT*, 16 May 1918.

100. "Mafia Murder No. 28 Has Unusual Feature," *CDT*, 8 December 1916; "Italian Slain; 29th on List of Black Hand," *CDT*, 20 December 1916; "Murder in Chicago," *CDT*, 5 December 1916.

101. Jeffrey Adler, *First in Violence, Deepest in Dirt: Homicide in Chicago 1875–1920* (Cambridge: Harvard University Press, 2006), 173.

102. Adler, *First in Violence*, 174; "12 Slain in 13 Months," *CR-H*, 28 April 1910.

103. "Boys Jailed as Imitators of Black Handers," *CDT*, 1 January 1917.

104. "Throw Bomb When Refused Girl's Hand?" *CDT*, 31 December 1917.

105. "'Over the Top' Lessons Smash Black Hand Line," *CDT*, 21 December 1919; "The Deposition of Nicola Braccio at the Trial of the Black Hands," *L'Italia*, 7 March 1920, CFLPS; "Hunt Black Hand Chief Hitting Trail to Italy," *CDT*, 22 December 1919; "Convict Women and One Man as Black Handers," *CDT*, 21 March 1920; "Three Black Handers Given Ten-Year Prison Terms," *CDT*, 16 May 1920.

106. "Friend of Years Pays a Tribute to Schuettler," *CDT*, 23 August 1918; "Chief of Police H. F. Schuettler Taken by Death."

107. "Chicago Thousands Pay Last Tribute to Schuettler," *CDT*, 27 August 1918.

108. "Gabriel Longobardi, Police Investigator of Mafia, Dies," *CDT*, 23 October 1932; "Slash and Beat Black Hand's Foe," *CDT*, 2 May 1909; "Captain Bernacchi, 34 Year Police Vet, to Retire Today," *CDT*, 12 May 1940; "Bernacchi, 83, Retired Police Captain, Dies," *CDT*, 5 February 1961.

109. "Police Mafia Ace Dies of Mystery Ill," *CDT*, 20 February 1923; "Death Solved," *CDT*, 20 February 1923.

110. "Welcome De Mar to Chicago Ave. Police District," *CDT*, 4 July 1928; "Lieutenant Riccio of Black Hand Squad Is Dead," *CDT*, 10 January 1935; "Deportation or Death Seen as Gangster Fate," *CDT*, 17 February 1926.

Chapter 4. The Prohibition Years

1. "Bloody 20th's Past Written by Gun Play," *CDT*, 3 February 1946.

2. Italians in Chicago Oral History Project, National Endowment for the Humanities, DEF 60, box 9, folder 1, LOG-94#46-47, University of Illinois, Chicago Library, 1980.

3. Italians in Chicago Oral History Project, DEF 60, box 9, folder 1, LOG-94#21 and 46.

4. "Two Are Shot When Bullets Rake Bakery," *CDT*, May 29, 1927.

5. "Panic Grips 'Little Sicily,'" *CDT*, September 9, 1928.

6. "'Murder Clique' Admits Killing 4 and Robbing 250," *CDT*, 25 November 1919; "Ten Others Are Condemned," *L'Italia*, 7 December 1919, CFLPS.

7. Francis McNamara, "Drama in the Death House," *CDT*, 29 November 1936; "Hangman's Noose Halts Il Diavolo's Long Reign of Terror," *CDT*, 25 November 1951.

8. Ibid.

9. Ibid.

10. "Seize Brothers on 'Black Hand' Threat Charge," *CDT*, 30 January 1920.

11. "Water Carrier to Café Nero," *CDT*, 12 May 1920; "Colosimo Murdered," *Chicago Herald and Examiner* 12 May 1920.

12. "Colosimo Slain by Black Hand for $150,000," *CDT*, 14 December 1920.

13. "Colosimo Slain; Seek Ex-Wife Just Returned," *CDT*, 12 May 1920; "Colosimo Death Mystery Baffles Police," *CDN*, 12 May 1920.

14. "Take Three as Extortion Gang," *CA*, 17 February 1913; "Poison Shot in Black Hand Guns," *CA*, 18 February 1913.

15. *People of the State of Illinois v. Michael Carozzo and Frank Cozzo*, Indictment, Term No. 2691 G. J. No. 133 P.G.D. No. 101172, 30 April 1913, Cook County Circuit Court Clerk; "Slain from Street Ambush," *CDT*, 18 February 1913; "Cosmano Shot Enright, Says Prosecutor," *CDT*, 11 February 1920; "Expose Labor Feud Between 'Moss' and Tim," *CDT*, 5 February 1920.

16. "Traces Death of Colosimo to Camorra," *CDT*, 15 May 1920; "Divorced Wife's Brother Tells of Family Rows," *CDT*, 12 May 1920.

17. "Victims Wipe Out Black Hand Gang," *CDT*, 23 November 1911; "Shooting a Clew to Four Murders," *CDT*, 4 December 1911.

18. "The Passing of Colosimo," *L'Avanti*, 22 May 1920, CFLPS; "Courts, Opera, Underworld to Bury Colosimo," *CDT*, 14 May 1920; "Hold Four New Suspects in Colosimo Murder," *CDT*, 14 May 1920.

19. "Chief of Black Hand Gang Shot in Police Trap," *CDT*, 25 October 1921.

20. "'Black Hand Ring' Smashed by U.S.; Six Men Arrested," *CDT*, 28 June 1923.

21. "Blackhanders Shot as Victim 'Digs Up,'" *CDT*, 23 September 1923.

22. "Black Hand Duo Nabbed; One Shot," *CDT*, 21 October 1923.

23. "Find King of Black Handers Slain in Road," *CDT*, 14 May 1928.

24. "Mafia Strikes as Kidnapping Trial Starts," *CDT*, 18 December 1928; "Ranieri's Tell Death Threats in Kidnap Trial," *CDT*, 19 December 1928; "Mafia Strikes as Kidnapping Trail Starts."

25. "Mafia Strikes as Kidnapping Trail Starts."

26. "Fake Mediums Found Aiding in Mafia Extortion," *CDT*, 24 September 1928.

27. Ibid.

28. "Slain by Victim as Black Hand Plot Is Foiled," *CDT*, 22 February 1931; William Brashler, *The Don* (New York: Harper and Row, 1977), 27; John Landesco, "The Life History of a Member of the '42' Gang," *Journal of Criminal Law and Criminology* 23 (1933): 964–98.

29. "Comerford in Court Urges Chief to Act," *CDT*, 21 September 1928.

Chapter 5. The Causes of Black Hand Extortion

1. "Two More Dead: Mafia Tentacles Spread over City," *CR-H*, 27 March 1911; "Police Hope to Solve Puzzle of Black Hand," *CDT*, 21 April 1911; "Grim Methods of the 'Mafia' Not All Romance," *CR-H*, 15 September 1912.

2. "Scoff at Black Hand: Letters are Derided," *CR-H*, 20 Nov 1907; "Black Hand Is a Hoax," *CR-H*, 14 April 1909.

3. "Origin of La Mafia," *CDT*, 28 July 1895.

4. Francis Marion Crawford, *Southern Italy and Sicily and the Rulers of the South* (New York: Macmillan, 1905), 368.

5. "The Origin of the Mafia," *CDT*, 5 May 1891.

6. Francis Ianni and Elizabeth Reuss-Ianni, *A Family Business: Kinship and Social Control in Organized Crime* (New York: Russell Sage Foundation, 1972), 25; Charles Heckethorn, *The Secret Societies of All Ages and Countries* (New York: University Books, 1965), 188.

7. Henner Hess, *Mafia and Mafiosi* (New York: New York University Press, 1998), 1; Gaia Servadio, *Mafioso* (New York: Stein and Day, 1976), 24.

8. Pino Arlacchi, *Mafia Business* (London: Verso, 1986), 3.

9. Ibid.; Hess, *Mafia and Mafiosi*, 10.

10. Arlacchi, *Mafia Business*, 21–22.

11. Joseph Albini, *The American Mafia* (New York: Appleton Century Crofts, 1971), 110.

12. Ibid., 127; Raimondo Catannzaro, *Men of Respect* (New York: Free Press, 1992), 39.

13. Anton Blok, *The Mafia of a Sicilian Village 1860–1960* (Prospect Heights,

Ill.: Waveland Press, 1988), 62; Tom Behan, *The Camorra* (New York: Routledge, 1996), 27.

14. Catanzaro, *Men of Respect,* 19; Blok, *The Mafia,* xvii.

15. Hess, *Mafia and Mafiosi,* 19.

16. Gus Tyler, *Organized Crime in America* (Ann Arbor: University of Michigan Press, 1962), 348; Catanzaro, *Men of Respect,* 33; Blok, *The Mafia,* 147.

17. Moses Finley, Dennis Smith, and Christopher Duggan, *A History of Sicily* (New York: Viking Press, 1987), 183; Blok, *The Mafia,* 177; Hess, *Mafia and Mafiosi,* 66.

18. Catanzaro, *Men of Respect,* 15; Diego Gambetta, *The Sicilian Mafia* (Cambridge: Harvard University Press, 1993), 95–96; Luigi Barzini, *The Italians* (New York: Athenaeum, 1964), 259; James Fentress, *Rebels and Mafiosi: Death in a Sicilian Landscape* (London: Cornell University Press, 2000), 166; Crawford, *Southern Italy and Sicily,* 374.

19. Hess, *Mafia and Mafiosi,* 31.

20. Ianni and Reuss-Ianni, *A Family Business,* 29; Tyler, *Organized Crime,* 349.

21. Thomas Hobbes, *Leviathan* (New York: Meridian, 1966); Desmond Ellis, "The Hobbesian Problem of Order," *American Sociological Review* 36 (1977): 692–703.

22. Hess, *Mafia and Mafiosi,* 185.

23. "Taken as Camorra Slayer," *CDT,* 14 January 1912; Hess, *Mafia and Mafiosi,* 25, 134, 152.

24. Arthur Train, *Courts, Criminals, and the Camorra* (New York: Charles Scribner's Sons: 1912), 147; Heckethorn, *Secret Societies,* 255.

25. Tammaso Sassone, "Italian Criminals in the United States." *Current History* 25 (1921): 23; Train, *Courts,* 147; Hess, *Mafia and Mafiosi,* 101; Behan, *The Camorra,* 10.

26. Vincenzo Ruggerio, "The Camorra," in *Global Crime Connections,* ed. Frank Pearce and Michael Woodiwiss (Toronto: University of Toronto Press, 1993), 144; Train, *Courts,* 148.

27. Sassone, "Italian Criminals in the United States," 23.

28. Heckethorn, *Secret Societies,* 269; Train, *Courts,* 147; John Mooney, "The Two Sicilies and the Camorra," *American Catholic Quarterly* 12 (1891): 745.

29. Train, *Courts,* 145; Behan, *The Camorra,* 12; "The Camorra," *Saturday Review of Politics, Literature, Science, and Art* 54 (1885): 70.

30. Mooney, "The Two Sicilies," 738; Train, *Courts,* 148–50.

31. Heckethorn, *Secret Societies,* 271; Train, *Courts,* 158; Behan, *The Camorra,* 19.

32. Train, *Courts,* 163.

33. Behan, *The Camorra,* 25; Ruggerio, "The Camorra," 151.

34. *WHSC,* 5.

35. Stuart Hall, Charles Critcher, Tomy Jefferson, John Clarke, and Brian Roberts, *Policing the Crisis* (London: Macmillan, 1978), 58.

36. Thomas Philpott, *The Slum and the Ghetto: Immigrants, Blacks, and Reformers in Chicago, 1880–1930* (New Haven: Yale University Press, 1978), 139; Harvey Zorbaugh, *The Gold Coast and the Slum* (Chicago: University of Chicago Press, 1983), 5; "Death Corner Wedding Grows Riot de Luxe," *CDT,* 4 September 1916.

37. University of Chicago, Local Community Research Committee, Lower North End, "History of the Lower North Side," vol. 3, no. 27a, Chicago Historical Society, 1928.

38. WHSC, 6; "New Black Hand Murder, Eight since December," *CDT,* 26 March 1916.

39. "100 Black Hand Brigands Terrorize 100,000 Italians and Sneer at the Chicago Police," *CDT,* 6 March 1910.

40. "Victim of Black Hand," *CR-H,* 9 April 1908; "Sicilians Pay Toll in Lives to Vendetta," *CDT,* 22 June 1914; "Kill Another Sicilian," *CR-H,* 27 April 1910.

41. "Sales, Swank, and Soot: Tale of Near North Side," *CDT,* 21 February 1954; Edith Abbott, *The Tenements of Chicago* (New York: Arno Press, 1936), 106.

42. Zorbaugh, *Gold Coast and the Slum,* 165; Rudolph Vecoli, "The Formation of Chicago's Little Italies," *Journal of American Ethnic History* 2 (1983): 7–20.

43. Bruce Zummo, *Little Sicily* (Chicago: Near North Publishing, 2001), 99; Zorbaugh, *Gold Coast and the Slum,* 165.

44. Frank Beck, *The Italian in Chicago* (Chicago: City of Chicago Department of Public Welfare, 1919), 7; Zummo, *Little Sicily,* 44; Marie Leavitt, "Report on the Sicilian Colony in Chicago," quoted by Harvey W. Zorbaugh, *The Gold Coast and the Slum* (Chicago: University of Chicago Press, 1983), 159–81.

45. Helen Day, Sicilian Traits, quoted by Zorbaugh, *The Gold Coast and the Slum,* 159–81.

46. "Misguided Love of the Fatherland," *La Parola dei Socialisti,* 31 May 1913, CFLPS; "Exploit Italians and Guard Them," *CDT,* 21 August 1910.

47. Grace Norton, "Chicago Housing Conditions, VII: Two Italian Districts," *American Journal of Sociology* 18 (1913): 509–42; Abbot, *Tenements,* 109; "One in Four in 'Little Italy' Had Phthisis," *CDT,* 22 April 1917.

48. Philpott, *The Slum and the Ghetto,* 7; "Citizens Fight Housing Plan: Charge Deceit," *CDT,* 15 February 1940.

49. Ernest Burgess, Robert Park, and Robert McKenzie, *The City* (Chicago: University of Chicago Press, 1967); Beck, *The Italian in Chicago,* 7; "Fine Chance for Good Fellows on North Side," *CDT,* 17 October 1914.

50. City of Chicago, *First Semi-Annual Report of the Department of Public Welfare to the Mayor and Aldermen of Chicago* (Chicago: Municipal Reference Library, 1915).

51. Beck, *The Italian in Chicago,* 25–28; Local Community Research Committee, University of Chicago, Lower North End, vol. 3, nos. 13, 27a, and 57, Chicago Historical Society, 1928; Zorbaugh, *Gold Coast and the Slum,* 181.

52. Zorbaugh, *Gold Coast and the Slum,* 165; WHSC, 6.

53. Robert Park, preface to Louis Wirth, *The Ghetto* (Chicago: University of Chicago Press, 1928).

54. Reports of the Immigration Commission, *Emigration Conditions in Europe,* 61st Congress, 3d Sess., Senate Document No. 748 (Washington D. C.: U.S. Government Printing Office, 1970), 209; Crawford, *Southern Italy and Sicily,* 366.

55. Hess, *Mafia and Mafiosi,* 108; Servadio, *Mafioso,* 5.

56. Tommaso Sassone, "Italy's Criminals in the United States," *Current History* 15 (1921): 26; Crawford, *Southern Italy and Sicily,* 367.

57. "Poison Kills Girl; Arsenic in Flour," *CDT,* 11 April 1908; "Silence Balks Police Seeking Mafia Gunmen," *CR-H,* 23 January 1912.

58. "The Police and Alien Ways," *CR-H,* 20 March 1911.

59. Louis Pojman and Jeffrey Reiman, *The Death Penalty: For and Against* (London: Rowman and Littlefield, 1974), 21; Thorsten Sellin, *Culture, Conflict, and Crime*, Bulletin 41, Social Science Research Council, 1938; "Italian Kills When Law Fails," *CDT*, 25 December 1916.

60. Joseph Albini, *The American Mafia* (New York: Appleton Century Crofts, 1971), 127; Edward Banfield, *The Moral Basis of a Backward Society* (Glencoe, Ill.: Free Press, 1958), 9; Rudolph Vecoli, *Chicago's Italians Prior to World War I: A Study of Their Adjustment* (Ann Arbor: University Microfilms International, 1963), 122.

61. Beck, *The Italian in Chicago*, 29.

62. Cairoli Gigliotti, *Toward the Danger Mark: Administration of Justice in the U.S.* (Chicago: self-published, 1916), 35, 163–64.

63. "Victim of Black Hand," *CR-H*, 9 April 1908; "Fourth Man Victim in Camorra War within 72 Hours," *CR-H*, 17 March 1911; "Police at Wits' End in 'Black Hand' War," *CR-H*, 18 March 1911.

64. Graham Taylor, *Pioneering on Social Frontiers* (Chicago: University of Chicago Press, 1930), 204.

65. "Saloon Black Hand Retreat," *CR-H*, 23 September 1908; Perry Duis, *The Saloon: Public Drinking in Chicago and Boston 1880–1920* (Urbana: University of Illinois Press, 1983), 147; "The Italian Saloons," *CDT*, 4 June 1873; "Hunt Black Hand Slayer," *CDT*, 7 January 1910; *WHSC*, 6.

66. "Call to Fight Black Hand," *CDT*, 22 September 1908; "Saloon Black Hand Retreat"; Lincoln Stephens, *The Shame of the Cities* (New York: McClure, Philips, 1904), 23.

67. *WHSC*, 7; "Slain by Black Hand; Little Italy Raided," *CR-H*, 7 January 1910.

68. *WHSC*, 7.

69. "Shots Miss Spy; Wound Three Others," *CR-H*, 20 December 1911; "Get Two in 'Black Hand' Case," *CR-H*, 24 December 1911; "Charged with Murder Plot," *CR-H*, 29 December 1911.

70. "Graft in the Police Department," *L'Italia*, 31 August 1901, CFLPS; "'Black Hand' Cop Acquitted," *CDT*, 19 October 1910; "Gambling Inquiry May Hit Three New District Rulers," *CDT*, 16 September 1911.

71. William T. Stead, *If Christ Came to Chicago* (Chicago: Laird and Lee, 1894), 307–11; L. O. Curon, *Chicago Satan's Sanctum* (Chicago: C. D. Phillips, 1899).

72. Stead, *If Christ Came*, 307–11.

73. "A Warning to Chicago," editorial *CDT*, 3 October 1890; "Police, Crime, and Vice in Two Cities," *CR-H*, 2 June 1911.

74. "Says Police Fix Limits to Crime," *CDT*, 6 April 1911.

75. "Big Map Locates Dives in Chicago," *CDT*, 25 February 1912.

76. James Doherty, "Hot Stove Jimmy Quinn!" *CDT*, 21 September 1952; "Big Map Locates Dives in Chicago," *CDT*, 25 February 1912.

77. "'Manny' Shakes Up Police," CDT, 6 June 1913; "Charges Are Filed against Revere, Baer, and Hanley," *CDT*, 23 November 1911; "Gambling Inquiry May Hit Three New District Rulers," *CDT*, 16 September 1911.

78. "The Black Hand Under Control," *Outlook*, June (1916), 347–48; "The Police and the Black Hand," *Outlook* June (1916): 347–48.

79. *People of the State of Illinois v. Joseph Bertucci and Bruno Nardi*, Indict-

ment, Term No. 3373 PGD No. 90592A, 1 March 1909, Cook County Circuit Court Clerk; "Two Men Placed on Trial; Sequel of Black Hand Deed," *CDT*, 22 June 1909; "Blackmail Peril Stalks in Court," *CDT*, 23 June 1909.

80. "Good and Bad Italians," *CDT*, 4 October 1911; "Crimes of the Italian Colony," *L'Italia*, 1 April 1911, CFLPS.

81. Gino Speranza, "Petrosino and the Black Hand," *Survey* 22 (1909): 11–14.

82. Robert Watchorn, "The Black Hand and the Immigrant," *Outlook*, 31 July (1909): 794–97; "Two Detectives Shot," *CDN*, 4 March 1910; "Detective Dying; Hunt Black Hand," *CA*, 4 March 1910; "Detective Shot Is Dying," *CA*, 5 March 1910.

83. "Little Sicily's Murders Go All over City," *CDT*, 27 December 1916; "'Death Corner' Slayer Will Be Freed by State," *CDT*, 8 November 1920.

84. "Little Sicily's Murders Go All over City."

85. David Neubauer, *America's Courts and the Criminal Justice System* (Belmont: West Publishing, 1999), 32.

86. Arthur Woods, "The Problem of the Black Hand," *McClure's* 33 (1909): 42–43; WHSC, 8–9.

87. "Little Sicily's Murderers go All Over City."

88. "Parole Abuses Laid to Politics in Penal Survey," *CDT*, 25 January 1928.

89. John Landesco, "Chicago's Criminal Underworld of the '80s and '90s," *Journal of Criminal Law and Criminology* 25 (1935): 928–40.

90. "Detective Shot as Mafia Warning in Zone of Death," 5 May 1915; "Black Hand Chief Is Killed with Sawed-Off Gun," *CDT*, 15 September 1918; "Jury Convicts Italian: Chief 'Black Hander' Flees," *CDT*, 16 October 1915; "Terrible Joe, Blackhand King, a-Shooting Goes," *CDT*, 29 October 1915.

91. *People of the State of Illinois v. Sam Ciminello et al.*, Indictment, Term No. 16080 G. J. No. 198 P.G.D. No. 16082, 19 March 1919, Cook County Circuit Court Clerk; "Defy Death and Race Tradition to Trust in Law," *CDT*, 1 March 1919; "Code of Sicily Seals Lips in Park Shooting," *CDT*, 3 September 1919.

92. "Code of Sicily Seals Lips in Park Shooting"; "Sends Man to Prison; Pays with His Life," *CDT*, 9 September 1919; "Grand Jurors Jar Black Hand by Indictments," *CDT*, 16 March 1919; "Code Is Murder Syndicate Clew in Morici Death," *CDT*, 29 January 1926.

93. WHSC, 9.

94. Ibid., 8.

95. Ibid., 9.

96. "Rich Men as Victims of the Black Hand," *CR-H*, 3 April 1908; WHSC, 10–12.

97. *United States of America v. Gianni Alongi*, Indictment, December Term A.D. 1910, U.S. District Court, Northern District of Illinois, Eastern Division, 23 January 1911.

98. WHSC, 14–16.

99. Ibid., 15.

100. Ibid., 15.

101. Ibid., 17; "'Black Hand' Suspect Talks, *CDT*, 27 July 1909.

102. "100 Black Hand Brigands Terrorize 100,000 Italians and Sneer at the Chicago Police," *CDT*, 6 March 1910.

103. Ibid.

104. "Kills Himself to End Fear after Getting Black Hand Letter," *CDT*, 25 April 1928.

105. *L'Eco deli Emigrazione* quoted in "Two Sicilian Journals Devoted to Emigration," *CDT*, 31 May 1910.

106. Arrigo Petacco, *Joe Petrosino* (New York: Macmillan, 1974), 111–12.

107. "No Need of Emigrating from Italy's Large Towns," *CDT*, 18 June 1910; WHSC, 9.

108. Petacco, *Joe Petrosino*, 112.

109. "Caught after Nineteen Years' Hunt," *CDT*, 13 April 1910; "Held as 'Black Hand' Gang," *CR-H*, 14 April 1910.

110. Frank Marshal White, "The Passing of the Black Hand," *Century Magazine* 95 (January 1918): 331–37; Immigration Act of 1907 34 Stat. at L. 898, chap. 1134, U.S. Comp. Stat. Supp. 1907; Petacco, *Joe Petrosino*, 112; Frank Marshal White, "How the United States Fosters the Black Hand," *Outlook* 30 (October 1909): 495–500.

111. White, "How the United States Fosters the Black Hand."

112. George Dorsey, "Law Fails to Keep Out Men Convicted of Crime," *CDT*, 19 April 1910; Gino Speranza, "Petrosino and the Black Hand," *Survey* 22 (1909): 11–14.

113. "Gunmen, Seeking Victims, Shoot One, Peril Many," *CR-H*, 11 May 1914.

114. "Two More Slain: Council Acts on Gunmen Tonight," *CDT*, 11 May 1914.

115. "Come to War on Criminals," *CDT*, 7 June 1909; "Acquits Man Who Armed Against Black Hand Ire," *CDT*, 25 June 1909.

116. "Swift Punishment the Remedy," editorial, *CDT*, 4 August 1909.

117. "The Police and 'Black Hand' Gangs," *CR-H*, 21 February 1911.

118. White, "How the United States Fosters the Black Hand."

Chapter 6. The Social Construction of Deviance

1. Gaetano D'Amato, "The Black Hand Myth," *North American Review* (April 1908): 544.

2. Gary Potter and Victor E. Kappeler, *Constructing Crime* (Prospect Heights, Ill.: Waveland Press, 1996), 3–5.

3. Ibid., 18.

4. Richard Quinney, *The Social Reality of Crime* (Boston: Little, Brown, 1970).

5. Victor Kappeler, Mark Blumberg, and Gary Potter, *The Mythology of Crime and Justice* (Prospect Heights, Ill.: Waveland Press, 1996), 4.

6. Mark Fishman, "Crime Waves as Ideology," in Gary Potter and Victor Kappeler, *Constructing Crime* (Prospect Heights, Ill.: Waveland Press, 1996).

7. Henry Brownstein, *The Social Reality of Violence and Violent Crime* (Boston: Allyn and Bacon, 2000), 168.

8. Potter and Kappeler, *Constructing Crime*, 9–13.

9. Charles Washburn, *Come into My Parlor: A Biography of the Aristocratic Everleigh Sisters of Chicago* (New York: Arno Press, 1974), 58–59.

10. George Murray, *The Madhouse on Madison Street* (Chicago: Follett, 1965).

11. "The Fine Italian Hand: How the Black Hand Came Out of Little Italy," *CDT*, 24 November 1918.

12. Ibid.

13. "Black Hand Death Society," *CDT*, 23 June 1914.

14. Sidney Kobre, *The Yellow Press and the Gilded Age of Journalism* (Tallahassee: Florida State University, 1964), 2, 15.

15. Gino Speranza, "How It Feels to Be a Problem," *Charities* 12 (1904): 457–63; "The Italian Electoral Vote," *L'Italia*, 17 August 1889.

16. Joel Best, "'Road Warriors' on 'Hair Trigger Highways,'" in Potter and Kappeler, eds., *Constructing Crime*; "Slain in His Bed," *CR-H*, 27 July 1911.

17. "Black Hand," letters to the editor, *CR-H*, 14 August 1911.

18. "Suppressing Mention of the 'Black Hand,'" *CR-H*, 15 August 1911.

19. Michael Woodiwiss, *Organized Crime and American Power: A History* (Toronto: University of Toronto Press, 2001), 8.

20. "Chief Hennessy's Assassination," *CDT*, 15 March 1891.

21. "Assassins in the Toils," *CDT*, 20 October 1890; "A Proposito Di Mafia," *L'Italia*, 25 October 1890, CFLPS.

22. "Another Victim of the Mafia Society," *CDT*, 25 October 1890.

23. "Work of the New Orleans Citizens," *CDT*, 28 October 1890.

24. "Mafia Secrets May Come Out," *CDT*, 9 March 1891; "Mafia Murderers Slain," *CDT*, 15 March 1891; "O'Malley Must Die or Decamp," *CDT*, 14 March 1891.

25. "May Lynch Mafia Thugs," *CDT*, 14 March 1891.

26. "Mafia Murders Slain"; "The New Orleans Horror," *CDT*, 15 March 1891; "Horrible Scenes in the Prison," *CDT*, 15 March 1891.

27. "Had to Lynch Them," *CDT*, 27 March 1891; "To Vindicate the Law," *CDT*, 18 March 1891; "Crescent City Press Opinions," *CDT*, 14 March 1891; "A Review of the Lynching," *CDT*, 27 March 1891.

28. "Uphold the Lynchers," *CDT*, 17 March 1891.

29. "New Orleans Lynching of 1891 and the American Press," *Louisiana Historical Quarterly* 24 (1941): 187–204.

30. "Sanctioned by Public Opinion," *CDT*, 15 March 1891; "O'Malley in Memphis," *CDT*, 21 March 1891.

31. "Was There a Corruption Fund?" *CDT*, 15 March 1891; "Current Notes," *CDT*, 15 March 1891.

32. "They Appeal to Italy," *CDT*, 15 March 1891.

33. "The New Orleans Horror"; "The Mafia," *CDT*, 18 March 1891.

34. "Blame Only the Southern Mob," *CDT*, 17 March 1891; "Chicago Contributed Nothing," *CDT*, 14 March 1891; "Raising the Call for Revenge," *CDT*, 15 March 1891.

35. "The Mafia Must Go," *CDT*, 19 March 1891.

36. "The Italian Question," *CDT*, 19 March 1891.

37. "Says the Mafia Must Be Killed," *CDT*, 23 March 1891.

38. "Italy Will Be on Hand," *CDT*, 17 March 1891; "The United States Will Have to Foot the Bill," *CDT*, 16 March 1891; "Uncle Sam Not to Blame," *CDT*, 17 March 1891; "The United States Not Liable," *CDT*, 18 March 1891; "Ru-

dini Calls for Help," *CDT,* 9 May 1891; "Money for the Slain," *CDT,* 4 April 1891.

39. "Will They Be Punished?" *CDT,* 18 March 1891; "O'Malley Surrenders," *CDT,* 4 April 1891; "Mafia's Work Disclosed," *CDT,* 13 April 1891.

40. "Mafia's Work Disclosed"; "The Revelations of the Mafias Methods," *CDT,* 14 April 1891.

41. "Your Turn Will Come," *CDT,* 18 March 1891; "May Call a Mass-Meeting," *CDT,* 18 March 1891; "Cheering the Stars and Stripes," *CDT,* 16 March 1891; "Mafia Meeting Mobbed," *CDT,* 23 March 1891; "Methodist Ministers Excited," *CDT,* 24 March 1891.

42. "Called the 'City-Hall Mafia,'" *CDT,* 3 April 1891.

43. "Rudini Calls for Help."

44. "The Mala Vita Dagos at Home," *CDT,* 2 June 1891; "Evil Life in Italy," *CDT,* 13 June 1891; "Trial of Mala Vita Members," *CDT,* 11 July 1892.

45. "Mafia Methods Exposed," *CDT,* 6 May 1891.

46. "Disappointed with the Report," *CDT,* 7 May 1891; "Consul Corte Speaks His Mind," *CDT,* 8 May 1891.

47. "The New Orleans Grand Jury Mafia Report," *CDT,* 7 May 1891.

48. "Says He Is a Mafia Victim," *CDT,* 18 March 1891.

49. John Kendall, "Who Killa de Chief?" *Louisiana Historical Quarterly* 22, no. 2 (1939): 492–530.

50. "The Origin of the Mafia," *CDT,* 5 May 1891; "Reputed Origin of the Mafia," *CDT,* 6 July 1891; "To Drive Out the Italians," *CDT,* 6 May 1891.

51. "No Case against Detective O'Malley," *CDT,* 9 October 1891.

52. "Black Hand Kills Its Greatest Foe," *CDT,* 14 March 1909; Arrigo Petacco, *Joe Petrosino* (New York: Macmillan, 1974), 123.

53. "Italian Version of Crime," *CDT,* 15 March 1909; "Fears for Roosevelt," *CDT,* 16 March 1909; "Eleven Taken in Petrosino Case," *CDT,* 15 March 1909; "Band to Fight Black Hand," *CDT,* 16 March 1909.

54. "Denies Black Hand Body Exists," *CDN,* 16 March 1909.

55. "Italy Hunts Slayers Afar," *CDT,* 18 March 1909; "Palermo Police Head Let Out," *CDT,* 9 July 1909.

56. "Petrosino Victim of Plot," *CDT,* 21 March 1909; "Sleuth's Slayers Known in Palermo," *CDT,* 4 April 1909; "Petrosino Suspect Known in New York," *CDT,* 7 April 1909.

57. "Slayers of Lieut. Petrosino Traced to Ohio Black Hand?" *CDT,* 7 August 1909; "Black Hand Plot Likened to Mafia," *CDT,* 16 June 1909; "Dens of Black Hand Found in Many Cities," *CR-H,* 10 June 1909.

58. "Secret Meeting Is Bared," *CDT,* 29 August 1909.

59. "Doom of Black Hand to Avenge Detective," *CR-H,* 14 March 1909; "Italians Anxious over Rumor," *CDN,* 24 August 1909.

60. "Doom of Black Hand to Avenge Detective."

61. Petacco, *Joe Petrosino,* 5.

62. "City Mourns as Body of Petrosino Arrives," *CR-H,* 10 April 1909; "Bring Victim of the Black Hand Home," *CDT,* 10 April 1909; "City Mourns for Petrosino," *CDT,* 13 April 1909; "Monster Candle to Burn Five Years," *CDT,* 19 April 1909; Petacco, *Joe Petrosino,* 163.

63. "Italy Acts on Tragedy," *CDT*, 19 March 1909; "Italy Asks Crime Conference," *CR-H*, 19 March 1909.

64. "Studies Sources of Immigration," *CDT*, 14 November 1909.

65. "Off to Sunny Italy to Study Immigration," *CDT*, 28 March 1910.

66. Robert Loerzel, *Alchemy of Bones: Chicago's Luetgert Murder Case* (Urbana: University of Illinois Press, 2003), 130.

67. George Dorsey, "Culture of Sicilians That of Ancient Greece," *CDT*, 13 April 1910.

68. Dorsey, "Procession of Rulers in History of Sicily," *CDT*, 14 April 1910.

69. Dorsey, "Sicilian Code of Honor Serves to Hide Crime," *CDT*, 15 April 1910.

70. Dorsey, "Centuries of Fighting Leaves Mark on Sicily," *CDT*, 16 April 1910.

71. Dorsey, "Mafia Mysteries Terrorize Sicily," *CDT*, 17 April 1910.

72. Dorsey, "Some Ways of Sicilians Due to Long Oppression," *CDT*, 18 April 1910.

73. Dorsey, "Law Fails to Keep Out Men Convicted of Crime," *CDT*, 19 April 1910.

74. Dorsey, "How Emigrants Evade Laws That Bar Them," *CDT*, 20 April 1910.

75. Dorsey, "Sicilians Are Inspired by Grim Determination," *CDT*, 22 April 1910.

76. Dorsey, "Sicily's One Hope in Its Emigrants," *CDT*, 8 May 1910.

77. Dorsey, "Sicilian Emigrant Brings Ideas Strange to America," *CDT*, 2 June 1910.

78. Dorsey, "Sicilian Emigrant Has Strong and Weak Points," *CDT*, 3 June 1910.

79. Dorsey, "Ideas of East and West Rub Elbows in Naples," *CDT*, 7 June 1910.

80. Dorsey, "Big Output of Colonists Doesn't Depopulate Italy," *CDT*, 10 June 1910.

81. Dorsey, "Calabria the Habitat of Extremest Poverty," *CDT*, 11 June 1910.

82. Dorsey, "Camorra, Once Protective, Now levying Blackmail," *CDT*, 18 July 1910.

83. Dorsey, "Immigration of Italians May Bring Big Results," *CDT*, 19 August 1910.

84. Dorsey, "America a Fertile Field for Criminals of Italy," *CDT*, 22 August 1910.

85. Dorsey, "Pray in Hungary to Aid Emigrants," *CDT*, 11 December 1909; Dorsey, "Slavs the Greatest People of Europe," *CDT*, 15 February 1910; Dorsey, "Emigrants from Bulgaria Are the Best of People," *CDT*, 10 March 1910; Dorsey, "People of Roumania Are a Primitive Race," *CDT*, 12 February 1910; Dorsey, "Rouomanian Ideas Unlike American," *CDT*, 13 February 1910; Dorsey, "Oriental Minds Use Devious Ways," *CDT*, 15 December 1910; Dorsey, "Revolt a Jump From Pan to Fire," *CDT*, 17 May 1911; Dorsey, "Lazy Streak in Philippines," *CDT*, 7 July 1917.

86. "An Italian in Reply to Dorsey," Voice of the People, *CDT*, 30 July 1910.

Conclusion

1. *WHSC*, 19; "Old Joe Gives Fatal Lead in Place of Silver," *CDT*, 25 April 1917.

2. *WHSC*, 20.

3. Gino Speranza, "How It Feels to Be a Problem," *Charities* 12 (1904): 457–63.

4. C. Webb, "The Lynching of Sicilian Immigrants in the American South: 1886–1910," *American Nineteenth Century History* 3, no. 1 (2002): 45–76.

5. "Mob Lynches Two Italians," *CDT*, 21 September 1910.

6. "Beat It or We'll Beat You, Aliens Told Downstate," *CDT*, 7 August 1920; "Drive Italians from Town," *CR-H*, 29 January 1908.

7. "Defends Italian Race," *CR-H*, 26 March 1910.

8. "Black Hand Is a Hoax," *CR-H*, 2 April 1908.

9. Cy Egan, *The Mafia Curse* (Philadelphia: Xlibris, 2008), 11; T. J. English, *Paddy Whacked* (New York: Harper Collins, 2005), 6.

10. "Hist! Black Hand for Primary Law," *CDT*, 31 October 1907; "Senators Maul Charity Reforms," *CDT*, 12 May 1909.

11. "Gary Vice Ring Uses Fire in Fight on Reformers," *CDT*, 29 July 1909.

12. Luciano Iorizzo and Salvatore Mondello, *The Italian Americans* (New York: Twayne, 1971), 164.

13. Michael Hughes to the Honorable William E. Dever, interoffice memo, 26 May 1923.

14. Grace Abbott, "The Treatment of Aliens in the Criminal Courts," *Journal of the American Institute of Criminal Law and Criminology* 2, no. 4 (1911): 554–67.

15. Massachusetts Commission on Immigration, *The Problem of Immigration in Massachusetts* (Boston: Wright and Potter, 1914), 105.

16. Herbert Asbury, *The Gem of the Prairie* (De Kalb: Northern Illinois University Press, 1986), 231; Stephen Longstreet, *Chicago: 1860–1919* (New York: McKay: 1973), 393; Michael Lyman and Garry Potter, *Organised Crime* (Saddle River, N.J.: Prentice Hall, 1997), 118.

17. Erich Goode and Nachman Ben-Yehuda, *Moral Panics* (Oxford: Blackwell, 1994), 108; "Kill Two in Black Hand War," *CA*, 15 March 1911; "Slain in Own 'Black Hand' Plot, Report," *CA*, 16 March 1911.

18. Asbury, *The Gem of the Prairie*, 231; Longstreet, *Chicago: 1860–1919*, 373; Lyman and Potter, *Organized Crime*, 118; "Uses Deadly Slug to Shoot Italian," *CDT*, 17 March 1911; "Two Men Are Slain in Camorra Plots," *CR-H*, 15 March 1911.

19. Carl Sifakis, *The Encyclopedia of American Crime* (New York: Facts on File, 1982), 200, 301.

20. Wikipedia, s.v. "Shotgun Man" (retrieved 31 January 2007, http://en.wikipedia.org/wiki/Shotgun_Man).

21. St. Philip Benizi, *Golden Jubilee Book*, n.p.

22. Chicago Area Project, Community Committee Reports 1933–1972, North Side Community Committee, box 93, folder 6, Chicago Historical Society.

23. William Foote Whyte, "Social Organization in the Slums," *American Sociological Review* 8 (1943): 34–39.

24. University of Chicago, Local Community Research Committee, Lower North End, "History of Lower North Side," vol. 3, nos. 35, 50, and 57, Chicago Historical Society, 1928.

25. Harvey W. Zorbaugh, *The Gold Coast and the Slum* (Chicago: University of Chicago Press, 1983); Whyte, "Social Organization in the Slums," 36.

26. St. Philip Benizi, *Golden Jubilee Book*, n.p.

27. "City's Public Housing Is Promise Unfulfilled," *CDT*, 15 October 1992; "Citizens Fight Housing Plan: Charge Deceit," *CDT*, 15 February 1940.

28. Bruce Zummo, *Little Sicily* (Chicago: Near North Publishing, 2001), 3; "Citizens Fight Housing Plan: Charge Deceit"; Candeloro, "Chicago's Italians: A Survey of the Ethnic Factor, 1850–1990," in Melvin Holli and Peter d'A. Jones, eds., *Ethnic Chicago* (Grand Rapids, Mich.: Wm. Eerdmans, 1995), 244.

INDEX

Abbott, Grace, 199
Abrahams, Emanuel "Manney," 143
Abrino, Nicholas, 104
Acci, Gaetano, 115
Accomando, Antonio, 42
Adams Elementary School, 40
Adams, Jane, 36
Adams, Lionel, 178
admonition, 147
Aiello, John, 54
Aiello, Joseph, 108
Albano, Angelo, 196
Albano, Giuseppe, 114
Albini, Joseph, 5
Alfano, Enrico, 79
Alito, Samuel, 8
Alongi, Gianni, 70, 75–76, 86, 151
Ambro, Frank, 73
amoral familism, 138
Antonucci, Katy, 115
Arlacchi, Pino, 122
Arquilla, Giorgio, 118

Baer, Bernard, 91
Baffa, Antonio, 53–56
Baijonotti, Paul, 12
Balzano, Frank, 75
Banfield, Edward, 138
Barasa, Bernard, 51, 91, 119, 197
Barbaro, Sam, 193
Barona, Modesto, 85
Barone, John, 148
Barone, Victor, 94
Barone, Vietro, 97
Barone, Vito, 141
Barsotti, Carlo, 28
Basso, Rocco, 78
Basso, Salvatore, 78

Basta, Jacob, 92
Battaglia, August, 98
Bell, Daniel, 5
Bellavia, Antonio, 65
Bergamo, Geatano, 24
Berkson, Samuel, 51
Bernacchi, Julian: attack on Longobardi, 52; Carlino arrest, 50; Carozzo Gang, 112; Catalanetto murder, 97; Crapa arrest, 43; creation of Black Hand Squad, 69; De Salbo arrest, 78; Geraci arrest, 49; Loungora arrest, 88; Lumia investigation 39; Morici arrest, 37; Rebella murder, 92; retirement and death, 106
Bertucci, Giuseppe, 52
Bertucci, Joseph, 144
Binzenza, Bruno, 24
Black Hand: affect on real estate values, 95; alien conspiracy theory, 4; anti Black Hand organizations, 35; apathy of city government, 47; Beniamino letter, 31; Cairo letter, 1; causes of Black Hand crime, 130–60; child offenders, 58–59, 104; creation of social problems, 163; demand for Italian police officers, 37, 40, 45–46, 62, 72; discrimination, 7–8, 44; disguise other crimes, 83; end of Black Hand, 194; ethnic succession theory, 5; federal involvement, 66, 71, 75–77, 92, 95–96; first Black Hand conviction, 38; first Black Hand letter, 26; first use of Black Hand name, 22; importation theory, ix; institutional legacy, 195–97; Italian origins, 2; journal-

Umbrello, John, 52
Umbrello, Vito, 144
Unione Siciliana, 30–31, 42
urban legends, 100
U.S. Commissioner of Labor, 19

Vacek, Joseph, 83, 166
Vachris, Antonio, 181
Vaiana, Michael, 100
Van Dine, Harvey, 105
vendetta, 17
Veriuso, Antonio, 24
Viana, Nicholas, 108–9
Vicario, Collogero, 181
vigilato, 147
Vitetta, Joseph, 84
Volini, Camillo: bombing, 104; committee to visit Chicago mayor, 45; death threat, 36; end of White Hand Society, 67; fled to Montana, 42; founding of White Hand Society, 30–34; Guinta kidnapping, 44; list of Black Hand offenders, 39; need for Italian police officers, 46; New Orleans' lynchings, 172, 176; Shotgun Man murders, 74

Walrus, 165
Walsh, James, 40
Walsh, Michael, 94
Washburn, Charles, 163
Washburn School, 40
Watchorn, Robert, 145
Waters, William, 48, 49
Wechaler, Isaac, 142
White, Frank Marshall, 156, 159
White Hand Police, 33
White Hand Society: articles of incorporation, 34–35; attempt to revive White Hand Society, 61; Beniamino letter, 31; Black Hand letters sent by friends, 110; call for renewed efforts, 66; call for resumption of White Hand Society, 80, 82; causes

of Black Hand crime, ix, 6, 9; committee to visit elected officials, 32; complexities of Black Hand prosecutions, 150; condition of Little Sicily, 131; demand for Italian police officers, 45; demise of White Hand Society, 67; discrimination against Italians, 49; executive committee, 32; failure, 42; formation of White Hand Society, 30; fugitives from Italian justice, 156; headquarters, 32; hiring of investigators, 33; improper definition of Black Hand crime, 7; increase in Black Hand crime, 71; Italian newspaper endorsements, 30–31; lack of cooperation from city of Chicago, 46–47; method of crime, 130; national attention, 35; notice to Black Hand criminals, 33; poor police cooperation, 77; report, 47; saloons and Black Hand crime, 93, 94; *Unione Siciliana* endorsement, 31
White Wings, 110
Whyte, William Foote, 203
Wickliff, John, 170
Williams, Ann, 75
Williams, Rev. Elmer, 89
Women's Association of Commerce, 95
Woodiwiss, Michael, 5, 167
Woodrick, Albert, 118
Woods, Arthur, 3
Wren, John, 146

yellow journalism, 165
yellow press, 30
York Palace Theatre, 104

Zabel, Robert, 59
Zagone, Mariano, 36, 86
Zapullo, Frank, 78
Zavello, Dominico, 85
Zorbaugh, Harvey, 131, 203

ROBERT M. LOMBARDO is an assistant professor
of criminal justice and a member of the graduate
faculty at Loyola University, Chicago. He received
his PhD from the University of Illinois in 1994.
Dr. Lombardo is also a thirty-three-year police
veteran, having served twenty-eight years with the
Chicago Police Department and five years as the
deputy chief of the Cook County Sheriff's Police
Department. He has worked in all areas of policing
including patrol, investigations, narcotics, and
organized crime. In addition, Dr. Lombardo has
taught, as a visiting scholar, at numerous police
training academies including the Chicago Police
Academy, the Illinois State Police Academy, and
the Police School of Catalonia, Barcelona, Spain.

The University of Illinois Press
is a founding member of the
Association of American University Presses.

Composed in 9.5/12.5 Trump Mediaeval LT Std
with Dear Sarah display
at the University of Illinois Press
Manufactured by Cushing-Malloy, Inc.

University of Illinois Press
1325 South Oak Street
Champaign, IL 61820-6903
www.press.uillinois.edu